KEN O'C

Foreword by

A REPAIR KIT FOR GRADING

15 FIXES FOR BROKEN GRADES

Ken O'Connor
A Repair Kit for Grading: ***15 Fixes for Broken Grades***

Published by:
FIRST Educational Resources, LLC
Winneconne, Wisconsin
www.firsteducation-us.com
info@firsteducation-us.com
ISBN: 978-1-7332390-7-3

Printed in the United States of America
(EnvisionInk Printing Solutions, Neenah, WI)

"As a Social Studies teacher, when I finally realized that the purpose of my grades was to reflect student achievement, I reached for A Repair Kit for Grading: 15 Fixes for Broken Grades *by Ken O'Connor and it acted as a rudder when navigating the array of grading decisions teachers make every day. As an administrator, I regularly lent out my copy to teachers who were in the same boat as I. As an author, speaker and consultant, I've recommended Ken's writing to thousands of educators needing alternatives to grading group projects, using zeros or deducting the grade for late submissions. As demonstrated with the sinking of the mighty Bismark, without a functional rudder we all go in circles. Thankfully, Ken O'Connor provides the rudder, the compass and the map."*

Myron Dueck, Educational consultant and author of
Giving Students A Say and Grading Smarter Not Harder

"If you are looking for a book to translate over 100 years of grading research into classroom practice, this is it! O'Connor provides 15 practical fixes to help teachers make their grades more consistent, accurate, learning-focused and meaningful. The educator vignettes and school policies provide clear examples of bridging theory with practice. I highly recommend A Repair Kit for Grading *to any educator interested in improving their grading practices."*

Dr. Matt Townsley, author and assistant professor of educational leadership at the University of Northern Iowa.

"If you are looking for a user friendly book that gets to the heart of how to provide accurate grades to your students, this is the book for you! In the third edition of Ken's A Repair Kit for Grading: 15 Fixes for Broken Grades, *Ken takes the technical side of grading presented in his first edition, blends it with the implementation of the repairs that he presented in the second edition, and marries the science and art of grading with new concepts such as the CALM criteria for accurate and effective grades. The readability of this text helps support a clear understanding of the missteps that can occur when determining a grade, and provides teachers the guidance on what to think about as they reflect on and repair those missteps in their grading practices. This is a must read for teachers, administrators, and school board members."*

Dr. Nicole Roorda, Ed.D., Associate Superintendent, Johnston Community School District and International Consultant on Assessment and Grading Practices

"Schools and learning communities around the world are embracing the opportunity to reflect and re-examine policies, programs and practices. A Repair Kit for Grading: 15 Fixes for Broken Grades *has arrived at just the right time. The references are updated so that research and evidence are reflective of current thinking and learning. I found the new Educator Vignettes and the Policy/Procedure examples to be helpful to "paint the picture" for teams and teachers. We will be using this book as a primary resource during our Assessment, Grading and Reporting policy review process next year. Thank you, Ken!"*

Jennifer Knight DeLashmutt, Director of Curriculum and Professional Learning International School Bangkok

"This book is essential for any teacher, school, or district looking to implement healthier grading practices. Full of simple shifts, A Repair Kit for Grading, *is a quick-reference guide full of easy-to-use concepts. The teacher and school examples get the wheels turning and help anyone take their grading practices to the next level."*

Katie Budrow, Science Teacher, Author of
Moving Beyond Classroom Management, #sblchat moderator.

"The world is changing as must our assessment practices! Ken O'Connor challenges educators to self-assess their views and current assessment procedures. This book is a "why-we-must" as much as it is a "how-to." We already know that students learn more when they know why *they are learning. Ken O'Connor persuades us to consider the same insight and core beliefs of what is best for learners and the eventual integration into the world that awaits them outside school. The connections made between what we teach and how it is of use to students goes so far beyond content, we cannot lose."*

Denine Laberge, High School Math Teacher
Division scolaire franco-manitobaine

"A perfect catalyst for professional dialogue - an ideal anchor text for school and/or district-based study groups to continue and sustain the difficult conversations about the purpose of assessment, and how it can be used to build the competence and confidence of students."

Rosalind Poon, Vice Principal, Richmond School District
British Columbia, Canada

"I loved and was influenced by A Repair Kit for Grading: 15 Fixes for Broken Grades *when it first came out. The "Grade Doctor" continues to push the reader's thinking about how we synthesize grading, marking, and scoring while maintaining a focus on Learning. I always have a copy to give to educators when they ask questions about assessment practices and am thrilled to have an updated version! Great vignettes and examples from educators, schools and districts that were clearly inspired by earlier editions provide a lens into environments that show how these fixes keep the focus on Learning."*

Ian Landy, Principal, School District 47 (Powell River)

"The beauty of this book is the mix of foundational evidence, research and rationales for each of the 15 fixes, the honest and comprehensive arguments for the pundits and the examples of the 15 fixes in practice in schools. Ken provides plenty of resources to guide those educators who are pushing the boundaries in their schools. It is refreshing to see how schools have moved beyond traditional approaches to practices that better support students."

Blair Peterson, Ed.D., Secondary Principal
The International School of Tanganyika

AUTHOR

Ken O'Connor is an independent consultant and author who specializes in issues relating to communicating student achievement, specifically grading and reporting. He is a strong advocate for creating in schools a culture of learning, not a culture of grades.

A graduate of the University of Melbourne (B.A. Hon) and the University of Toronto (M. Ed), he has been a staff development presenter and facilitator in 47 states in the USA, 10 provinces and two territories in Canada, and in 35 countries outside North America.

His twenty-three year teaching career included experience as a geography teacher and department head at 6 schools in Toronto and Melbourne (Grades 7-12).

Ken was a Curriculum Coordinator responsible for Student Assessment and Evaluation and Geography for the Scarborough Board of Education (and then the Toronto District School Board) from March 1990 to June 1999. He also worked (half time) as a consultant on Secondary Assessment at the Ontario Ministry of Education from November 1998 to December 1999.

He is the author of *How to Grade for Learning: Linking Grades to Standards*, Fourth Edition. Corwin, Thousand Oaks, CA, 2018, *The School Leaders Guide to Grading*, Solution Tree, Bloomington, IN, 2013, and *Fifteen Fixes for Broken Grades: A Repair Kit*, Pearson, Toronto, 2012. Articles written by Ken have appeared in the NASSP Bulletin, Educational Leadership and School Administrator.

Ken is husband to Marilyn (they will celebrate their 50th wedding anniversary in May 2022), father to Jeremy (Charlene) and Bronwyn (Rob), his married children and a grandfather to 14-year old twins Elliot and Vivian O'Connor, and 3-year old Emmeline Mason.

Ken is a sports fanatic. His lifelong sport is field hockey; he has been involved in administration, playing, coaching (his teams won two provincial high school championships and three of his players went on to represent Canada in the Olympics), and umpiring, including umpiring men's matches at the 1984 Olympic Games and the 1990 World Cup. More recently he has become an avid pickleball player and a keen golfer. He can often be found watching his favorite teams and sports - the Buffalo Bills in the NFL, Arsenal in the English Premier League, Duke basketball, ATP and WTA tennis, and the Australian Football Leagues for men and women.

Website: oconnorgrading.com
Email: kenoc@aol.com
Twitter: @kenoc7

FOREWORD

I'm not sure of the story's veracity, but it's told often here in Virginia, and it goes like this: The power plant in Norfolk went down one evening, and all power in the area stopped, 'a true emergency. The technicians were called in, and they worked around the clock, but could not figure out how to fix the problem and return power to the electrical grid. So, the plant manager contacted the company in Ohio that built the plant, and that afternoon, one of their experts flew down to Norfolk to see if he could help.

The expert arrived at the plant and walked about a fourth of the way into the plant, followed by plant technicians and supervisors. He stopped suddenly, and stood quietly, listening, tilting his head in different directions, to try to get a sense of things. Suddenly, he marched into a far right corridor, then under subsequent pipe junctions and on through the plant, turning here and there, following a schematic only he could see in his mind's eye.

Finally, at the back of the entire plant, he reached up and inserted a flathead screwdriver into an unmarked screw in the distribution box before him, and he turned it a quarter of a turn. The lights, power, and electricity roared back to life, the city's electrical grid returned to normal. Relieved, the supervisors smiled, shook his hand, took him to dinner, and drove him back to the airport.

A week later, the plant manager received the bill for the expert's service: $5,000. Stunned, the manager called the expert and inquired why the price was so high when all he did was turn a screw a quarter of a turn. The expert replied, "Oh, I'm only charging 5 cents for turning the screw. I'm charging $4,999.95 for knowing which screw to turn."

Knowledge is power.

Power, for educators, is tooled by our ethics, instructional and assessment repertoire, skillful use of cognitive science principles, and professionalism. It is manifest ultimately in robust student achievement among the most diverse of pupils, in the most challenging of times. If knowledge is power, then, through a funky transitive property, knowledge in our education world equals profound student achievement.

This is what we have here in Ken's updated edition of A Repair Kit for Grading: 15 Fixes for Broken Grades, 3rd Edition. The ideas contained herein are about student achievement as each "fix" for a grading challenge furthers our cause: accurate, ethical, equitable grading, which ultimately yields higher student achievement than is obtained via antiquated, and candidly, unethical and ineffective grading practices. Dare we open the toolbox and imagine the power its contents wield? Yes, and with all alacrity!

Particularly potent in this third edition are educator stories (vignettes) of how teachers and leaders were able to use the fixes to respond successfully to grading and reporting challenges. They are, of course, practical, but more importantly, they model principled approaches that yield effective solutions. Many educators read books such as this and look for quick recipes for their grading cookbooks: What does that look like in my physical education class? How do I turn 'almost proficient' into a calculated percentage for the gradebook? How many grades do I have to record each week? What's the highest grade I should allow on a re-do?

When we are principled in grading, however, we move from grades as transactional, coercive tools of ineffective teachers to grades as helpful, accurate communication of student proficiency used by effective teachers to facilitate student growth and achievement. Just as standardized test scores from provincial and state exams can be used punitively or diagnostically (helpfully), grades can be used to create despair, categorize falsely, and undermine learning progress, or they can be used as markers that summarize where students are as of one calendar date, helping to identify success thus far and illuminate the path ahead.

Hope and achievement here are energizing; students commit to learning's cause. A promising school experience is far more demanding of students, and they achieve more than antiquated grading practices provide. Teachers applying uncoverable labels, hiding behind a one-size-fits-all, uniform timeline, using grades as rewards, and diluting the accuracy of grades by including elements in a grade not indicative of the evidence we claim to be reporting via that grade are uninformed, and in some cases, invoking an unprofessional "dodge" from our corporate ethics.

When principled, we see clearly, and we summon the stamina needed to navigate grading mechanics that initially elude us. Without the bigger picture of why we do what we do, i.e., purpose, it's easy to scuttle early efforts and return to the familiar, rationalizing that the system is just too big for one person to alter, and gosh, the way we used to grade wasn't really so bad as to be worth the hard evolution. In this, we sacrifice student learning and thereby, futures, upon the alter of convenience and, perhaps, local politics or collegial peer pressure to conform. Students are counting on us to get it right and struggle through these challenges, however, as meaningful lives, job and adult functionality are at stake, and we are professionals who claim expertise in the craft and science of teaching.

Through these educator stories in this third edition and both his compelling analysis and the wisdom gained from ceaseless work in North America and around the world, Ken provides clear articulation of these stamina-building principles and how to use them to inform our responses to grading dilemmas. These "broken" grades are some of the biggest and most common concerns we encounter in our schools today. In an increasingly anxious world with sometimes conflicting information passing our screens each day, it's a relief to have such a clear, CALM (see chapter 1) compass to guide our next steps. On some days, it's outright Oxygen.

Here, we get the navigational charts for how to report students meeting or not meeting deadlines, how to handle extra credit, academic dishonesty, group projects, missing evidence, zeroes, formative vs summative reports, separating compliance from mastery, grading students against standards instead of each other, measures of central tendency, and using the most recent evidence when reporting. Ken uses a stunning number of real-classroom and district examples, adding practical insights on breaking down standards (outcomes) into learning targets for clear communication of student achievement, reporting character, work habits, career and college readiness skills, and how to address legal concerns in grading.

There is a tendency among experts in educational subjects to be so overly familiar with a topic that they can't understand why others don't see what they see.

It's so obvious and logical, how could you question the premise? Thankfully, Ken avoids that. He sees the hesitant educator's concerns as legitimate and responds to each one with due respect for the educator's professionalism and experience.

This is also one of Ken's deepest dives into motivation. The connection among grading, motivation, engagement, and equity is profoundly compelling. P.E. teacher Josh Ogilvie's story about his grading approach and his student Nina is the stuff that sparks inextinguishable fires in each of us, and whew, Tom Schimmer's reflection (Chapter 4) on zeroes and accountability – wow! Get to the reading of this new edition for the motivation and accountability sections alone. They're worthy of specific faculty discussion this very week.

And hey, I now know the mock Latin phrase, illegitimi non carborundum, which is coming in handy during these stressful times. Look it up or see it used in the pages ahead.

A Repair Kit for Grading: 15 Fixes for Broken Grades, 3rd Edition is not just for teachers and principals. This is the book for school board members, parents, business leaders, state legislators, and other stakeholders who venture into grading waters with their local schools. Reading it gets them up to speed on the modern era of grading, providing the fundamental understandings on which to discuss policy and practice. It's one of the books I'm sending to my own representatives (with an encouraging invitation to read it) in hopes securing ethical and accurate grading policies – and respectful discussion of the challenges we face, not arguments from myth and conspiracy.

Ken is keenly aware of what's happening in schools. With so many connections around the world, he proves his points fully, providing dimension and real-classroom classroom and school applications for all. He possesses the intellect and cogency to help us see ourselves doing the very things he promotes. This isn't a record of others' success so much as it is a road revealed, complete with its pavement markers, guard rails, traffic signs, clear views of the horizon, and a handy GPS. Honestly, it's one of the most helpful DIY education books I've ever read.

Grading dispositions, policies, and practices imbue everything we touch as educators. Deep engagement into their merits transforms pedagogy in wonderful ways, and we are renewed, realizing that we are part of something larger than ourselves. Indeed, in both the quiet moments of interpersonal connection and the louder moments of collective efficacy, it's epic.

So now, read the book, get the knowledge, and turn the screw: Embrace your power!

Rick Wormeli
Author, *Fair Isn't Always Equal*, 2nd Edition
March 2022

DEDICATION

In this third edition, I want to acknowledge the oldest and youngest women in my life.

First and most important, this edition is dedicated to my wife Marilyn who has been my strongest supporter and advocate. Her help and encouragement have made it possible for me to write this and my other books – and to indulge my passion for sports played, officiated, and watched live and on television. About the time the book is published, we will celebrate our fiftieth wedding anniversary and, while I can't understand why anyone would stay with me for fifty years, I just want to publicly say thank you – I couldn't have done it without you.

Next, I want to dedicate this edition to my youngest granddaughter, Emmeline Mason, who turned five on New Year's Eve 2021. Much of Emme's two years of kindergarten has been online, but she continues to show a sense of wonder and joy in her learning. My hope is that this will continue through the rest of her K-12 experience because her teachers know how to do assessment with her, not just to her, and they know how to grade for learning.

As with the previous editions, this book is also dedicated to all those brave teachers who have been pioneers in grading for learning. They know who they are, and they have fixed broken grades.

TABLE OF CONTENTS

FIGURES

EDUCATOR VIGNETTES

Fix 1
Josh Ogilvie, British Columbia

Fix 2
Lindsay Prendergast, Nevada

Fix 3
Brent Brayko, Hong Kong

Fix 4
Garnet Hillman, Illinois

Fix 5
Brian Shaw, Indiana

Fix 6
Ross Cooper, New York

Fix 7
Tanya De Hoog, British Columbia

Fix 8
John Stephens, Prince Edward Island

Fix 9
Shannon Schinkel, British Columbia

Fix 10
Katie White, Saskatchewan

Fix 11
Phil Stringer, British Columbia

Fix 12
Tom Schimmer, British Columbia

Fix 13
Amy Hodgson, Michigan
Leah Braman, Michigan

Fix 14
Becky Peppler, Wisconsin

Fix 15
Erin Beard, Oregon
Kristy Dolha, British Columbia
Janes Mattiace, International

POLICY/PROCEDURE EXAMPLES

Fix 1
Pewaukee High School, Wisconsin
Christel House Academy, Indiana

Fix 2
Prairie Spirit School Division, Saskatchewan

Fix 3
Pittsford Central School District, New York

Fix 4
Minnetonka Public Schools, Minnesota
Thomas Jefferson Middle School, Virginia
Grand Erie District School Board, Ontario

Fix 5
North East School Division, Saskatchewan

Fix 6
Pewaukee High School, Wisconsin

Fix 7
Solon Community School District, Iowa
Christel House Academy, Indiana

Fix 8
El Monte City Schools, California

Fix 9
Hong Kong International School, Hong Kong

Fix 10
Langley School District, British Columbia

Fix 11
Lambton Kent District School Board, Ontario

Fix 12
Urbana City Schools, Ohio

Fix 13
International Schools Group, Saudi Arabia
Winneconne School District, Wisconsin

Fix 14
Shattuck St. Mary's Forest City International School, Malaysia
International School of Kazan, Russia

Fix 15

Seoul Foreign School, South Korea
Rocky View Schools, Alberta
River East Transcona School Division, Manitoba

PREFACE

> The Committee on Grading was called upon to study grading procedures. At first, the task of investigating the literature seemed to be a rather hopeless one. What a mass and a mess it all was! Could order be brought out of such chaos? Could points of agreement among American educators concerning the perplexing grading problem actually be discovered? It was with considerable misgiving and trepidation that the work was finally begun.
>
> *(Middleton, quoted in Guskey, 1996, p. 13)*

This statement—or something similar—probably could have been made in almost any school or district in North America at any time in the last one hundred and twenty years. It was actually made by Warren Middleton in 1933. It can't be said quite as easily in 2021, but it still applies because, although many schools and districts have made considerable progress, grading still remains an aspect of school that is slow to change and poorly done in many schools, especially high schools.

It was with equal "considerable misgiving and trepidation" that I decided to take on this difficult topic in an article for the NASSP Bulletin (O'Connor, 1995). That misgiving continued when I wrote *How to Grade for Learning* (O'Connor, 1999, 2002, 2009, 2018), and continues to this day.

So, why a new edition, and why do I still have "misgiving and trepidation"?

This new edition is necessary because grading is still a "mass and a mess" in many schools. Although teaching has become increasingly standards based and we know more than we ever knew about how people learn, traditional grading practices persist, especially in middle and high schools. These practices often result not only in ineffective communication about student achievement, but may actually harm students and misrepresent their learning. Thus, I still feel the need for this "Repair Kit," in which I identify 15 ways to fix "broken" grades—15 things we should do if we want grades to be effective.

One of the major reasons for writing this edition is the role of standards or learning goals (also called learning outcomes) and the increasing emphasis that the mission of schools is the development of all students as lifelong learners. All American states and Canadian provinces have now had academic content standards for many years. The mandate is that schools are supposed to be standards based for curriculum, instruction, assessment, and grading and reporting, but what I often see, especially in middle and high schools, is some emphasis on standards for curriculum, instruction, and assessment but very little standards-based grading and reporting. My hope is that this book will help schools and teachers develop standards-based grading and reporting practices because such practices can make substantial contributions to improved student learning.

My "big book," *How to Grade for Learning*, is more detailed and more theoretical in its approach and is possibly more appropriate for administrators and curriculum leaders, while the focus of this intentionally much smaller book is on classroom implementation and is probably more appropriate for classroom teachers. The two books therefore complement each other, and my hope is that teachers and administrators will use them together to develop a deeper understanding of the issues in and solutions to concerns about grading. I also am pleased to report that my "misgiving and trepidation" continues to be reduced for four reasons:

1. Over the last ten years consensus about how grades should be determined in standards-based systems has been reached (see especially Feldman, 2019; Guskey, 2015; McTighe & Ferrara, 2021; Rinkema & Williams, 2019; Schimmer, 2016; Wormeli, 2018). An example of this consensus is found in Brookhart et al. (2020) who identified "Eight Essential Principles for Improving Grades," which are as follows:
    1. Clarify purpose (See Chapter 1)

2. Establish (learning) goals (Fix 7)
3. Base grades on a collection of evidence (Fix 10)
4. Reflect current achievement (Fix 14)
5. Use established criteria aligned to targeted learning goals (Fixes 7, 8, 9 and 11)
6. Set conditions for opportunities to learn (Fix 13)
7. Report achievement separately (Fix 1)
8. Use scales with fewer gradations (Fix 8)

2. The ever-increasing number of districts/schools (especially high schools) that are embracing standards-based grading. For example, Matt Townsley indicated that 54% of 195 schools reporting in Iowa indicated full implementation of standards-based grading, and 76 of the 195 schools indicated that they have a plan in place to implement standards-based grading (Townsley, 2019).

3. Many computer grading programs, both those that are part of Student Information Systems and those that stand-alone, are now designed for standards-based grading

4. Online and hybrid learning during the COVID-19 pandemic demonstrated the effectiveness of the standards-based approach to curriculum and instruction and led to greater acceptance of standards-based grading (See Saltzman, 2020)

For the bigger picture of how grading fits into classroom assessment, this book complements the books and videos produced by Rick Stiggins' Assessment Training Institute in Portland, Oregon and the work of Garth Larson's First Educational Resources in Winneconne, Wisconsin, especially the STAGR Center (Standards, Targets, Assessment, Grading and Reporting)

Examples in the text and the Educator Vignettes following each fix show how teachers and schools implement standards-based grading and reporting, how to fix broken grades, and how their use has impacted learning, learners, and teachers. I sincerely thank all those who provided these materials, but I must emphasize that they all should be seen only as examples, not as models.

My hope is that individuals and groups in schools and districts will use this book to help them to reflect on the grading practices they currently use. The description and explanation of each of the 15 Fixes begins and ends with quotations, which are designed to be used to begin or focus appropriate professional dialogue.

I would like to express my appreciation to Rick Stiggins and Steve Chappuis for agreeing that there was a place for the first two editions of this book as well as Garth Larson for enthusiastically supporting the idea and the development of this third edition. I thank Douglas Rife for his assistance in reverting the rights to the book from Pearson Education to me. I would like to thank Mark Bazata (mainly) and Garth Larson and Becky Peppler for the time and effort they put into reviewing drafts of the manuscript and for their many excellent suggestions that have made it a much better book. I would like to thank Mark for also being the copy editor and the designer Dionne Evans for their considerable help in crafting the final product. I must also thank my cover consultants, Becca Lindahl and Katie White, for their helpful suggestions. I would also like to thank those educators who sent me their assessment and grading policy and procedures, many of which are in the book. As the author, I take full responsibility for the ideas in the book, but the final product has been improved immeasurably by the contributions of those listed. I also express my gratitude to the thousands of teachers who have attended my workshops over the last twenty-two years, from whom I have learned so much.

There are many changes in the text of this edition that reflect the new understandings that have occurred in the eleven-plus years since the second edition was written and hopefully make the ideas clearer and more helpful. The major changes in the third edition are as follows:

- The fixes have been reworded so that they start with action verbs indicating what should be done (i.e., do first, don't second).
- The description and explanation of each of the fixes have all been rewritten to some extent with major revisions to fixes 1, 4, 7 and 8.
- All new Educator Vignettes and policy/procedure examples for each fix.
- The references have been updated; I have tried to only use references that are from 2016 or later. The exceptions are references kept due to not being able to find anything recent that is better and/or references from articles or books I consider to be "classics."

- The fixes in procedural language have been added.
- The survey and the rubric for grading practices have been revised, and
- the Discussion Guide has been expanded and is published as a separate document.

I also want to be clear about what this book is *not*:

- It does *not* provide a comprehensive treatment of any of the issues raised; for that, I would refer you to books that are more focused on specific issues. For example, if you want detailed information on self-assessment read White (2022) and Dueck (2021), on equity Feldman (2019), on relationships Wolcott (2019), and on assessment Chappuis and Stiggins (2020), McTighe and Ferrara (2021), and Cooper (2022).
- It is *not* research. I'm a compiler and analyst, not a researcher. I provide examples and evidence from research, but if you want research go to Guskey and Brookhart (2019) and/or Matt Townsley's website (http://mctownsley.net/standards-based-grading/).
- It is *not* "A Repair Kit for Grading After the Pandemic Guidebook." I make some references to what happened and what we learned during and from the pandemic, but I believe that individually and collectively the fixes were needed before the pandemic, during it, and will continue to be needed after the pandemic. The two mantras frequently heard during pandemic schooling "Grace before grades" and "Do no harm" are at the heart of the fixes and should always be in the forefront of teachers' thoughts and actions.

Ken O'Connor
Scarborough, Ontario, Canada
and The Villages, FL
March, 2022

CHAPTER 1
SETTING THE STAGE

School is indeed a kind of game, but it is a terrible game, with broken engagement and reward structures. Students are motivated to get good grades, but not to learn.

Professor Barry Fishman in the Introduction to the 50th Anniversary edition of Wad-ja-get?: The Grading Game in American Education (Kirschenbaum et al., 1971, 2021, xxiii)

Every state in the United States, every province in Canada, and almost every jurisdiction in most other countries has now had educational content standards for a number of years—public, published statements of the expected outcomes of learning; that is, what students are expected to know, understand, and be able to do. The primary goal of a standards-based system is for all students to "meet standards," or to be competent or proficient in every aspect of the curriculum. The key to reaching this goal is to evaluate every student's achievement using similar criteria, consistently applied at all levels.

The two essential questions that all educators should ask about their grades are,

1. How confident am I that the grades students receive in my classroom/school/district are consistent, accurate, learning-focused, meaningful, and (CALM)? and
2. How confident are we that we align what we believe (Purpose and Principles) with what we do (Policy, Procedures, and Practices)?

In many schools/districts, the answers to these questions twenty-six years after I first developed guidelines for grading, especially at the middle and high school levels, still range from "not very" to "not at all." Because of this, I believe that, very often, grades are "broken" and that teachers and schools/districts need a "repair kit." I offer such a kit here in the form of 15 Fixes that teachers and administrators alike can apply to repair broken traditional grading systems.

Caitlin Tucker (2020) identified these problems with traditional grades:

Traditional grades

- do not reflect mastery of grade level skills;
- are used like carrots to get students to complete "work" (practice and/or evidence of learning);
- place the focus on the product, not the process;
- do not clearly align grades entered into the grade book with specific skills;
- do not provide an incentive to revisit and improve graded "work" (evidence of learning);
- do not require students to *think* about their learning; and
- happen *to* students.

(Tucker provides a "deeper look" into each of these problems on pages 3–8.)

It is important to acknowledge that teachers who continue to use broken grading practices (as I did when I was a classroom teacher for 23 years) are not knowingly using broken practices— they are doing what was done to them, or they are following the advice of mentors who also don't know better. Now, however, we do know better, and as Carol Commodore said on Twitter on August 1st, 2014,

> "What we know now doesn't make yesterday wrong, it makes tomorrow better."

Another reason why we must abandon traditional grading practices is provided by this statement from Professor Christopher Dede of the Harvard Graduate School of Education:

> "The most dangerous experiment we can conduct with our children is to keep schooling the same at a time when every other aspect of our society is dramatically changing."

This was originally in a written statement by Professor Dede to the PCST (Public

Communication of Science and Technology) Panel in 1997, but it is even more relevant now as the pace of societal change and our knowledge base about how children learn and how to use assessment to improve learning has increased so dramatically over the intervening 20 plus years while so many aspects of "schooling," especially grading, have remained the same.

The COVID-19 pandemic that has impacted schools in so many ways has also provided us with a reason and an opportunity to examine and question traditional practices. As Jay McTighe said in a personal communication in the summer of 2021,

> "The aftermath of times of crisis inevitably offers an opportunity to step back and re-examine all facets of life, and it is thus an opportune time to scrutinize our current educational system."

CALM Grading

As the first "essential question" indicates, effective grades need to meet four overarching criteria for, or keys to, effectiveness: they must be consistent, accurate, learning-focused, and meaningful (CALM). Each of these keys is defined here and then woven into each of the 15 Fixes throughout the rest of this book. I believe that most teachers, students, and parents would agree that these are reasonable and necessary expectations and that it is therefore reasonable for administrators to mandate the basic principle of each fix while reaching agreements with educators and other stakeholders about the 'how,' the 'how much,' and the 'when' to implement each fix.

Grades need to be *consistent* across teachers. The grades students receive should not be a function of whether they are in teacher X's or teacher Y's class. The question "How good is good enough?" needs to be the same from classroom to classroom; that is, performance standards must be the same from teacher to teacher. Students achieving at the same level should receive the same grade regardless of context. This clearly is not the case in schools where some teachers are identified as "hard", and others are labeled as an "easy A." This should never be acceptable. To "fix" grades, especially in standards-based systems, it is essential that all teachers in every school teaching the same grade or same subject/course should determine grades in similar ways and apply similar— or the same—performance standards. This consistency in the meaning of grades should be systemic at all levels—school, district, and, ideally, state/province.

Grades need to be *accurate* reflections of student achievement. Inaccurate grades lead to poor decisions being made by and about any student whose grades are used as the basis of those decisions. When determining grades, many teachers continue the traditional practice of combining a large amount of evidence/data into a single summary symbol. This may involve literally hundreds of decisions; if even one is wrong, the grade inaccurately reflects student achievement. Inaccurate grades most commonly result from teachers determining them by blending achievement with behaviors (e.g., effort, participation, adherence to class rules—Fix 1), poor-quality assessment (Fix 10), and inappropriate use of the mean (average) in combining data (Fix 11). For grades to be *accurate*, each of these practices and others, discussed in Fixes 2, 3, 4, 5, 6, 9, & 12 needs to be eliminated.

The assessment and grading process needs to be *learning-focused*. Students and parents need to understand that achieving in school is not only about compliance/completion or accumulating points. When teachers assign a point value to simply turning in evidence of learning or put a mark or number on everything students do, the message sent to students is clear: success lies in the quantity of points earned. Any intended message about valuing the quality of the learning is blurred. We want students to understand that school is about learning.

Grades are also learning focused when the purpose of each assessment is clear. Formative assessments are designed to help students improve, and in almost all cases, should not be used to determine grades. This allows students to perceive learning as a process that takes time and struggle and in which they have risk-free opportunities to learn from their mistakes. Summative assessments are designed to measure student achievement and are used to determine student learning status at a point in time. With some limited exceptions, only evidence from summative assessments should be used when determining grades (Fix 13). We also must allow new evidence to replace old evidence when it is clear that a student knows or can do something today that they didn't or couldn't previously (Fix 14). Finally, and perhaps most importantly, for grades to be learning focused, students must be involved in assessment and grading (Fix 15).

Grades need to be *meaningful*. They must communicate useful information to students and to everyone interested in or needing to know about their learning. Traditionally, teachers have collected evidence using various assessment methods and have organized their grade books by type of evidence such as tests, projects, and assignments. Thus, the grading link to learning outcomes has been tentative at best. The "fix" needed for grades to be *meaningful* is that they must directly reflect specified learning goals. This requires that teachers set up and organize their grade books around those goals or standards and do not simply summarize multiple marks into a single grade or organize grades by the date administered, type of assignment or activity, or type of test by using the standards or some organizational structure arising from or related to the standards (Fix 7). The evidence categories for Mathematics, for example, may include "develops and uses number strategies," "compares and orders whole numbers to 100," and "uses estimation strategies." The evidence structure for English may use strands such as reading, writing, listening, speaking, language, and literature

Words Matter

For this book to be useful, the reader must understand my intended meaning. For clarity right from the start, I provide the following definitions and ideas:

Mark/Score/Grade

Mark/ Score: the number or letter placed on any single student assessment (test or performance) to indicate the quality of achievement demonstrated.

Grade: the symbol (number or letter) reported at the end of a period of time as a summary statement of student performance.

(N.B., this is different from the definition provided by Brookhart (2016) in which she states, "Grading refers to the symbols assigned to individual pieces of student "work" OR to composite measures of student performance on student report cards" [Emphasis added]). As these are completely different processes, I think we communicate more clearly if we distinguish between them with my definitions above.)

Learning activities/Evidence of learning, not "work"

This is what students do/provide; they don't *work* or submit *work*, they participate in learning activities and they provide evidence of learning through formal and informal assessments. Throughout the book, I attempt to be consistent with never using "work" in my writing, as I would like to see it eliminated from the vocabulary of education. "Work" will, however, appear in quotes from other writers, usually with what I believe to be the more appropriate word choices in parentheses (i.e., "learning activities" or "evidence of learning").

Standards = Learning Goals = Outcomes = Expectations = Competencies

I realize fine distinctions between these terms are made by some educators, but I use them interchangeably.

Assessment/Evaluation

Assessment is now commonly used to include both the gathering/describing (assessment) and making judgments (evaluation) of/about student achievement, although it is important to note that the two components are fundamentally different and there was a time not very long ago when both words were always used. For example, when I was reappointed as a Coordinator in the Curriculum department in my school district in 1997, my title was "Coordinator of Assessment and Evaluation"; if the same position existed today, the title would almost certainly just be "Coordinator of Assessment."

Policy/Procedures

Policy: broad statements of general intent that require school/district Board approval. For example, "Grades shall be consistent, accurate, learning-focused and meaningful."

Procedures: administrative regulations that specify what employees are required to do; they don't require Board approval, so they can be changed by administrators. The specifics of how teachers are to determine grades are often called "Policies" but generally are more accurately labeled as "Procedures." For example, teachers often share their grading practices with students and parents and are labeled as "Mr. O'Connor's Grading Policy" when they should be identified as Procedures. It is important to note that procedures must be consistent with state/provincial, and district/school policies.

What We Believe

Purpose(s) for Grades

Purpose is critical in everything we do because it is—or should be—our compass or rudder steering us to our desired destination. If we have any difficulty in deciding what to do to reach our destination, we should go back to purpose. Traditionally, grades have served a number of purposes—communication, providing information for student self-assessment, sorting and selecting, motivation and punishment, and teaching/program evaluation. As Schneider (2020) pointed out,

> "A-F grades serve several different purposes, and those purposes are too often in conflict with one another."

He goes on to say the following:

> "Letter grades do several different things, none of them well, and the result undermines student learning. . . Our present use of grades is the result of historical accident, not design. The result is that grades fail to advance the multiple purposes they ostensibly serve."

For example, for communicating effectively in a standards-based environment where the objective is all students succeeding, we need to communicate the highest possible achievement in the narrowest possible range. For the sorting and selecting purpose, however, these same students need to be spread along the widest possible range, ranking some high and some low. These two purposes are clearly in conflict, but the problem is solved when we identify primary and secondary purposes for grades. McTighe and Ferrara (2021) stated,

> "the primary purpose . . . of grades [is] to communicate student achievement based on clearly articulated learning goals and established criteria."

This requires that the other purposes for grades—providing information for student self-assessment, sorting and selecting, motivation and punishment, and teaching/program evaluation—to be seen as secondary purposes.

A central premise of this book is that, in agreement with McTighe and Ferrara, the primary purpose of grades is communication about achievement, with achievement being defined as performance on learning outcomes measured against accepted performance standards. I believe that at the district and school levels there must be a shared vision of the primary purpose of grades and that it must be public and published so that it is understood by all stakeholders. I accept that a school/district may choose a primary purpose different from mine, but it is critical that it be available to anchor any dialogue and decisions about grading practices.

Principles

Principles are the values that orient us as individuals or as organizations and drive what we do every day. School and district principles are stated in mission and vision statements. When I visit school websites, I find that the first thing that comes up is often the mission statement, and when I visit schools in person, I frequently see the mission statement on a wall in the entrance foyer or the main office. When I start to discuss current assessment and grading practices in the school, however, misalignment with the mission statement is often clear. Mission statements need to be more than nice words on a wall or on a website. For example, this is the mission statement of a school district in New Jersey:

> The mission of the Township of Franklin Public Schools is to *develop the unique potential* of *each individual student* and *create global learners* through a *challenging and diverse curriculum* in a *positive learning climate* that promotes the *development of the whole child* and fosters *respect for all students*.

There are no italics in the original, but I have italicized words for emphasis. Each italicized word or phrase has implications for what schools in that district do in curriculum, instruction, assessment, grading, and reporting. For example, with the emphasis on *developing* the "unique potential of each student," students should receive lots of descriptive feedback, and there should be not even the slightest suggestion of using the bell curve.

What We Do

Practice(s)

There are three areas of teachers practice that have had a huge impact on how teachers have approached grading and how they have determined grades. They are fairness/equity, motivation, and professional judgment.

Fairness/Equity

> The term "equity" refers to fairness and justice and is distinguished from equality: Whereas equality means providing the same to all, equity means recognizing that we do not all start from the same place and must acknowledge and make adjustments to imbalances. The process is ongoing, requiring us to identify and overcome intentional and unintentional barriers arising from bias or systemic structures.
>
> (National Association of Colleges and Employers)

This description of equity is powerfully illustrated in this graphic:

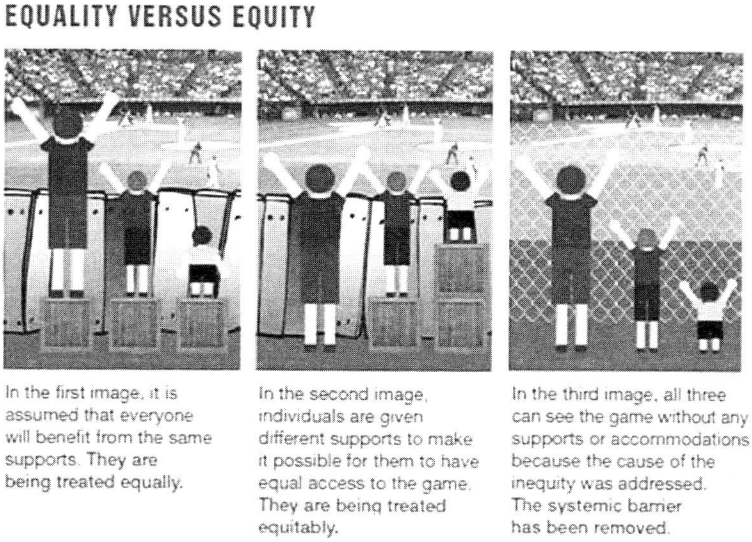

Figure 0.1. Equality vs. Equity
Permission provided by City for All Women Initiative (CAWI), Ottawa.

In education, we have tended to think of fairness as equality. All students have been required to do the same assessments in the same amount of time, and their grades have been calculated in the same way from the same number of assessments. But students are different in many different ways, and so treating them the same can actually be unfair. As the description and graphic above illustrate, fairness is much more about equal opportunity than it is about equality. For example, some students need to wear glasses, and for equal opportunity they wear their glasses when they need them. For fairness we do not say, "You are doing a test today, but you cannot wear your glasses because everyone is not wearing glasses" or "Some students in this class need glasses, so you will all wear them" (whether you need them or not).

The leader in promoting equity in grading is Joe Feldman. His book, *Grading for Equity* (Feldman, 2019), is a must read for all educators. He states the following:

> Our grading practices must promote the best and most aspirational thinking of what each of our students are capable of as learners, *regardless of their race, their first language, their family's income, or their previous educational experiences.* [Emphasis added]
>
> (p. 65)

This points us to the third panel in Figure 0.1 – equity isn't just about equal opportunity; it is also about the removal of systemic barriers. Feldman expands that basic principle when he says,

> We want our grading to
>
> - be truthful, dignifying our students by telling them exactly where they are academically and what they need to be successful
> - interrupt the structures and patterns that have made high achievement of some student groups, and the underachievement of other groups predictable. . .
> - continue to facilitate the success of those student populations who have been relatively well-served
> - specifically support those groups that have been historically undeserved and therefore have underperformed in our schools; students of color, students of low income, English learners, and students with special needs. (pp. 65-66)

To achieve the equity in grading that is described in this list, Feldman identifies accuracy, bias-resistant, and motivational as the three pillars for equitable grading. I believe those pillars are provided for in the fifteen fixes as indicated below:

ACCURATE

- not "omnibus" (*Fix 1*)
- mathematically correct and sound (*Fixes 11 and 12*)

BIAS-RESISTANT

- practices that give all students the opportunity to succeed regardless of circumstance (*Fixes 2, 3, 4, 5, 6, 9*)
- resistant to biases based on student's race, gender, family income, first language, or special needs (*Fix 10*)

MOTIVATIONAL

- practices that orient students to the value of learning rather than point collecting (*Fixes 7 and 8*)
- practices that support a growth mindset, encouraging students to take risks and to recognize the value of prolonged practicing and mistakes (*Fixes 13, 14 and 15*)

Perhaps one of the most telling examples of inequity in grading practices is the inclusion of homework in grades. This became particularly clear during the COVID-19 pandemic when teachers were able to more clearly observe the difficulties faced by some students who were the caregivers for younger children, had to work to support for their family, didn't have a space or the resources to complete homework, or didn't have an adult to help them. These difficulties existed before the pandemic and will continue after the pandemic, so for equity, it is essential that teachers not include homework in grades.

Another aspect of inequitable grading practices that must be addressed is the variability of teachers' grading practices that often occurs within one school and even between teachers at the same grade level or teaching the same course. This variability means that grades are often a game of chance that further disadvantages marginalized students. To overcome this variability, schools and districts must develop and insist on consistent implementation of school/district grading procedures that are required of all teachers. Joshua Starr captured this in his article in the May 2021 *Kappan* titled "Too much autonomy can mean too little equity," in which he said the following:

> Let's face it, pursuing equity in K-12 education can also be hard work. It requires constant attention, like tending a campfire that keeps burning through logs. Staff need to question old assumptions

> and embrace new priorities. Teachers need to learn new skills and be held accountable to new goals. Resources need to be reallocated. Students and families need to be kept informed and engaged. Given such complex and ongoing challenges – not to mention pushback from angry parents and, perhaps resistant teachers and staff – it's easy to see why a principal would give up on the district's equity agenda and retreat to the comfort of the status quo.

Starr was referring to a district's overall equity agenda, but what he said particularly applies to equity in grading procedures because of teacher, student, and parent sensitivities to changes in grading practices. It is for this reason that equity in grading requires that administrators take a hands-on approach to supporting and supervising teachers' grading procedures.

This book is primarily about grading and secondarily about assessment, both of which require planning and are part of the larger plans for instruction and learning. It is therefore also important to acknowledge that those larger plans must also consider and provide equity. In the past, those plans have often prescribed the same learning pathways for all students: "Every student is expected to read the same book at the same pace, listen to the same lectures, and complete the same math problems using the same materials" (Novak, 2021). However, as Novak points out, "When we design the same learning pathways for all learners, we might tell ourselves we are being fair, but in fact, single pathways are exclusionary." So, how can or should we plan differently? Novak stated,

> Luckily, there is a framework that rejects these one-size-fits-all solutions and empowers educators to proactively design learning experiences so all students can increase their brainpower and accelerate and own their learning. The framework is **Universal Design for Learning** (UDL). UDL is a framework for designing learning experiences so students have options for how they learn, what materials they use, and how they demonstrate their learning. When implemented with a lens of equity, the framework has the potential to eliminate opportunity gaps that exclude many learners, especially those who have been historically marginalized. If we want all students to have equal opportunities to learn, we have

> to be incredibly purposeful, proactive, and flexible. UDL creates a learning environment that is the least restrictive and most culturally responsive, trauma-informed environment for all students.

This isn't the place for detailed information about UDL, but to improve equity in our schools, it is a very worthwhile framework. Teachers should read Meyer et al. (2014) and Jung (2021) and consider using Katie Novak's (2021) UDL Flowchart (https://www.novakeducation.com/hubfs/Resources/UDL_FlowChart.pdf)

Motivation

Grades are often used as extrinsic motivators, meaning that their power to influence student behavior derives from outside the student. Many teachers—and parents, grandparents, and other adults—have used grades as extrinsic motivators ("Everyone who gets an A on this quiz can skip the next homework assignment"; "Get a B or better on that test or you can't go to the concert"). But as Klein (2020) stated,

> There is little to no evidence or research that proves that grades make students learn more or work harder in school. In fact, there is ample evidence that grades actually do the opposite: they hurt academic motivation and inhibit learning.

Many schools and school districts have mission or belief statements that state their desire to develop students who are "self-directed, lifelong learners." To achieve this goal, students need to be intrinsically motivated, meaning that their desire to achieve and improve must arise from within themselves. Intrinsic motivation conflicts with the use of grades as extrinsic motivators. Anderson (2021) put it this way: "if you want students to be motivated from within, you need to stop trying to motivate them from without" (p. 24). Thus, as we think about our current and future grading practices, it is important that we examine and apply our knowledge and beliefs about what does and does not motivate students.

The research on motivation shows that continued use of extrinsic motivators leads to two main results. First, extrinsic motivators increase students' focus on the reward or punishment rather than on the desired behavior. Second, they give rise to the need to continuously increase the amount of the reward or punishment to elicit the desired behavior (Kohn, 1993). Thus, it is inappropriate to use grades as extrinsic motivators, either to reward desirable behavior or to punish undesirable behavior. The primary "reward" for learning should be intrinsic—the positive feelings that result from success. Actual success at learning, then, is the single most important factor in intrinsic motivation, and it is important to recognize that success is relative—success for each individual is seeing oneself improving.

Daniel Pink (2009), the renowned author of best-selling business books, mainly does two things in his classic book *Drive: The Surprising Truth About What Motivates Us*: he summarizes modern psychological research on motivation and describes the motivational practices of innovative companies, but he also provides an eleven-page section of "Tips for Parents and Educators." In that section, he says a number of things that educators (and parents) need to think deeply about. Consider the following:

> "All kids start out as self-directed Type Is" (intrinsically motivated).
>
> "But many of them end up as disengaged, compliant Type Xs" (reliant on extrinsic motivation).
>
> "We need to break Motivation 2.0's (extrinsic motivation) grip on education and parenting."
>
> "There is a mismatch between what science knows and what schools (and parents) do."
>
> "We're bribing students into compliance instead of challenging them into engagement."
>
> (Pink, 2009, p. 174)

These powerful statements lead to the conclusion that teachers and parents must recognize the following:

> "Type I behavior is made, not born" (p. 78);
>
> "Type I's almost always outperform Type Xs in the long run" (p. 79);
>
> "Type I behavior does not disdain money or recognition" (p. 79);
>
> "Type I behavior is renewable resource" (p. 80);
>
> "Type I behavior promotes greater physical and mental well-being" (p.

> 80) and finally,
>
> "Ultimately, Type I behavior depends on three nutrients: autonomy, mastery and purpose" (p. 80).

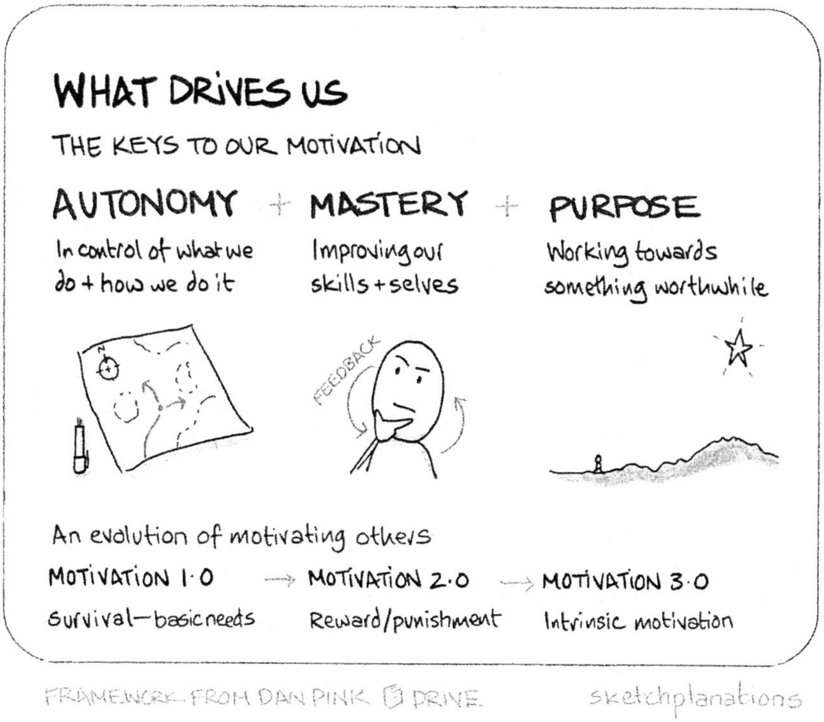

Figure 0.2. Daniel Pink's Three Keys to Intrinsic Motivation
Permission provided by Jono Hey

Teachers must know how to provide the three nutrients or keys to intrinsic motivation shown in Figure 0.2. Students are granted autonomy when they are provided with real choices about what they learn, how they learn, and how they show evidence of learning. Autonomy leads to engagement, which Pink says is critical for mastery. Mastery for Pink is not, however, necessarily achieving at high levels, but is witnessing improvement within oneself. This means students have to know what better is, both the what and the how well (Fixes 7 and 8), and they have to be able to self-assess and use feedback effectively (Fixes 13 and 15). The third key is purpose, which requires that students understand the significance and value of what they are learning and doing. The best classroom practices are based on these three keys and thus maximize intrinsic motivation and minimize extrinsic motivation. Teachers in these classrooms help students to the critical understanding that "30 years from now, it won't matter what grades you got. What will matter is what you learned and how you used it" (Poster seen on the wall of a high school cafeteria in Council Bluffs, IA).

Professional Judgment

> Teachers' professional judgments are at the heart of effective assessment, evaluation and reporting of student achievement. (Ontario Ministry of Education, 2010, p. 8)

This statement rightly acknowledges that teachers are professionals who have craft knowledge that they use to make judgments about student achievement. There are, however, two problems with this. First, teachers often say that they are striving to be objective (or "more objective") in their assessment and grading, but that is impossible because, although some of the things they assess are objective—namely facts, spelling, and calculation—assessment is a subjective process. Teachers create assessments based on their professional judgment of what is to be assessed and how, which is a subjective process. We need to acknowledge this and not apologize. As Wiggins (1997) noted,

> All scoring by human judges, including assigning points and taking them off math homework is subjective. The question is not whether it is subjective, but whether it is defensible and credible. The Advanced Placement and International Baccalaureate assessments are subjective and yet credible and defensible, for example. So-called objective scoring is still subjective test writing.

Thus, the real issues are accuracy and consistency, not objectivity versus subjectivity. We need to develop approaches to help teachers both assess and grade more accurately and consistently so that the subjective judgments they make may be credible and defensible. One key to accomplishing this is shared understanding of performance standards— agreement on "how good is good enough?" Another is educators use of words. For example, they should stop using subjective pejoratively and stop saying they are trying to be objective.

The second problem is that some teachers, sometimes supported by their union leaders, insist that professional judgment is each teacher 'doing their own thing,' which simply isn't the case. One of the defining characteristics of being a professional is that, because of their great responsibilities, professionals are subject to ethical constraints and core values specific to their profession. Thus, this definition by Cooper (2011) brilliantly captures what professional judgment is for educators:

> "decisions made by educators, in light of experience, and with reference to shared public standards and established policies and guidelines" (Cooper, 2011, p. 13).

The "shared public standards" and "established policies and guidelines" come from state/provincial, district, and school policies and procedures, and teachers are required by professional ethics to adhere to those policies and procedures. What is needed is a set of guidelines such as the 15 Fixes this book provides. Making these fixes part of district or school policy, providing teachers frequent opportunities both for professional learning and dialogue about these guidelines, and carrying out shared marking to arrive at a common understanding of performance standards will greatly enhance the probability of consistent grading across teachers and classrooms. The time has come to be clear that teachers are not independent contractors— grading must not be a private practice; it must be a shared practice based on public, published procedures.

It is essential that schools/districts align what they do (i.e., policy, procedures, and practices) with what they believe (i.e., principles and purpose). For example, if a district has in its mission/vision that it will provide "A learning environment and professional culture of caring and support," it must have procedures requiring multiple opportunities for students to demonstrate their achievement on standards (including reassessment, when appropriate) and support, not penalties for students who have difficulty in meeting timelines. Further, all teachers must provide the multiple opportunities and support because these are "established policies and guidelines." This was reinforced by Dwyer and Hiscock (2019) who put it this way:

> If you truly want to change the learning environment for students, your grading policies must align with your goals. If your goals include actual student growth, higher-order thinking, self-reflection, goal-setting and perseverance, a traditional grading system is not adequate. (p. 125)

In Fix 11, I recommend that grades for standards should be determined by mode + more recent + professional judgment. It is important to recognize that this honors the professionalism of teachers, which is taken away when grades are simply the product of calculations done by a computer grading program.

What We Know

We know that for schools to achieve their mission in this 21st century when our goal is success for all, we have to create in our schools a culture of learning, not a culture of grading. To do that, we need to follow an order of operations that we have always known is absolutely necessary but perhaps had become somewhat forgotten until the needs became so great during the first few months of pandemic schooling in 2020. That order of operations is as follows:

- Basic needs
- Relationships
- Learning
- Engagement and Equity
- Feedback
- Grades

Children can't learn if their *basic needs* for food and shelter aren't met. Thus, we must attend to those needs first. Then we have to look after *relationships*, especially those between teachers and students. Wolcott (2019) wrote, "The answer to student success won't be found in a box... The answer to success is right in front of us...looking up at us each day with hopeful eyes" (p. 2). And that answer is positive teacher-student relationships. He further states that, These relationships lead to greater academic outcomes, including marked improvement in the areas of reading, math, student participation, student motivation, critical thinking ability, and engagement. (pp. 2-3) Next comes *learning*, or clarity about the what and the how well, and teachers and students knowing how we learn. Clarity about the what and how well is addressed in Fixes 7 and 8. Judy Willis (2018), a neurologist and a teacher, stated,

> Understanding the neuroscience of how their brains learn, and what influences its most successful acquisition and application

> of learning, is a powerful tool for helping students confront the increasing demands of school. This knowledge also better equips students, parents, and educators to recognize applications and implications from the rapidly expanding research. Further, these insights can enhance students' effectiveness, creativity, and enjoyment of learning.

One example that illustrates this is provided by Tomlinson and Sousa (2020) who describe how the pairing of neuroscience and psychology offers new insights into the principles of effective instruction. They wrote,

> "Studies in neuroscience reveal the strong influence past learning has on the acquisition of new learning" so " the more teachers can do to connect new learning to students' past learning, the greater the chance students will understand and remember that new knowledge." (p. 17)

Successful learning/achievement for all requires *engagement and equity*; engagement will occur when we maximize intrinsic motivation, and equity will be greater when we recognize that is about equal opportunity and the removal of systemic barriers, not equality (see sections above on motivation and fairness/equity).

Feedback is what helps any learner, young or old, improve when it is descriptive, not evaluative. Nobody gets better if they get 7/10 on an assessment, but if they get two stars and a wish, they have the information that can propel them to greater learning (see Fix 13).

And last in the order of operations comes *grades*. As this book is about how to grade effectively, I'm not diminishing the significance of grades by placing them last in the order of operations; I'm simply recognizing that students can learn well and teachers can teach well without grades. Having said that, for the foreseeable future in most schools—especially high schools—grades aren't going to disappear. Thus, we need to ensure that they are effective in meeting their primary purpose of communicating student achievement, meaning grades have to be CALM: Consistent, Accurate, Learning-focused, and Meaningful (see Figure 0.4).

What we know makes grading reform critical, but be warned it isn't easy. Zerwin

(2020) revealed this when she wrote,

> The grading system seems too pervasive, too embedded in the required grade books and official records that come out of our classrooms. It seems risky to go against what most of our colleagues are doing. We worry about our classrooms. Will everything fall apart if remove the center that students have become accustomed to? What if they stop doing anything at all without the usual reward of points for grades? (p. 12)

Non illegitimi carborundum.

Student Involvement

It has become increasingly clear that student involvement in learning, assessment, grading, and communication can make significant contributions to improved achievement and positive attitudes about learning/school. This issue is so significant that I incorporate suggestions about it into all of the Fixes. Fix 15 is a synthesis and summary of these ideas as presented throughout the rest of the book with some additional information.

There is nothing more important than helping students become confident learners. . . In the end nothing else that we do in school really matters.

- Ferriter, 2021b

The 15 Fixes

The 15 Fixes are organized into four categories—fixes so that grades are about achievement only, fixes for evidence, fixes for grade determination, and fixes to focus on learning.

FIXES FOR PRACTICES THAT DISTORT ACHIEVEMENT

Fix 1 Include only achievement; don't include student behaviors in grades.

Fix 2 Support learners to meet timelines; don't reduce marks on late assessments.

Fix 3 Use only evidence of achievement; don't provide extra credit or use bonus points.

Fix 4 Apply behavioral consequences and reassess when academic dishonesty occurs; don't reduce marks.

Fix 5 Report absences separately; don't consider attendance in grade determination.

Fix 6 Use individual achievement evidence; don't include group scores in grades.

FIXES FOR LOW QUALITY OR POORLY ORGANIZED EVIDENCE

Fix 7 Organize and report evidence by standards/learning goals or targets; don't organize by assessment methods or report a single subject grade.

Fix 8 Provide clear descriptions of proficiency levels; don't assign grades using inappropriate or unclear performance standards.

Fix 9 Compare each student's performance to preset standards; don't assign grades based on student comparisons.

Fix 10 Use evidence from high quality assessments; don't use evidence from low quality assessments.

FIXES FOR INAPPROPRIATE GRADE DETERMINATION

Fix 11 Consider several measures of central tendency and use professional judgment; don't rely only on the mean.

Fix 12 Use incomplete or insufficient evidence and reassess when evidence is missing; don't include zeros in grade determination.

FIXES TO SUPPORT LEARNING

Fix 13 Use evidence primarily from evaluative assessments to determine grades; don't use evidence from formative assessments.

Fix 14 Emphasize more recent achievement; don't just summarize evidence accumulated over time.

Fix 15 Involve students; don't leave students out of the assessment and grading process.

Figure 0.3. The 15 Fixes

CALM Grading

Consistent – Fix 8
Accurate – Fixes 1, 2, 3, 4, 5, 6, 9, 10, 11 and 12
Learning-focused – Fixes 13, 14 and 15
Meaningful – Fix 7

Figure 0.4. CALM Grading and the 15 Fixes

CHAPTER 2

FIXES FOR PRACTICES THAT DISTORT ACHIEVEMENT

Fix 1 Include only achievement; don't include student behaviors in grades.

> Any summative assessments of habits of success should be separate from grading of academic competencies. The longstanding, traditional practice of raising or lowering academic grades based on behavior, participation, or perceived effort leads to the serious problem of students and families being unable to judge their academic progress accurately.
>
> *(Levine, 2021, p. 23)*

The primary purpose of grades is—or should be—to communicate achievement. Thus, grades are broken if they include a mixture of achievement and behaviors. The fix for this is to make grades as pure a measure as possible of student achievement; that is, make them reflect only student performance in mastering the public, published learning goals of the state/province/district/school, and report separately on valued behaviors. This is the only way that grades can act as clear communication. Everyone who has a need to know about a student's performance in school certainly can be told that she/he is "a nice student who tries hard" or is "a pleasure to teach," but they also have a right to know the specific level of her/his achievement level on each standard at a given point in time.

The grading practices required by schools/districts have contributed to grade inflation for some students by including desired behaviors unrelated to achievement, while other students who achieve at a high level have received deflated grades because of their failure to exhibit these same behaviors. For example, consider this example that would be typical for many American high schools:

> **Participation Grade** – A daily participation grade may be given in a class. Students with an excused absence must be given the opportunity to make up their participation grade. The classroom teacher will determine what make up is acceptable. Students with unexcused absences, truancies, or those who choose to not make up participation points, will lose their daily participation grade.

Teachers combine achievement and other variables, such as behavior, into grades for several reasons. One is the belief that this practice appropriately rewards students who are well behaved and punishes those who do not behave as required. When combined in this way, grades are used as extrinsic motivators to control student behavior. A second reason, particularly prevalent at the high school level, is that teachers have had no way to communicate separately about the behaviors they think are important, so they have blended them together with achievement. The solution for this faulty communication is to use standards-based expanded format report cards where the desirable behaviors are listed and evaluated. In my experience, this has become common at the elementary level and is becoming more common for middle schools but is not yet as widespread a practice as it should be in high school reporting. This is somewhat ironic because it is only at the high school level that grades serve high-stakes purposes (e.g., scholarships, college admissions, rank in class, athletic eligibility). Therefore, high schools especially should depict achievement as accurately as possible to ensure good decisions

When a school/district decides to report behaviors separately there are several aspects on which decisions need to be made. These aspects include:

- How many?
- What?
- Description/explanation,
- Performance standards
- Who reports - overall or by subject?

How many? To some extent, this will depend on the "what" and how that is decided; like so many aspects of grading and reporting, however, I think "less is more." It is best practice to choose three to six behaviors that are highly valued by all stakeholders rather than a long list of all the valued behaviors.

What? There needs to be a very clear sense of what behaviors and attitudes are really valued by the school/district/community. One approach is to use the student attributes identified in mission or vision statements. For example, an international school in Asia had this mission statement:

> The International School . . . is a community that is committed to excellence. We inspire students with a challenging, international education, based on an American curriculum, in a *nurturing learning environment* that promotes *responsibility* and *respect*. We aim to develop *socially engaged, self-motivated, creative, compassionate* individuals who will be a force for positive change in their communities and the world.

With this mission statement, it should be easy for stakeholders to agree that the behaviors reported separately would be responsibility, respect, social engagement, self-motivation, creativity, and compassion. Another approach for schools/districts that have developed a "Portrait of Graduate" (i.e., the attitudes and skills that students will need to be successful beyond high school), would be to include information about each student's demonstration of those attitudes and skills on the report card. As an example, Fairfax County, Virginia identifies these characteristics in its Portrait of a Graduate: Communicator, Collaborator, Ethical and Global Citizen, Creative and Critical Thinker, and Goal-directed and Resilient Individual (Fairfax County Public Schools, n.d.).

Another good example of the "what" is provided by the provincial report cards in Manitoba that identify three categories of "Learning Behaviors"—Personal Management Skills, Active Participation in Learning, and Social Responsibility—which allow schools/districts to add up to two local options (Manitoba Education, 2021, p. 34).

There are many other approaches to the "What." British Columbia and Yukon identify three "Core Competencies": Communication, Thinking, and Personal and

Social Awareness and Responsibility (British Columbia Ministry of Education, n.d.). Some schools use the 21st Century Skills developed by the Partnership for 21st Century Learning (Partnership for 21st Century Skills, 2012 pp. 3-4) while others utilize the sixteen Habits of Mind developed by Art Costa and Bena Kallick (The Institute for Habits of Mind, n.d.). Comprehensive coverage of a large number of approaches to the "what" is found in Eliot Levine's (2021) *Habits of Success* (pp. 8 - 12).

Description/Explanation. It isn't sufficient to simply have the titles and categories for behaviors; description or explanation in considerable detail of the components of each category is necessary so that there is consistency in teacher interpretation and assessment of the behaviors, and so that students and parents understand what is included in, for example, Manitoba's three categories of Learning Behaviors: Personal Management Skills, Active Participation in Learning, and Social Responsibility. The Manitoba Ministry of Education provides this explanation through the following descriptors and lists of indicators:

> **PERSONAL MANAGEMENT SKILLS**
>
> The student self-monitors their own behaviours and personal growth, Organizes for learning, contributes positively to the learning process, and takes responsibility for work completion.
>
> - organizes materials (e.g., study notes)
> - uses class time productively
> - works independently
> - completes homework and assignments on time
> - persists when faced with challenges
> - seeks help when needed
> - demonstrates a strong work ethic
> - shows patience
> - makes a consistent effort
> - demonstrates on-task behaviours
> - sets personal management goals and monitors growth

ACTIVE PARTICIPATION IN LEARNING

The student participates actively in learning, is curious, sets learning goals, self-assesses, provides feedback, and uses feedback for improvement.

- shows interest; asks questions
- takes initiative
- is curious—investigates questions, hypothesizes, estimates, analyzes
- self-assesses work quality based on quality criteria
- uses descriptive feedback to improve learning
- uses criteria to provide descriptive feedback
- explores themes and enriches topics through interest-based learning
- uses a variety of media for communications

SOCIAL RESPONSIBILITY

The student demonstrates citizenship and social skills that contribute to making the classroom, school, and larger community a positive, safe and caring environment.

- works and interacts well with others
- is welcoming and positive
- shares resources, materials, and equipment with others
- respects classroom and school values and routines
- responds positively to the values and traditions of others
- respects self, others, and the environment
- shows empathy and compassion
- contributes to making the community a better place
- takes initiative and leadership in community service
- works for a sustainable planet
- takes an equitable share of work in a group
- is courteous
- respects the need for safety for self and others – physical and emotional

(Manitoba Education, 2021, p. 36)

These Learning Behaviors are reported on for grades 1 to 12 so schools/districts can choose the indicators that apply by grade level.

Performance Standards

Performance standards can describe quality or quantity and can be used for behaviors, but it is generally recommended that frequency descriptors like Almost Always, Frequently, Sometimes, and Rarely should be used for behaviors.

Who reports?

Commonly for elementary schools, the behaviors are reported on once by the core teacher, which is the teacher who sees them for most of the day. High school reporting of behaviors is almost always done on a subject-by-subject basis, and middle schools are truly in the middle— in some it is done once, while in others it is done for each subject. Depending on the extent to which students are on a rotary timetable, it is usually better for it to be done for each subject.

One of the best examples of this type of reporting is from the American School of Bombay shown below in Figure 1.1.

American School of Bombay

High School Semester Report Card 2019-2020

Student Name: **Grade:** 10 **Date:**

Course: World History 2 **S1** **S2** **Teacher:**

Criteria	S1	S2
Developing Questions and Planning Inquiries	EX	EX
Applying Disciplinary Concepts and Tools	GD	EX
Evaluating Sources and Using Evidence	GD	GD
Communicating Conclusions and Taking Informed Actions	EX	GD

ATLs	S1	S2
Managing Complexity	NA	C
Collaboration and Social Skills	C	NA
Critical Thinking	C	NA
Creative and Innovative Thinking	NA	S

Teacher Comment: Semester 2

Course: Chemistry 2 **S1** **S2** **Teacher:**

Criteria	S1	S2
Knowledge and Understanding		EX
Application of concepts and methodologies		EX
Analysis and Evaluation		EX

ATLs	S1	S2
Managing Complexity		C
Collaboration and Social Skills		C
Critical Thinking		C
Creative and Innovative Thinking		C

Teacher Comment: Semester 2

Figure 1.1. American School of Bombay High School Report Card

Permission provided by the American School of Bombay

Further, an excellent example of clearly articulated behaviors is provided in Figure 1.2 below.

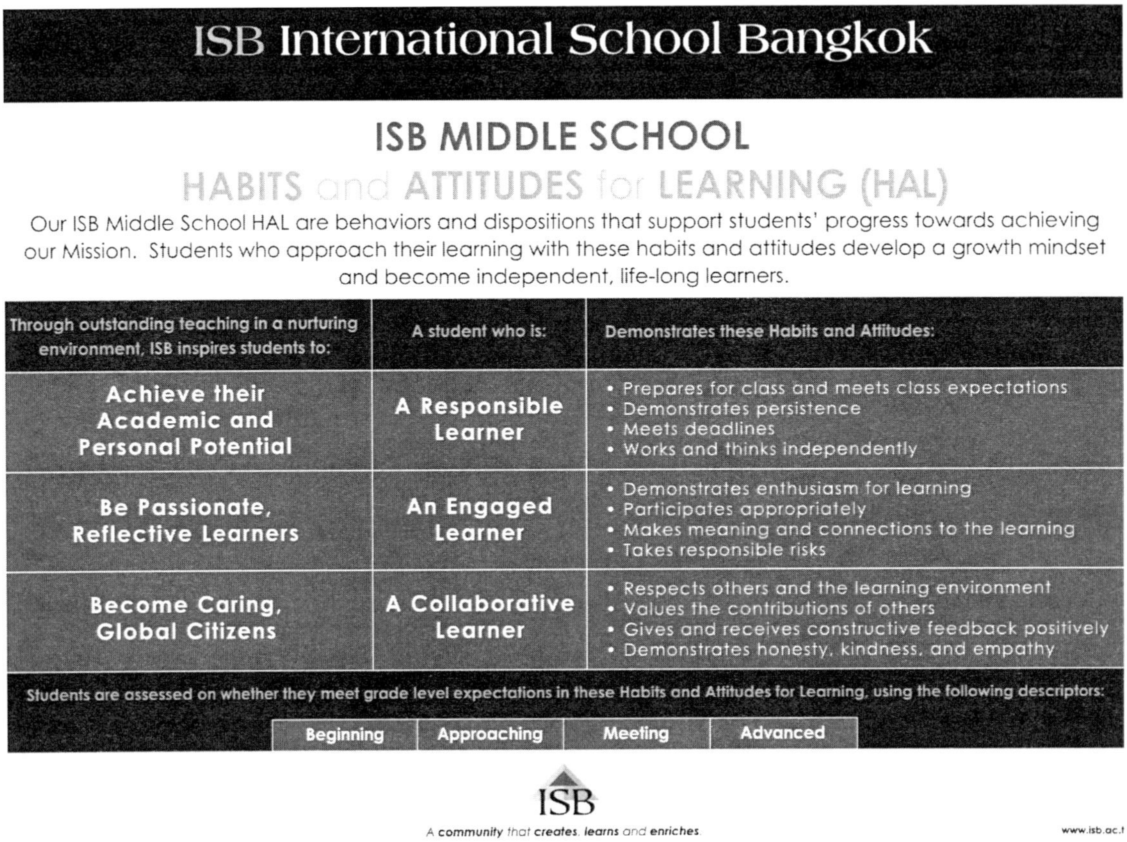

ISB International School Bangkok

ISB MIDDLE SCHOOL

HABITS and ATTITUDES for LEARNING (HAL)

Our ISB Middle School HAL are behaviors and dispositions that support students' progress towards achieving our Mission. Students who approach their learning with these habits and attitudes develop a growth mindset and become independent, life-long learners.

Through outstanding teaching in a nurturing environment, ISB inspires students to:	A student who is:	Demonstrates these Habits and Attitudes:
Achieve their Academic and Personal Potential	A Responsible Learner	• Prepares for class and meets class expectations • Demonstrates persistence • Meets deadlines • Works and thinks independently
Be Passionate, Reflective Learners	An Engaged Learner	• Demonstrates enthusiasm for learning • Participates appropriately • Makes meaning and connections to the learning • Takes responsible risks
Become Caring, Global Citizens	A Collaborative Learner	• Respects others and the learning environment • Values the contributions of others • Gives and receives constructive feedback positively • Demonstrates honesty, kindness, and empathy

Students are assessed on whether they meet grade level expectations in these Habits and Attitudes for Learning, using the following descriptors:

Beginning	Approaching	Meeting	Advanced

ISB

A community that creates, learns and enriches

www.isb.ac.t

Figure 1.2. International School of Bangkok Habits of Learning (HAL)
Permission provided by the International School of Bangkok

As you read and think about Fix 1, keep in mind that it is the "big idea," and Fixes 2-6 are subsets of the larger issue of separating behaviors from achievement. They each address specific behaviors that lead to inflated or deflated student grades, both inaccurate measures of achievement.

Legal Issues (USA)

Educators must also think about whether grading policy/procedures are legally sound. According to Link and Kauffman (2021) in the *School Administrator*, "courts expect schools to ensure that students receive a *fair* grade" (p. 46). They further stated,

> While having a written grading policy is important, simply having one doesn't guarantee courts will side with school districts. In fact,

> the recent trend signals that courts are more willing to rule on cases with less deference to the policies of school officials, especially when policies are deemed unfairly applied. (p. 46)

This is especially true when behavior is conflated with achievement grades. In several cases, judges have ruled that reducing grades for disciplinary reasons (i.e., consuming alcohol off-campus and being suspended) is unacceptable because it results in "misrepresentation of academic achievement." Courts have been clear that non-academic factors such as attendance are unacceptable in the determination of grades because they have taken "grade accuracy to mean the *extent to which it permits someone to estimate the extent of a student's knowledge and skills in a given area* (Link & Kauffman, 2021, p. 47). This means that inflating and deflating students' grades by including behavioral factors as a percentage of grades is legally unacceptable as it results in a misrepresentation of achievement. Students must also be provided with due process; according to Link and Kauffman (2021), this means that

> "grading policies be accurately communicated to students and their parents in advance, that a grievance procedure for grades be in place and conducted fairly and consistently, and that grading policies are reasonable and have a *valid academic focus*" [Emphasis added] (p. 48).

Link and Kauffman concluded their article with this advice:

> "By understanding the impact that court decisions have had on school grading policies and practices, school leaders will save potential legal expenses and avoid entanglements that come with parent school conflict (p.48)

Additional useful information about grading and the law, especially as it relates to special education, can be found in Freedman (2020).

Student Involvement

Students benefit from frequent opportunities to identify both the behaviors that help and those that hinder their achievement. They also can self-assess their achievement and behaviors and set goals for both. In furtherance of this, teachers can identify the components of desired behaviors and help students to develop specific goals. For example, students often hear that they "need to improve their effort," but effort is a vague concept. To help clarify this concept for students, teachers can identify the components of effort, such as persistence, striving for accuracy, time on task, and trying alternate methods, which students may then focus on to identify their relative strengths and weaknesses.

As educators, our beliefs and practices about motivation will greatly impact students. Students who have a sense of control because they know they can make choices, and who receive frequent descriptive feedback instead of rewards and punishment linked to their behaviors, are much more likely to exhibit the desired behaviors and to value the separation of achievement and behavior.

Summary

Grades are broken when they include a mix of achievement and non-achievement elements. The fix is to report variables such as behaviors separately from achievement, thereby ensuring that the grades reflect student achievement as accurately as possible.

> "Grades are not and have never been a valid measure of academic achievement. Rather, they are a multidimensional assessment of both academic achievement (cognitive factors) and substantive engagement in the schooling process (non-cognitive/conative factors)."
>
> *(Bowers in Guskey and Brookhart (Eds) 2019. p. 44)*

Educator Vignette

Josh Ogilvie
Physical and Health Education Department Head and teacher,
Burnaby South Secondary School,
Burnaby, British Columbia

In my career as a physical education teacher and a department head, I have noticed a common perception of physical education being a class where students go to *do* something, but not necessarily to *learn* something. One way this notion is reinforced is when work habits, or learning behaviors, are included in the assessment and grading practices used to communicate student learning achievement. By including this information, students receive a distorted grade that combines academic and non-academic factors creating uncertainty about how successful they were in their learning and/or how they might have grown as learners. As a result, a focus on learning is lost, and the act of doing receives more attention, further perpetuating the belief that physical education is about doing, not learning.

To help shift this perspective in my classes, I developed a physical education report card and personal learning chart to use with students throughout the year that outlines the intended learning standards for the class, charting individual progress and achievement, a separate section on their work habits, and information related to grading purposes. We use the report card and learning chart throughout the year to discuss and reflect on how they are progressing in their learning, how their work habits can support them, and how this information is used during grading and reporting time.

When it is time to determine a grade, I meet with students individually and we consider the most recent and/or consistent evidence of learning achievement recorded on their learning chart to determine their grade. We transfer this agreed upon information onto their physical education report card, as well as in my gradebook, which is also used for grading and reporting purposes for the school report card. Additionally, students use their work habits to reflect on and discuss how they influenced their learning, and what areas, if any, they could improve upon with a plan to do so.

Separating student learning achievement from work habits has helped students to gain clarity regarding what they are learning and how successful they are in it. It has also helped them develop a deeper understanding of how work habits influence their learning experiences and how they as learners can grow in these areas, too. Collectively, these practices have helped them to realize that learning is a focus and does happen in physical education class, and that their grades are based on what they have been able to achieve in their learning.

The processes I used to separate academic achievement from student behaviors in the grading process are easily replicated in all subject areas. I've used this approach with human anatomy and physiology classes, sports science classes, and with learning support classes. A key step to remember is to be clear and transparent regarding the intended learning standards as well as supportive work habits for the class. Separating these from each other makes it easier to understand how students are progressing, and eventually achieving, and what supports, if any, can help them make improvements.

Nina: *"I didn't think I could ever be good at PE"*

Since I began using the PE report card and the personal learning chart, and by separating academic achievement and work habits, I have seen a wide range of positive impacts on students and their learning. A particular example that stands of a dramatic impact is with a Grade 10 student named Nina (this is not their real name).

> Nina was a student who indicated that she never had a positive experience in her previous PE classes and that she was looking forward to it being over so that she never had to take a PE class again (in British Columbia, PE classes are optional after Grade 10). Through further discussion, Nina mentioned that she felt embarrassed, ashamed, incompetent, and could never keep up with her peers in PE class, leading her to simply give up trying at anything. When I asked what takeaways she had from her previous classes, or what she had learned prior to our class, her response was, "*nothing.*"
>
> As the term went on, and the entire class learned about the assessment and grading processes we used in class, including the separation of work habits from their level of academic achievement, I noticed Nina's demeanor and body language shift in class. Like everyone in the class, she received ongoing feedback (from me, herself, and her peers) on her progress in learning as well as her work habits. At first, Nina was reluctant to receive any feedback, and when she began to hear and see strengths being associated with her learning and work habits, she became more energized and focused in class and became more open to using feedback to guide her efforts. Nina began to understand her strengths and areas for growth in both her learning and her work habits, and this helped to create clarity and understanding for her regarding where she was and how to move forward in each area.

When it came time to determine grades for the first report card, I met with Nina to talk about her progress in the class and how we would form a grade for both her learning achievement and her work habits. Nina sat across from me with a disheartened look and said, "*I know, I'm not doing well.*" I asked her to bring out her personal learning chart so we could discuss how she was doing in class. Nina looked at her personal learning chart, then at me, and then again at her chart, seemingly in disbelief that she was indeed performing quite well with her learning and with her work habits. She had a hard time to form a full sentence at this realization, and then she said with a high level of enthusiasm, "*I didn't think I could ever be good at PE.*"

For Nina, having a clear understanding of her learning and work habits helped her to understand how they are connected and how they are different. Nina benefitted from receiving separate feedback on these specific areas, as it allowed her to challenge her pre-conceived notions of who she was in a PE class and what she was capable of. It wasn't until the first report card that she was able to fully understand this, and when she did, it was a transformative experience for her. Throughout the rest of the year, Nina excelled even more in the PE class, taking on leadership roles in the class that she likely never thought of before. Also, Nina chose to take a PE class in her Grade 11 year and plans to do so in her grade 12 year, too. She cited this experience as the turning point for her in strengthening her self-esteem, self-efficacy, and an enjoyment of being physically active.

Nina shared these revelations with me at the end of her Grade 10 year. For her, knowing how she was progressing with her learning separate from her work habits really helped shift her perception of herself. She felt her previous experiences in PE class reflected who she was as a person and as a student, and she was ready to give up. I remember her saying that separating learning from work habits was something so simple, yet had such a profound impact on her, and that she wished this was more common is school. To Nina, "*It just makes sense.*"

Pewaukee High School
Pewaukee, Wisconsin

GUIDELINE 9: Separate grades will be given for academic and non-academic (Success Skills) proficiency.

- Non-academic factors will not be included in academic grading.
- Teachers will monitor and report student Success Skills each term. (Pewaukee High School, 2015, p. 9)

Christel House Academy
Indianapolis, Indiana

Academic and non-academic achievement are scored and reported separately. Non-academic achievement, such as citizenship and behavior, are scored and reported using the CHOW (Character and Habits of Work) Targets (Christel House Academy, 2018, p. 5).

Fix 2 Support learners to meet timelines; don't reduce marks on late submission of assessments.

> My relationship to deadlines, like that of almost everyone I know, is full of contradictions. I crave them and avoid them, depend on them and resent them. . . . The time-sensitive obligations that add both structure and suspense to our lives . . . can inspire nauseating dread as much as plucky action.
>
> *(Syme, 2021)*

Syme captures accurately the relationship of students to time deadlines; some students depend on them, some resent them, and some suffer incapacitating dread while others are pushed to "plucky action." The issue that teachers face, then, is what to do that will most likely result in students meeting timelines, and what is educationally appropriate when some students inevitably don't meet timelines for submitting assessments.

Let's start with what *not* to do. Traditionally, we have used penalties such as a reduction of one letter grade or of several points for each day a required piece of assessment evidence is late. Penalties distort the achievement record the grade is intended to communicate, may harm student motivation, and for many students, do not result in changes in behavior. The fix is to not use penalties but to set up support systems that reduce or eliminate the problem of late submission.

Many teachers believe that they need procedures with penalties to ensure that students turn in assessment evidence on time so the teacher can maintain the pace of instruction necessary to meet tight curricular requirements. Many also use penalties because they believe that it communicates fairness to students: everybody receives the same amount of time. There are, however, at least four problems with this practice. First, and most damaging, is that they distort the grade's representation of the student's true achievement. Second, they can motivate exactly the opposite behavior than what was intended. At some point in the grade reduction scenario, accumulating penalties leads students to conclude that it no longer makes sense to complete that assessment. If it is an important piece of assessment evidence, it is better that the student submits it late than not at all. Third, my own classroom teaching experience along with anecdotal evidence from many teachers leads me to conclude that penalties don't work because they do not change behavior—the same student who is late with required evidence in week 2 is frequently late in weeks 18 and 36. Similarly, Dueck (2014) suggested four CARE guidelines that must be met before late penalties are applied as follows:

> Care: The student must *care* about the consequences of the penalty.
>
> Aims: The results of the penalty must complement my overall *aims* as a teacher.
>
> Reduction: The penalty must result in a *reduction* of the negative behavior.
>
> Empowerment: The student must feel *empowered* regarding the actions for which he or she is being penalized. (p. 6)

Fourth, having absolute deadlines (and penalties) for everything does not prepare students for the world beyond school. In the "real world," timelines are frequently negotiated (i.e., real estate, legal matters) or adjusted to circumstances (i.e., contractors and consultants); deadlines range from fixed to considerably flexible (Ironically, "You can't deliver 'work' late in the real world" is the very reason some teachers tell students they have the requirement!). We prepare students better for that world when we offer a variety of deadlines in school; learning that is part of an instructional sequence may need to be done tonight for tomorrow, but timelines for long-term assignments should be framed more flexibly.

Furthermore, if adults in the world beyond school are not able to meet a timeline, we often can communicate with the person/institution to whom we are responsible, arrange a new mutually agreeable timeline, and then work to meet it. This is the responsible, adult behavior that we need to encourage in students, and we do this by allowing them to request extensions. This is preferable to students "hiding in the back corner," as they often do when they have late or missing assessment evidence. If we want students to be responsible and timely, then we can teach them and help them along the way, rather than assume they will learn the lessons through punitive policies.

What policies and procedures are most likely to get them to learn as much as possible and exhibit the desired behaviors? Teachers should not condone or ignore lateness in submitting required evidence. Teachers should keep records of students' timeliness and report on this behavior in expanded format report cards. They also can assign consequences as they would for any other unacceptable classroom behavior. Direct parent contact may also be necessary, especially if the lateness is chronic. Students who are late with important assessment evidence should at first be invited to come in before school, at lunchtime, or after school where they will receive both the assistance and time they need. Then, if they don't respond to the invitation, they should be required to attend. This is like the approach suggested by those who use Response to Intervention (RtI) in which the "pyramid of interventions" to help students succeed moves from "limited and voluntary" to "significant and compulsory." One high school in Georgia made this time from 4 PM to 6 PM on Friday afternoons and, while I'm not recommending this time frame, they found that after students attended only once there was no repetition of late submission.

In the final analysis, how we approach late submission depends on our beliefs about our role as educators. In this regard, I think a very helpful way to think about this is provided by seeing the teacher's role as a "warm demander." Matt Alexander (2016) citing Lisa Delpit (the originator of the concept) says,

> "Warm demanders are teachers who expect a great deal of their students, convince them of their own brilliance, and help them to reach their potential in a disciplined and structured environment."

In other words, once teachers have created a safe, caring, supportive culture in their classroom they can—and should—have high expectations for student behavior and academic achievement. Alexander suggests a four-part framework for how to become a warm demander:

1. Belief in the impossible.
2. Build trust.
3. Teach self-discipline, and
4. Embrace failure.

The consequences for submitting required assessment evidence late should be as positive and supportive as possible, although some "negative" consequences may be warranted for repeated or chronic lateness. Supportive approaches do not distort achievement or motivation and more closely mirror practices in the world beyond school. Support should also include identifying at the beginning of the school year students who are organizationally challenged and providing them with assistance and structure in assignments.

It is important to recognize that support must be a collaborative action by all faculty, so whether the support time is before school, during the day, or after school, it must be a shared responsibility so that there isn't an unreasonable burden on individual teachers. Partly for that reason, and partly because of the message it sends to students about the school having a 'success for all' orientation, I think the best way to provide support for students who have difficulty submitting evidence on time is to have a support period in the timetable at least several times each week. This is becoming increasingly common, and there are many examples of this approach (see O'Connor, 2018, pp. 110-113)

One example of providing regular support time is the Advisory program at Lake Braddock Secondary School in Burke, Virginia. Advisory is structured time built into the school day to "develop meaningful connections with students and address the social and emotional learning needs of students." The school timetable has four periods each day with periods 1, 3, 5 and 7 on Purple Day and periods 2, 4, 6, and 8 on Gold Day. Advisory take places during period 4 and has been split into 2 parts: Advisory and WIN (What Individuals Need) time. The bell schedule for the high school for Gold Day is as follows:

Period 2	8.00 - 9.28
Break	9.28 - 9.43
Period 4	9.43 - 10.30 WIN
	10.30 - 11.09 Advisory
Break	11.09 – 11.16
Period 6	11.16 – 1.12 includes lunch
Break	1.12- 1.19
Period 8	1.19 - 2.45

Advisory time is used for lessons from Project Wayfinder, from the county school system, and from Lake Braddock curriculum writing teams. Students move up with their Advisory teacher from seventh to twelfth grade. WIN time is for academic support/intervention and enrichment. Students get WIN passes from the teacher they want to see or are requested to see. Students are required to report to their Advisory teacher with their WIN pass, and then they proceed to the classroom of the teacher who issued the WIN pass. More specifically, WIN time is used for students to complete late and missed assignments, retake assessments, or to engage in intervention or enrichment opportunities. The school sees WIN time as "an opportunity for all students to become a goal-directed and resilient individual, an opportunity to increase student autonomy and self-efficacy, and to create a community of more effective independent learners."

Providing support time every second day sends a clear message that the school wants students to learn and be successful. David Wickham, a social studies teacher at Lake Braddock, says that it provides an amazing opportunity to build strong relationships with a group of students over several years, and that it is a great safety net for students.

Some teachers (and parents) will see the emphasis on support and communication suggested here as too "soft," but they are wrong. Insisting that students submit important assessment evidence even when it is "late" is "hard," not "soft." In a brilliant blog responding to those who support penalties, Bill Ferriter (2021a) makes it clear that "students who struggle with 'work' behaviors continue to struggle, no matter how many point consequences you assign" (p. 6) and that,

> Once you know the reasons kids are struggling with 'work' completion, you can develop systematic schoolwide interventions . . . (and) classroom practices that are responsive to the realities that some of our students wrestle with day in and day out. (p. 6)

The principle that should be applied to late submission is to separate achievement from behavior and communicate both to those who have a right to know about the student. For example, if Rory is a brilliant writer who always hands assignments in late, both aspects are hidden if she gets a C or a D for Writing. But if she gets an A and the report says, "Brilliant writer, but always late," then we have accurate information. A daily newspaper or an advertising agency may not want to employ Rory, but she may be perfect to write features in a monthly magazine or as a novelist or playwright.

Student Involvement

Students should have input into decisions about timelines for required assessment evidence: when they have input, they have ownership, and ownership leads to meeting timelines. This is attested to Siobhan Buckman, a middle and high school drama and theater teacher, who stated,

> I find that giving students authentic ways in which they can feel in control goes a long way to shifting the dynamic in the room. . . How due dates are agreed upon can be a starting point. I find that when I model authentic negotiation, students don't abuse the system - their ownership of the timeline places them at the center, and negates any need to dodge a due date, or panic over the 'work'. . . In my classroom, this approach has consistently led to higher quality 'work,' fewer missed due dates, and increased motivation. (Gonser, 2021)

If a student is not able to meet a timeline, the teacher should not use mark penalties, but should encourage the student to acknowledge the lateness and request an extension and/or suggest other appropriate consequences.

Summary

Penalties distort achievement and motivation and, in my experience, are generally ineffective. The fix for late student submission of assessments is a positive, supportive approach that directly affects student behavior, leaving the scores and the resulting grades as pure measures of achievement.

> – When we encounter a student who cannot read, we teach that student to read
> – When we encounter a student who struggles in math, we teach that student math
> – When we encounter a student who does not behave, we punish that student.
>
> *(Fisher & Frey, 2019, p. 84)*

Educator Vignette

Lindsay Prendergast
Former Secondary School Principal
School Improvement Coach, NWEA
Portland, OR

The crucial practices that facilitate a successful, embedded implementation of a policy to eliminate point-deductions for missed deadlines at the secondary level, like much of our work as leaders, require both proactive and responsive actions. Some of these actions take the form of procedures to ensure fidelity to Fix #2, while others are applied in daily decision-making and support culture shift beyond just words in a handbook, as these examples describe.

In two schools where I have worked as an administrator, adopting a policy of not deducting points for late submissions of student learning sets the stage for countless conversations around our vision for student learning and contributes to substantial improvement to both teaching and learning. Simply put, Fix #2 can support the systemic improvement of many critical practices beyond only grading.

Providing support for students to meet deadlines must extend beyond verbal encouragement, so adjusting time structures is often a necessity. In a high school in Colorado, when we endeavored to increase the rigor and academic demands of our courses, we determined we could not simply ask more of the students without creating support structures as well. This led to the creation of biweekly Supplemental Studies periods wherein students visited teachers for assistance, reassessment, or reteaching opportunities. When I was Principal of an international school, we established thirty minutes after school every day as a designated reinforcement opportunity. Teachers could require students to attend but, over time, and in conjunction with other broader shifts in grading practices, student perception began to change that the reinforcement time was an opportunity. "I have to go" became "I need to go" as we moved away from a penalty system for not learning and towards a common understanding that the learning was non-negotiable.

At the high school in Colorado, there were pre-existing policies that allowed for point deduction on late assignments, and we still had a chronic issue with students not completing learning activities. Our leadership team also observed a troubling dynamic developing amongst teachers. Students who frequently submitted work after deadlines, or not at all, had become the targets of stereotypes such as lazy, disorganized, or apathetic, and teacher behavior towards them could not be characterized as supportive. As Dr. Devin Price (2021) suggests in her book, *Laziness Does Not Exist,* "for many of us, our first instinct is generally to blame a person for their own misfortune, especially if we can pin that misfortune on laziness," so we were moving further away from our goal of learning for all students and remaining in a cycle of blame and punishment. After initiating a larger shift towards grading for learning, including the elimination of deducting points for late work, our staff underwent an inventory across departments of what was being asked of students inside and outside the classroom and examined hidden root causes of behaviors such as missing deadlines (i.e., organization skills, anxiety, uncertainty, too many activities) that would go on to become a framework of areas we could proactively address. We articulated the goal that the teacher and student (and parent, where appropriate) should work together to identify the root cause of the behavior; thus, teachers began including a form on late assignments which immediately opened up opportunities for targeted support:

With late work, students will attach responses to the following questions:

I turned my work in after the deadline - oops! The reason this happened (I think) is because:

Check all that apply:

____ *I didn't quite understand what to do*

____ *I got busy and just forgot!*

____ *Personal events kept me from being able to work on it*

____ *Something else (add details here if willing)*

[Optional add-on]: My guardian(s) know(s) that I missed this deadline:
___*Yes* ___*No*

Though this is simple in nature, the subsequent conversations held with students after teachers received this form yielded constructive actions rather than useless penalties. A collaborative decision could then be made to determine next steps: reinforcement time, a review of their organizational strategies, or even a one-on-one conversation about something affecting their life. The lasting impact of decisions such as providing time and space for students to receive support in the school day and creating opportunities to understand the root cause of behaviors such as missing deadlines or not completing work exemplified an enhanced focus on learning by both teachers and students. When the adults overcame their deep-rooted beliefs in using points as carrots and sticks, the students quickly adapted and, in both schools, significant improvements were made on overall learning outcomes.

Policy/Procedure Example

Prairie Spirit School Division
Warman, Saskatchewan, Canada

ADMINISTRATIVE PROCEDURES

AP-414 Assessment

l) Late "work"

i) Penalties that affect grades (removing marks because of a submission timeline) will not be applied.

ii) Teachers will put supports in place for students to complete and hand in work on time. Student refusal or inability to complete work (lack of evidence of learning) is a behavior problem that should be addressed through interventions and non-academic consequences. (Prairie Spirit School Division, 2020, p. 5)

Fix 3 Use only evidence of achievement; don't provide extra credit or use bonus points.

> Somewhere today students are receiving extra credit in Mathematics for contributing boxes of tissues to the classroom supply, for cleaning up the chemistry lab, for turning off their cell phones in English, and for bringing cans of green beans to history class in support of the school's food drive.
>
> *(Westerberg, 2016. p. 17)*

WARNING: This fix is for those countries and cultures where the use of extra credit and/or bonus points/questions are common practice.

Extra credit (points for doing things that have nothing to do with the learning goals) and bonus points can distort a student's record of achievement. Grades are broken as a communication tool if we give points for actions like those listed in the introductory quote as these actions do not demonstrate achievement of specific academic standards. The fix for this is to eliminate the of use extra credit or bonus points. If students want to receive a higher grade, teachers should require them to provide "extra" evidence that demonstrates a higher level of achievement.

Over the years, I have heard of an amazing array of extra credit activities including cleaning blackboards, bringing in classroom supplies, supplying food for the food drive, or bringing a Mexican dish for Spanish class. My favorite story was from someone who said her high school Physics teacher believed, very appropriately, in students identifying examples of physics in the "real world." He provided them with a "worksheet" with six questions, and for each worksheet they completed, one percent was added to their grade. Her final grade in Physics was 91 percent and she did 60 extra credit sheets! It is interesting to speculate on her level of physics knowledge. One high school Science department even had an "Extra Credit Counter" (like a counter or merchandise display in a store) for each course on the school's website.

I have also heard many stories about the availability of bonus points on tests and exams and, in some instances, students finish with grades of 110 percent! The main problem with bonus points is that the questions for bonus points are frequently the conceptual or higher order thinking questions that enable teachers to tell the difference between students who are proficient and those who are excelling. These questions should not be a matter of choice; all students should attempt them so that teachers have the evidence they need to make that critical distinction. Another problem with bonus points is that can hide weaknesses. One of my grandchildren received 28 out of 25 on a Grade 4 math test and she was appropriately pleased and proud; closer examination, however, revealed that she received the ten points for the bonus questions, but she got all three questions on one math concept wrong. Wormeli (2018) supported this view of bonus points:

> If a student falters in her demonstration of mastery with the regular test items, but overcomes those scoring losses with points from a bonus section, then we have to reconsider whether the new, bonus-inflated grade really represents what the student knows and is able to do. This is especially problematic if the bonus questions or prompts are unrelated to the test's topic, such as the spurious bonus questions used by some teachers: "What's Mr. Terwilliger's favorite sport?" "What famous person died on this day in 1939?" "What was the score of last night's Orioles game?" Or "Who's buried in Grant's tomb?" (p. 200)

The basic problem with weaving extra credit and bonus points into a grade when they reflect something other than the expected learning is that they distort the record of achievement. Extra credit and bonus points stem from the belief that school is about doing the "work," accumulating points, and that quantity is the key—with more being better—rather than about achieving higher levels of learning. In standards-based systems, though, the main issue should be having enough quality evidence to accurately determine each student's achievement. Extra credit and bonus points come from a culture that emphasizes extrinsic motivation. As with other non-achievement factors that find their way into the grade, they have frequently been used to manage student behavior.

Students should, of course, be able to provide additional evidence of their understanding, knowledge, and/or skill. However, this additional evidence must reveal new or deeper learning and should be considered along with the previous evidence to determine the student's level of achievement. For example, if previous evidence was a mixture of the achievement levels of "proficient" and "approaching proficiency" and a student's additional evidence was all "proficient," this would allow the teacher to justify assigning this student a final achievement level of "proficient" with the appropriate letter grade (see Fix 8 for more on levels of achievement and performance standards).

The shift in thinking is illustrated in the following example. Imagine that a student receives the following scores for a series of tests and assignments:

5/10, 66/100, 39/50, 27/35, 37/50, 8/10, 15/20, 20/25, 8/10, 75/90

The total would be 300/400, and if the grade were calculated as a mean in the traditional way, the grade would be 75 percent, which, in most schools/districts, would be a grade of C. The student then completes three extra credit assignments (which may or may not be in any way related to the learning goals) for which he receives scores of 14/20, 7/10, and 3/5. The total is now recorded as 324/400 (although it is really 324/435) with a mean of 81 percent, so the student receives a final grade of B, which is an inflated grade.

Now imagine that a different student has a teacher who is truly standards based; this teacher records scores as proficiency levels, with 3 as proficient (meets the standard). The scores this student receives on a series of tests and assignments are 1, 2, 2, 1, 2, 2, 2, 2, 3, and 3. The mean, median, and mode for these scores are the same—2—so this student would normally receive a grade of C. The teacher, however, notes that the two more recent scores are 3s, so they ask the student to provide extra evidence on specific learning goals to confirm that this is now her level of achievement. The student receives 3, 4, and 3, which shows she is now proficient, so her final grade is a well-deserved B.

Student Involvement

Through self-assessment and teacher communication, students can acquire a clear sense of their level of achievement. If it is less than proficient, or lower than they (or their parents) are willing to accept, teachers can offer students opportunities to provide additional evidence. It must be clear that this will not result merely in points being added to a total. If students can show that they now know, understand, or can perform at a higher level, their grade must reflect this. At minimum, students should be partners in identifying appropriate evidence of additional learning, providing suggestions about what they will do to show a higher level of achievement. For some, it may be a traditional test; for others, it will be a product. For others, still, it will be a performance or a personal communication such as an interview or oral exam. If they have participated appropriately in student-involved assessment, they will make the right choice(s).

Summary

Grades are broken when teachers provide extra credit or bonus points that are simply about acquiring more points and fail to acknowledge higher levels of proficiency. The fix is to eliminate extra credit and bonus points that do not relate to achievement and to communicate clearly to students and parents that better grades come from evidence of higher levels of performance, not just from more points.

> "Extra credit (is) inequitable because it reflects a student's environment over which she has no control. Extra credit, although it is optional and open to all students, doesn't allow all students to take equal advantage because it requires extra resources beyond the course requirements. Extra credit is extra, . . . and often requires money (materials, tickets to a movie), time, or adult support beyond what the school provides. . . Without us realizing it, extra credit not only devalues a teacher's curriculum, but actually increases the achievement gap – offering opportunities that only those students who have resources, supports, or stronger education backgrounds, can take advantage of."
>
> *(Feldman 2019, p. 114)*

Educator Vignette

Brent Brayko
Former Associate Principal for Teaching and Learning
Hong Kong International High School
Hong Kong

Current Adjunct Instructor for Teacher Education
St Norbert College
De Pere, Wisconsin

As an administrator supporting a faculty that was working to "fix" the inconsistencies and misalignment in our assessment, grading and reporting structures, I found that telling personal stories from my own background as a student, and then as a teacher, made the issues more personal and relevant, and I would often see nods of heads in acknowledgement from their own experiences.

After auditing our grading practices, it became clear that there was much inconsistency in what teachers were including while factoring their grades. Note that I used the word "factor" because we were not yet at the point of teachers determining grades based on professional judgment. Based on research, it was clear that we must only use evidence from academic achievement against the standards when determining a grade. We created what we called "Approaches to Learning" for Self-Motivated Learning, Collaboration, and Respect and Responsibility and reported on them separately four times a year versus reporting an academic achievement grade twice a year. However, even after doing this, we still had a few teachers who were offering extra credit or bonus questions with the old mentality that these were ways of either rewarding hard work or those who wanted to go "above and beyond." These extra points would be used to "boost' their grade. As I talked to teachers and students, I gave them a personal story from my own high school days that seemed to bring the point home that adding extra credit or bonus points distorted actual achievement and rendered grades not only inaccurate but was potentially harmful.

Here is my story:

> In high school, I enjoyed math through "Advanced Algebra," but I hit a wall in my understanding and ability to conceptualize trigonometry and pre-calculus concepts. I knew if I wanted to get to college, I had to do all I could to succeed and be able to "check it off." I had a tough time in my Advanced Mathematics course during my junior year, but I was a "good student" who always did my homework and smiled in class and even raised my hand once in a while. I "did" school well and took every offer of extra credit that I could. Many times, these opportunities had nothing to do with math, but any chance to get a few extra points was how I learned to keep my grade up. I even got a few points for bringing in boxes of tissues in the winter for the classroom. The point is that I

really was no stronger than a “C” student in terms of my knowledge and ability to apply the math, but I ended up with a “B.” As a result, I was WAIVED from a college math course because of a “B or better in high school math classes.” Sounds great; however, I ended up failing the math section on the exam to get into the College of Education the first time because I lacked the necessary skills and understanding. I should not have been waived because the B was not accurate. If I had taken the college math course I needed, I believe I would not have failed that part of the College of Education exam. I ended up struggling through with math tutoring and extra independent work because I did not have the necessary skills. The extra credit and bonuses had distorted my achievement and abilities, and it caused greater problems for me down the road.

This story seemed to hit home with both students and teachers as we worked toward fixing this broken grading practice. Instead of extra credit points being added to a grade, what had been bonus questions became another opportunity for students to demonstrate their level of proficiency and gave teachers another chance to provide meaningful feedback.

Policy/Procedure Example

Pittsford Central School District
Pittsford, New York

Agreed upon practice #2

We believe this: ***Grades will reflect a student's individual academic achievement.*** *Learning behaviors are important but they should be reflected separately, not in an individual's academic grade.*

Therefore, we agree that: ***No extra-credit will be awarded.***

Grades should not be used to award extra-credit to students. Working within teacher parameters, students may be allowed multiple opportunities to demonstrate their learning of essential academic standards, but this is not to be confused with students doing "extra credit work" to boost their academic average. Some examples to consider:

Not Allowed **This is extra credit which *is not aligned* with our Grading Philosophy or our agreed upon grading practices.**	**Allowed** **This would not be considered extra credit as this *is aligned* with our Grading Philosophy and supports student learning.**
Not Allowed: Awarding additional points in the grade book for attending an after school club meeting, or an evening concert as a spectator or audience member, or any similar event, on a specific date.	**Allowed:** Expecting students to attend or participate in an activity outside of class time that is directly aligned to the essential learning of the course; all students have access to this activity either through district provided transportation or due to multiple opportunities over the duration of the course; students are expected to demonstrate learning related to the academic standards as a result of this experience.
Not Allowed: Completing an extra activity in order to "raise their grade" or get "extra credit"	**Allowed:** Giving students another opportunity to demonstrate their mastery of essential learning standards.
Not Allowed: Awarding points in the grade book for meeting with a teacher to do "test corrections" without any additional learning being demonstrated.	**Allowed:** Giving students an opportunity to re-do all or a portion of an assessment after demonstrating additional learning.
Not Allowed: Awarding additional points in the grade book, or receiving any academic award, for bringing in supplies, contributing to a food drive, wearing spirit wear, etc.	
Not Allowed: Awarding bonus or challenge points on an assessment.	

Figure 3.1. Pittsford Agreed Upon Practice #2
Permission provided by the Pittsford Central School District
(Pittsford Central School District, 2019, p. 3)

Fix 4 Apply behavioral consequences and reassess when academic dishonesty occurs; don't reduce marks.

"When kids cheat on assignments it is because they have been taught that grades outweigh the importance of knowing things. We need to fix this."

Brian Aspinall on Twitter 05/10/21

"You cheated, so you get a zero on this test, assignment." This has been the typical response to the discovery of academic dishonesty. It is another example of broken grades because it uses an assessment/grading procedure as a tool to discipline students for inappropriate behavior, thus distorting student achievement. The fixes for this are to articulate an academic honesty policy with clear behavioral consequences for breaches and, because untainted evidence of student achievement is needed to determine grades, to require students to redo the test or assignment without cheating or plagiarizing.

Academic dishonesty is an ongoing problem in middle and high schools and colleges. According to the International Centre for Academic Integrity "More than 60 percent of university students freely admit to cheating in some form," and their surveys of over 70,000 high school students demonstrated that 64 percent of students admitted to cheating on a test, 58 percent admitted to plagiarism, and 95 percent said they participated in some form of cheating, whether it was on a test, plagiarism or copying homework. (ICAI, 2022)

Dealing with academic dishonesty is difficult; probably like many of you, it has been the subject of many emotional conversations. As with most behavioral concerns, there are two main issues: how to prevent it and what to do about it when it happens. Most schools try to deal with both of these issues together by having punitive policies that range from zeros on the assignment to loss of credit to expulsion. These policies arise from the belief that if the punishment is sufficiently severe, then students will not risk being caught. Continuing academic dishonesty, however, points to the need for viable alternatives. It is best to begin with how to prevent it and then to develop procedures to deal with it when it happens.

How to Prevent Academic Dishonesty

"Prevention is better than cure" is an old but true saying, and it certainly applies here; the better we educate and communicate, the less academic dishonesty that will occur. The first steps in prevention are as follows:

1. Explaining what academic integrity is and why it is essential, and
2. Describing what academic dishonesty is.

The International Center for Academic Integrity defines academic integrity as "a commitment, even in the face of adversity, to six fundamental values: honesty, trust, fairness, respect, responsibility, and courage" (ICAI, 2021, p. 4). As an example from K-12, Westwood Community High School in Fort McMurray, Alberta stated that academic integrity is "adherence to ethical and moral principles, soundness of character, honesty," and that it is "the moral code or ethical policy of education. Includes values such as the avoidance of cheating and plagiarism, maintenance of academic standards, honesty, and rigour in research" (Westwood Community High School, n.d.). Westwood states that are three reasons for academic integrity: (a) respect, pride, and character for self and others; (b) giving credit where credit is due; and (c) showing what *you* (my italics) know and can do.

After providing clarity about the what and why of academic integrity, schools then need to communicate effectively about what academic dishonesty is because, as educators, we often assume students know what we mean by, for example, plagiarism. This, however, isn't always the case, even for high school students. Babcock Neighborhood School in Charlotte County, Florida has this statement in its Student and Parent Handbook 2020-2021:

> Academic integrity is a cornerstone of any school's commitment to the principles of free inquiry. Students are responsible for learning and upholding professional standards at all grade levels as appropriate for research, writing, and assessment. Written or other work which students submit must be the product of their own efforts. Any form of dishonest or unethical behavior is prohibited.
>
> There are many different forms of academic dishonesty. The following kinds of honesty violations and their definitions are not

meant to be exhaustive. Rather, they are intended to serve as examples of unacceptable academic conduct.

- **CHEATING**
- **PLAGIARISM**
- **FABRICATION:** Falsifying or inventing any information
- **FACILITATING ACADEMIC DISHONESTY:** Aiding another person in an act that violates the standards of academic honesty.
- **FALSIFYING RECORDS AND OFFICIAL DOCUMENTS**
- **MULTIPLE SUBMISSION:** Submitting the same work in two or more courses.
- **COMPUTER MISUSE**: Using technology to plagiarize, violate copyright law, or tamper with another's work.

(Babcock Neighborhood School, 2020, p. 9)

This is a useful student-friendly statement, but I think they should have included brief explanations of Cheating and Plagiarism as they did for the other examples. Acceptable brief descriptions of cheating and plagiarism that could be added are the following:

CHEATING: Using dishonest means to obtain an unfair advantage (e.g., using a cell phone to find answers during a test).

PLAGIARISM: Using the words or ideas of others without acknowledgment; includes copying homework.

Also, as long as there is clear communication between the student and his/her teachers, I see no problem with submitting the same evidence of learning in two or more courses when the same or similar standards are being assessed.

Two additional steps are necessary or desirable to maximize the prevention of academic dishonesty. It is necessary that students and parents know that there will be behavioral *and* assessment consequences for academic dishonesty, and it is desirable that students make a commitment to academic integrity by requiring them to attest that they will be or have been academically honest. For example, students at Silver Spring International Middle School sign this pledge:

> Academic Honesty and Integrity promote a system of values that brings out the best in a group of individuals, provides for an orderly, effective, and positive academic community, and supports the idea of learning promoted in the IB learner profile and mission statement.
>
> Academic Dishonesty leads to a loss of credibility and trust within the community and the learning process.
>
> I acknowledge that I have read and discussed the purpose of the Academic Honor Code.
>
> I have been made aware of the policies set out within the document.
>
> I understand that the Academic Honor Code is the expected standard for all academic work.
>
> I, ________________________________ (student name), pledge to follow the Silver Spring International Middle School Academic Honesty Policy.
>
> **Student Name:**______________________________________
>
> **Student Signature:**__________________________________
>
> **Date**:______________________________
>
> (Silver Spring International Middle School, n.d.)

Further, students in the Senior School at Crofton House School in Vancouver sign this statement on each evaluative/summative assessment:

> **Academic Integrity** means **honesty** and **responsibility** in scholarship. My signature below shows my commitment to and obligation that all of my academic work is from my own efforts unaided except where specified.
>
> __________ (initial here)

Procedures to deal with Academic Dishonesty

When academic dishonesty is suspected, students can be interviewed privately in an attempt to determine whether the transgression actually occurred and whether it was inadvertent or deliberate. If it was inadvertent, the student may be counseled and may revise the assessment as appropriate. School/district procedures should describe the prescribed behavioral and assessment response(s) to deliberate dishonesty.

Effective procedures first and foremost recognize that academic dishonesty is very serious inappropriate behavior and, as such, requires behavioral consequences. Second, and very importantly, effective procedures also recognize that the appropriate academic consequence is to have students redo the assessment with honesty and integrity, and NEVER use mark reductions, especially zeros. Effective procedures also acknowledge that teachers can make it easier for students to be academically dishonest when their summative assessments are primarily about right and wrong answers and when they use the same assessments year after year. To this end, teachers should avoid prompts that are easy to Google and use prompts that aren't easy to Google, as illustrated in Figure 4.1.

Easy to Google	Not Easy to Google
Define	Evaluate
Memorize	Justify
Repeat	Design
List	Generate
Duplicate	Create

Figure 4.1. Googleable or Not
Adapted from the original seen in a Myron Dueck presentation

In late 2021, I looked through ten pages of results on Google for a search on "academic dishonesty policies for high schools" and read the procedures for approximately forty high schools. Only two did not have a requirement for mark reductions. I see this as a failure on the part of school/district administrators to recognize that the primary consequences for academic dishonesty should be behavioral and that, while those consequences should align with the philosophy of the school/district code of conduct, they can be as "soft" or as "hard" as it is considered necessary for students to understand that it is an unacceptable behavior. This is reinforced with the double consequence of requiring that the assessment be redone honestly. Three examples of school procedures for academic dishonesty can be found in the Policy/Procedures section at the end of this fix. They are presented as examples, not models. It is worth noting that the Minnetonka procedures (a) emphasize encouraging understanding of academic honesty and supports behavior change, and (b) do not identify specific consequences but require that the consequences are considered separately for each infraction. I'm confident that none of the consequences after 7.12 would be used for academic dishonesty! The Thomas Jefferson Middle School Procedures interestingly distinguish between Accidental, Deliberate, and Repeated malpractice with escalating consequences. The Grand Erie District School Board shows differences in the "Continuum of Behavioural and Academic Responses to Cheating and Plagiarism" for Primary/Junior and Intermediate/Senior (note the Canadian spelling of "behavioural"). The New Berlin School District in Wisconsin is another excellent example (O'Connor, 2018, pp. 101-103).

Student Involvement

One way to involve students in academic honesty is for schools to have frequent age-appropriate discussions with students about the why and what of the school's procedures using specific examples. Having the requirement that students sign an academic honesty pledge or a signed statement on each evaluative assessment causes students to reflect on this issue for each assessment so that they are likely to develop a clearer understanding of what academic honesty requires.

Summary

Academic dishonesty is unacceptable and must not be tolerated. Grades are broken, however, if the response to cheating is a lowered score or grade, as this renders the student's record of achievement inaccurate. The fix is to remove grading as the vehicle for assigning a consequence to students who are academically dishonest and to have an academic honesty procedure that clearly describes inappropriate practices and the consequences for breaches without impacting grades. To emphasize that the learning is most important, the procedure would also require that students must redo any assessment that involved academic dishonesty—without cheating or plagiarizing.

Copying is cheating.
Homework is not supposed to be copied.
Education relies on each student's integrity.
Attitude for learning is built upon honesty.
Teachers lose trust when you cheat.
Integrity for yourself is priceless.
Not learning to your full potential makes you lose valuable time.
Giving away answers is not cool and only hurts you and the other person.

Honesty is respected. Cheating should be rejected

Supplied by the Charlotte County Public Schools Superintendent's Academic Integrity Committee, a committee consisting of students from all four (4) county high schools (Charlotte County Public Schools, 2020, p. 7).

Educator Vignette

Garnet Hillman
Former High School Spanish Teacher
Author and Educational Consultant,
Crest Hill, Illinois

As an educator, academic dishonesty is disheartening. When I began my teaching career, students who cheated on an assignment or assessment would receive a zero in the grade book and had no opportunity to remedy the situation. It was a response that made sense to me at the time—if something is not your work, you don't get credit. What I realized over time is that simply putting a zero in the grade book does not address the real problem that underlies the academic dishonesty, nor does it contribute in an accurate way to their grade. I discovered that I needed to consider two things when students cheated. First, I had to remind myself that when work was not from the student, I had no evidence of their learning. I needed that evidence to plan for future learning and to make an accurate inference about a score or grade. I also had to consider that the act of cheating is behavioral. I had to address the behavior separately from the academic side if I was going to effectively respond to the situation.

After I worked to understand the two different facets of academic dishonesty, I had the opportunity to put the thinking into practice. During a summative writing assessment, a student placed a notebook in her lap and proceeded to copy what she had in the notebook onto the paper I had provided. At first, my emotions rose. I was disappointed and felt like part of our relationship broke at that moment. So, I took a step back to think and process before I went and talked to the student. When I was ready, I approached the student and asked her why she didn't feel ready for the assessment. In my mind, there must have been some reason she didn't feel prepared because this student had shown proficiency in the practice leading up to the assessment. She looked surprised with the question but went on to tell me that there were circumstances that made it impossible for her to study the prior evening. I told her that she would have to reassess; this wasn't going to give me a true picture of her learning, and I asked when she thought she would feel ready. We worked out a time a couple of days later and scheduled the reassessment. Next, we addressed the behavior. In our student handbook, there were consequences for academic dishonesty. I let the student know that she would be referred to the dean for the behavioral infraction.

This separation allowed me to address both the academic and behavioral aspects that are involved when students cheat. This particular student came in on the day we had chosen for her reassessment and did well. She appreciated the opportunity to show her learning and in turn knew her grade would reflect that. Instead of building a wall between us, my response strengthened our relationship. She didn't shut down or feel embarrassed. She didn't disengage from class; rather, she gained confidence in her academic skills and didn't display the behavior again.

Policy/Procedure Examples

1. Minnetonka Public Schools
Minnetonka, Minnesota

From **Policy #636: SECONDARY ACADEMIC INTEGRITY POLICY**

V. CONSEQUENCES FOR ACADEMIC INTEGRITY VIOLATIONS

A. A violation of the academic integrity policy is a behavioral infraction and shall be treated as such. Therefore, consequences shall be developed for each violation of the academic integrity policy.

1. All violations are cumulative for all courses.
2. The infraction will be examined in the context of the student's record.
3. If the behavior warrants it, the consequences may be increased based on the facts and the violations of other policies and procedures.

B. The objective in dealing with any violation of the academic integrity policy will be twofold:

1. To educate the student about the severity of this ethical violation and its long-term implications; and,
2. To encourage a behavior change in a caring, consistent and instructive way with the purpose of preventing any future violations. The student, parents, teachers, counselors, and administrators all play a key role in this process.

C. The violation will be recorded into the student's official disciplinary record. (Minnetonka Public Schools, 2007, pp. 2-3)

From **Student Discipline and Code of Conduct #506**

7.0 DISCIPLINARY ACTION OPTIONS

It is the general policy of the school district to utilize progressive discipline to the extent reasonable and appropriate based upon the specific facts and circumstances of student misconduct. The specific form of discipline chosen in a particular case is solely within the discretion of the school district. At a minimum, violation of school district rules, regulations, policies or procedures will result in discussion of the violation and a verbal warning. The school district shall, however, impose more severe disciplinary sanctions for any violation, including exclusion or expulsion, if warranted by the student's misconduct, as determined by the school district. Disciplinary action may include, but is not limited to, one or more of the following:

7.1 Student conference with teacher, principal, counselor or other school district personnel, and verbal warning;

7.2 Parent contact;

7.3 Parent conference;

7.4 Removal from class;

7.5 In-school suspension;

7.6 Suspension from extracurricular activities;

7.7 Detention or restriction of privileges;

7.8 Loss of school privileges;

7.9 In-school monitoring or revised class schedule;

7.10 Referral to in-school support services;

7.11 Referral to community resources or outside agency services;

7.12 Financial restitution;

7.13 Referral to police, other law enforcement agencies, or other appropriate authorities;

7.14 Out-of-school suspension under the Pupil Fair Dismissal Act;

7.15 Preparation of an admission or readmission plan;

7.16 Expulsion under the Pupil Fair Dismissal Act;

7.17 Exclusion under the Pupil Fair Dismissal Act;

7.18 Other disciplinary action as deemed appropriate by the school district.

(Minnetonka Public Schools, 2002, pp. 7-8)

2. Thomas Jefferson Middle School, Arlington, VA

Levels of Malpractice	Description	Actions by Teacher & Department Head	Action by Counselors & Administrators
Level 1	**Accidental Malpractice** May occur due to inexperience and is limited to **the first.** May occur if a student submits work that is not entirely their own, with only instances of plagiarism. *An example may involve paraphrasing ideas or using material without MLA citation. It might not also be where a student has copied homework from a classmate or asked for "help" in a way that solicits answers, rather than understanding.*	If an assignment: -team conference with student to inform and guide future behavior -incident recorded in team notes, parent/guardian contacted -teacher allows the student to make up the assignment so that the student generates original ideas. Students may earn full-credit. If a test, exam, or quiz: -If the student is caught cheating in the midst of a test or the results of a test indicate student(s) have cheated, the teacher speaks with the student(s) involved to verify cheating has taken place. The same procedure as that for cheating on an assignment is followed and the student is allowed to retake a different version of the test for full-credit.	No intervention by counselors or administrators at this level.
Level 2	**Deliberate Malpractice** A student has one recorded instance of malpractice either within the same course or in other courses within the same academic **OR** it is clear that the dishonesty was intended. *In these cases, students may have completely copied work from another student, or used words that are not their own, without citing the source. A student may have copied from electronic sources and/or changed key words and phrases. If a student copies work on an assignment or test, it is assumed that they did so, knowingly.*	- Level 1 procedures for infractions involving assignments, tests and quizzes apply. AND - The classroom teacher makes a copy of the assignment, and any other documents related to the assignment for counselor AND - The student is presented with a choice of assignment to complete to promote Academic Honesty in the school community.	1) Parent or guardian is contacted. 2) Teacher submits materials and summary of incident to the grade level counselor. 3) Counselor meets with student to provide counseling. 4) Grade level assistant principal and principal are notified.

Level 3	**Repeated Malpractice** A student has more than one recorded instance of malpractice either within the same course or in other courses across academic years. *In these cases, students may have submitted plagiarized work, made up sources, submitted the same assignment more than once, stolen test materials, used electronics inappropriately, or shared or published answers.*	- Level 1 procedures for infractions involving assignments, tests and quizzes apply. AND - The classroom teacher makes a copy of the assignment, and any other documents related to the assignment for counselor AND - The student is required to serve in-school suspension (ISS) for 1 day.	

Figure 4.2. What happens if I do something considered to be malpractice?
(Thomas Jefferson Middle School, 2021, p. 4)

3. Grand Erie District School Board, Brantford, Ontario

CHEATING AND PLAGIARISM GRADES 1 TO 12

Component	Primary /Junior	Intermediate/Senior
Prevention of cheating and plagiarism	Students will be involved in plagiarism Awareness and Education.	Teachers will review the responsibilities of the student, the proper method for citing sources, and the school policy on cheating and plagiarism at the beginning of each course.
	Principals will ensure that information about the plagiarism and cheating policy is communicated to students and parents.	Principals will ensure that information about the plagiarism and cheating policy is communicated to students and parents. Students will be made aware of the consequences of cheating and plagiarism.
	Teachers should design evaluation activities to include checkpoints so that student progress and work can be monitored.	Teachers should design evaluation activities to include checkpoints so that student progress and work can be monitored.
	Teachers should change the topics or modify their approach to topics on assignments from one year to the next. Do not use the same topics so students are not tempted to copy or modify.	Teachers should change the topics or modify their approach to topics on assignments from one semester and year to the next. Do not use the same topics so students are not tempted to copy or modify.
	Teachers should propose assignment questions that employ "higher order thinking skills".	Teachers should propose assignment questions that employ "higher order thinking skills".
	Teachers should set an example — acknowledge the sources of the materials used in class.	Teachers should set an example – acknowledge the sources of the materials used in class.
	Teachers should ask students to submit rough notes and a list of sources with their final copy as proof of their work.	Teachers should ask students to submit rough notes and a list of sources with their final copy as proof of their work.
	Teachers should take note of the behaviour to use as evidence in the evaluation of learning skills.	Teachers should take note of the behaviour to use as evidence in the evaluation of learning skills.

Detection of incidents of cheating and plagiarism (including the use of online or electronic translators in submitting Foreign Language tasks) The following are some clues that academic honesty is in question: · shifts in style or quality of writing · references or quotations lacking or missing completely	For young students, it is important to keep the focus on developing an understanding of the seriousness of cheating and plagiarism in a supportive and nurturing manner. Upon detection of incidents of cheating and plagiarism, students will be counseled and re-educated about cheating and plagiarism.	There are a number of methods for determining if plagiarism has occurred. These include: · Searching for the occurrence of specific sentences or unusual phrases contained within a suspect assignment using Internet search engines · Searching Library full text databases for text taken directly from a journal article · Searching research papers available for purchase via "paper mills" · Checking students' work using plagiarism detection software, such as Turnitin. Turnitin allows students to review their work and provides teachers and students with a tool for

Component	Primary /Junior	Intermediate/Senior
· similar or identical assignments submitted · datedness · odd, complex, out-of-place sentences · documented references are very unusual and hard to locate · spelling or grammar does not match the student's writing abilities		checking the integrity of work submitted. Turnitin can also be used as a teaching tool – it is accessed through the Virtual Learning platform.
Consequences for students who cheat or plagiarize	The teacher will use professional judgement and work with the student to determine the course of action on an individual basis.	The teacher will conference with the student and contact the parent to explain the situation. The teacher will use professional judgement and work with the student to determine the course of action on an individual basis.
	Subsequent incidents of cheating and plagiarism will result in notification to the parent(s) and school principal.	Subsequent incidents will be reported to administration and tracked.
	Students will be expected to complete work to the best of their ability in a supportive and supervised school environment (work assigned should be developmentally appropriate and within their range of proximal development - incidents of cheating and plagiarism in young children most likely stem from a lack of understanding of the concept of academic property, or from a lack of understanding of the task at hand - both should be explored and considered a teachable moment).	Where the integrity of an evaluation activity has been compromised, a student is still responsible for meeting the missed expectations. For a first offence, the teacher should provide an opportunity for the student to re-submit the evaluation activity or an alternate assignment with no penalty. At the teacher's discretion, the student may be required to complete the evaluation activity under supervised conditions. In those instances, where a student demonstrates a pattern of behaviour, the school principal may determine an appropriate consequence.
	If the incidents continue to occur this moves from an assessment issue to a discipline issue and progressive discipline as outlined in SO11 Progressive Discipline and Promoting Positive Student Behaviour will take effect.	If the incidents continue to occur this moves from an assessment issue to a discipline issue and progressive discipline as outlined in SO11 Progressive Discipline and Promoting Positive Student Behaviour will take effect.

Figure 4.3. Continuum of Behavioural and Academic Responses to Cheating and Plagiarism (Grand Erie District School Board, 2018, pp. 4-5)

Fix 5 Report absences separately; don't consider attendance in grade determination.

> If the grade represents the number of days students attend school in addition to what standards they have mastered, it can no longer be used to accurately document mastery . . .
>
> *(Wormeli, 2018, p. 163)*

Grades are broken when they are directly or indirectly related to a student's attendance record. The fixes are to report attendance separately from grades and to determine grades only from evidence of achievement.

Most teachers would probably agree that all students should attend school regularly, as most students need to do so to be successful in their learning. However, standards-based learning is not about seat time—it is about what students know, understand, and can do. Grades should be accurate reflections of that and that alone. Attendance, therefore, is best recorded and reported separately simply as days present (or days absent).

The basic problem with attendance in the USA (and in some other countries) is that there have been mandated minimum number of hours for K-12 schools, and at the high school level credits have been defined by the required number of hours of seat time. This requirement in Texas was typical:

> In addition to compulsory attendance law, districts are required to enforce the 90 percent rule, which states that students in grades K-12 must attend class for 90 percent of the time it is offered to receive credit or a final grade. The 90 percent rule applies to most absences, including excused absences. If the student doesn't meet this requirement, an attendance committee may grant the student credit or a final grade, depending on the circumstances.
>
> (Texas Association of Public School Boards, 2022)

Fortunately, seat time requirements have been significantly reduced in the last five years, and that trend has been accelerated by virtual and hybrid learning during the COVID-19 pandemic. In November 2019, ExcelinEd stated that "examining seat-time requirements for awarding credit and graduation reveals that all 50 states and Washington, D.C., have either fully or partially authorized the awarding of credits based on mastery in lieu of seat-time" (ExcelinED, 2019, p. 1). According to their report at that time, 32 states had fully authorized mastery as the basis for credit, while 18 states plus the District of Columbia had authorized mastery but still had some restrictions in place. Examples of this can be found in Oregon and Maine:

> **Oregon**
>
> Oregon Administrative Code 581-022-1131 allows a school district or charter school to grant credit if a student demonstrates mastery by any one or more of the following ways:
>
> - Successfully completing classroom or equivalent work designed to measure proficiency in class or out of class, where hours of instruction may vary;
> - Successfully passing an appropriate exam designed to measure proficiency or mastery of identified standards;
> - Providing a collection of work or other evidence which demonstrates proficiency or mastery of identified standards;
>
>   and/or
> - Providing documentation of prior learning activities or experiences which demonstrate proficiency or mastery.
>
> (Oregon Department of Education, 2015)

> **Maine**
>
> The state education agency states that "A total of at least 175 instructional days are required" for Maine virtual students. However, "There is no hourly requirement, per day or per year. Local agencies and schools are asked to declare how they will determine this, but it is not prescribed by the state."
>
> (Patrick & Chambers, 2020, pp. 3 - 4)

Another attendance issue that relates to the determination of grades is the common practice of schools/districts to define excused and unexcused absences and then having different consequences on grades and the ability of students to “make up” for excused and unexcused absences. An example of this is from a high school in Minnesota:

> **Consequences of Excused Absences**
>
> 1. Students whose absences are excused are required to make up all assignments missed or to complete alternative assignments as deemed appropriate by the classroom teacher.
> 2. ‘Work’ missed because of absence must be made up within a reasonable time frame set by the teacher from the date of the student’s return to school (usually two days for each one day of absence).
>
> **Consequences of Unexcused Absences**
>
> Students with unexcused absences shall be subject to discipline in the following manner:
>
> 1. For the first 5 or more unexcused absences per quarter, the student will not be allowed to make up work missed due to such absences.
> 2. After the 3rd cumulated unexcused absence in a quarter, a student’s parent or guardian will be notified by mail that his or her child is nearing a total of 5 unexcused absences in a quarter.
> 3. Upon 10 cumulated unexcused absences in a semester, the administration may impose the loss of academic credit in the class or classes from which the student has been absent. However, prior to loss of credit, an administrative conference must be held between the principal, student and parent. An appeal conference may take place upon initiative by either the student or the parent.
>
> (South Koochiching-Rainy River School District, n.d.)

The distinction between excused and unexcused absences may be very important for behavioral, financial, and legal reasons, but it is irrelevant to learning and grades. From these perspectives, the only issue is whether students learn and demonstrate learning by providing appropriate assessment evidence. Students who have been absent require opportunities to learn what they have missed and subsequently to demonstrate what they know, understand, and can do, regardless of the reason for the absence. Some districts acknowledge this in their procedures, as can be seen in the following examples, but they still put inappropriate emphasis on absence in allowing make-up opportunities and the determination of grades.

> **Assignments for Excused Absences**
>
> Students with excused absences may complete assignments and tests missed during an excused absence provided that the work is completed in a timely manner.
>
> **Assignments for Unexcused Absences**
>
> Make-up work/tests for unexcused absences shall be at the discretion of individual teachers.
>
> (El Segundo High School, 2020)

> **12 – Day Absence Procedure:**
>
> – If a student accumulates more than 12 total excused or unexcused absences in any class period during a semester, he/she is in violation of the absence limit. If the student is passing the class with an "A", "B" or "C", he/she will receive credit; however, the letter grade will be reflected as a "P" for that class on their permanent transcript. This "P" will be calculated as a 2.0 toward the student's cumulative GPA. Students who have a "D" or "F" will maintain those grades.
>
> (Great Falls High School, 2020, p. 3)

(I cannot state strongly enough that, while I appreciate these procedures make no or limited distinction between excused and unexcused absences, these procedures are or should be seen as unacceptable.)

Another reason it is inappropriate to make the distinction between excused and unexcused absences is that the difference often depends on the "creativity" of the parent(s) or the student. This is a polite way of saying whether parents or students are willing to lie on behalf of their child, which is obviously an inappropriate basis for decisions affecting grades or "makeup" opportunities.

In some of the schools in which I have taught, it was a common practice (especially in Physical Education) to include a fixed number of points for attendance and to deduct one or two points for each absence. In subjects such as Physical Education, Drama, and Music active participation is essential, but with such a procedure a student would have zero for attendance after 10 absences even though they attended 35 out of 45 days in the grading period. Such procedures are illogical, distort the meaning of the grade, and should not be permitted.

One aspect of attendance and grades that presents a real dilemma is when there are requirements that students attend certain out-of-school activities or performances, such as concerts in a music course or performances in a drama course. When participation is required, however, for the program to function, it is reasonable to suggest that there should be consequences for failure to attend. Policies that simply state that students receive a failing grade if they miss performances are inappropriate. A student who is proficient or better in all the music or drama learning goals would have their grade distorted if it was lowered for failing to attend one or more performances. The best approach in standards-based schools is probably a behavioral consequence, but I acknowledge that it is difficult to determine what is appropriate. As schools/districts make the transition to a true standards-base, it may be necessary to establish a policy that students must attend X (or all) concerts/performances as a prerequisite to receiving a grade/credit, and that they will otherwise receive an Incomplete. This policy can be communicated in writing to students and parents at or before the start of the course. This issue for music concerts is addressed in the Educator Vignette for this fix below and in Shaw, 2018.

Summary

In standards-based systems, all marks and grades (pass/fail, A/B/C/D/F, %, etc.) should be determined by proficiency, not by seat time. Most students need to attend class to be successful, and teachers must ensure that engaging learning activities are being provided so that students feel it is worth their while to attend. However, absences should not directly affect students' grades. Grades are broken if there is a direct impact because a behavioral variable is being allowed to distort achievement. The fix is to deal with attendance separately from achievement by simply reporting days present (or days absent).

There is no legitimate purpose for distinguishing between excused and unexcused absences. For educational purposes, therefore, there need only to be recorded absences.

(Gathercoal, 2004, p. 163)

Educator Vignette

Brian Shaw
Assistant Professor of Music Education
Indiana University,
Bloomington, Indiana

A common practice in school music programs is assigning a grade for attendance at evening or weekend concerts, rehearsals, festivals, and other events. In many cases, students' final grades are largely determined through attendance. I have seen policies where concert attendance comprised 90% of the final grade or students were prescribed a deduction of two full levels for a missed performance (e.g., a student who earned an A receiving a C on the report card). Even though this is a common practice, it is an approach to grading that is "broken" and in need of repair.

The US National Coalition for Core Arts Standards and Canadian provincial curricula have enumerated a compelling set of power standards for music education. These include creating music, performing music, responding to music, and connecting through music. While not every music course has the same curriculum, music grades—like grades in all classes—serve as honest communication when they are based on the applicable power standards. However, no matter how many teachers treat it otherwise, concert attendance is not a content standard. As a result, music grades often fail to convey meaningful information about students' musical abilities or achievement. Instead, they mainly report about students' attendance and so-called "participation." This is undoubtedly why many colleges and universities disregard music grades when reviewing students' transcripts and contribute to the misperception that music is a less serious school subject.

Music teachers often describe a concert or performance as a summative assessment. Unfortunately, this is not quite correct. While it is true that a concert may serve as an assessment of the group's performance, or of a music program as a whole, the purpose of the concert is to *share*, not *evaluate*, what the individual students have learned. Teachers are busy leading the performance, not appraising each student's musicianship. Usually, if students arrive on time and wear black socks (also not a core arts standard), they receive a perfect score. If they are absent, there are catastrophic consequences for their grades, even though they have not suddenly become worse musicians. Their grades have been distorted. Making matters worse, these policies tend to affect already-marginalized students the most. Families who have access to concert attire, transportation, childcare, and agreeable work schedules have an easier time ensuring their children's attendance.

Thoughtful music educators can take several steps to alleviate these concerns. First and foremost, music grades should be determined by each student's individual performance on valid summative assessments of musical achievement. Not all music educators see themselves as competent assessors, so professional development may be an intermediate step. Concert attendance can be *encouraged* without being *graded*. Music educators can also take proactive steps toward achieving consistent turnout by identifying and removing barriers to student attendance, which may include ride sharing, uniform assistance, or personal communication with families. Concert attendance could also be treated under the school's existing attendance policy. Many workable solutions are possible.

Even though concert grades are widespread, they distort reports about student achievement. They are an object lesson in the harmful effects of also violating Fix #1: "Include only achievement; don't include student behaviors in grades." While old habits can be hard to break, students will benefit from changes to concert grading policies. Music education is a rigorous, multifaceted, enriching, worthwhile pursuit for students, and our gradebooks should reflect this truth.

Policy/Procedure Example

North East School Division
Melfort, SK

PRACTICE #5 Report absences separately; don't include attendance in grade determination

- Because outcomes-based learning is not about seat time, it is about what students know, understand and can do—grades should be accurate reflections of achievement and achievement alone.
- Record attendance separately.
- Have attendance policies that address ways to offer another opportunity, consider personal issues, and provide support.

(North East School Division, 2017, p. 4)

Fix 6 Use evidence of individual achievement; don't include group scores in grades.

> We don't grade group work! I have argued repeatedly that cooperative learning is for learning, not for grading.
>
> *(Kagan Online, 2022)*

Grades are broken when they include group scores for learning activities done in cooperative learning groups. The fix is to ensure that all evidence used to determine grades comes from individual evidence of achievement.

Cooperative learning is a very powerful teaching/learning strategy; when done well and used appropriately, it can lead to significant learning gains and more positive attitudes about learning and school. Collaborative skills and the ability to work in teams are very important skills to learn to prepare students for their life and work beyond K-12. Frequently in cooperative learning situations, however, students are required to produce a group product or presentation for which they receive a group score, which is then recorded for each member of the group. The reason this is often done is because it reduces the marking load of teachers; that is, however, a bad reason for a bad practice.

Let's take a look at five common practices for assessing a group project:

> **"Shared Group Grade**
>
> The group submits one product and all group members receive the same grade, regardless of individual contribution.
>
> **Group Average Grade**
>
> Individual submissions (allocated tasks or individual reports) are scored individually. The group members each receive the average of these individual scores.
>
> **Individual Grade - Allocated task**
>
> Each student completes an allocated task that contributes to the final group product and gets the marks for that task

Individual Grade - Individual report

Each student writes and submits an individual report based on the group's work on the task/project

Individual Grade - Examination

Exam questions specifically target the group projects, and can only be answered by students who have been thoroughly involved in the project."

(Carnegie Mellon University Eberly Center, n.d.)

I see the first two options as being completely unacceptable and the third as dubious, so teachers are left with the last two options in addition to individually assessing the collaborative skills of each student. Group scores are unacceptable primarily because they will almost always lack accuracy for each individual but also because they violate one of the key principles of cooperative learning – individual accountability – and their use results in cooperative learning being implemented incorrectly. Another reason for opposing group scores is that cooperative learning has encountered parental and student resistance in some schools/districts precisely because of group scoring. In the extreme, parents have taken teachers, principals, schools, and districts to court over this issue. The parents generally have won because judges followed the principle that no student's grade should depend on the achievement (or behavior) of other students. Cooperative learning can be a powerful teaching/learning strategy. We want to help students to be successful learners, and thus we need to have all such powerful strategies available. We do not want to impair any strategy's effectiveness by incorrectly measuring the achievement of students who use it.

There is yet another issue with providing scores for products or performance developed in cooperative learning groups. The strategy is cooperative *learning*, which implies that any activities that occur in groups are learning activities and any assessment of them is best considered formative assessment to help students improve their knowledge, understanding, and skill(s). Such assessment is *for* learning and should not produce scores that are part of grade determination (this issue is examined in depth in Fix #13). After a class has experienced cooperative learning, teachers should then assess students individually to find out what they know, understand, and can do as a result. An example (not a model) of how this can be done is shown in Figure 6.1:

Classroom groups, each with four students, have been given a project to investigate the impact of World War I on the social, cultural, and economic conditions in a region in North America.
The teacher shares the rubric she will use for scoring the project. Groups must find multiple sources, including multimedia resources, and must present the product of their collective investigation on a poster.
Students may choose the region they will investigate and may divide up the investigation as they choose. When they have collected their sources, they meet as a group to integrate their findings.
Each group exhibits their poster in a classroom gallery walk. The teacher and the students use the rubric to provide feedback about each group's poster and achievement of learning goals. Each group uses self and peer assessment for feedback about their group process and individual collaborative skills.
After the gallery walk, the teacher requires each student to write individual essays about the impact of World War I on the social, cultural, and economic conditions on a region of their choice in North America and North America in general. The teacher provides feedback on the first draft of each student's essay, and assigns individual scores based on a rubric for the final (revised) essay.

Figure 6.1. What a Well-Designed Cooperative Learning Project Looks Like
(Adapted from Rasooli & Brookhart, 2021, p. 48)

Summary

Grades are broken if they involve the use of group scores from cooperative learning or group activities. This is because group scores almost certainly will not accurately reflect the achievement of each student and therefore would be unfair for some members of the group. This problem can be addressed by recognizing that cooperative learning is essentially a learning activity, not an assessment tool, and students should be required to complete an individual assessment after the cooperative learning activities. (See also Kagan, 1995)

Should Projects Be Graded?
In short, the answer is a resounding "No!" Project based learning experiences should call for a great deal of student critical thinking and creativity. And, research tells us that "carroting and sticking" these types of skills isn't just ineffective, but detrimental.

If Not Grades, Then What?
In short, the answer is feedback

(Cooper, R, 2018)

Educator Vignette

Ross Cooper
Administrator,
Chappaqua Central School District
New York

As a fourth-grade teacher at Willow Lane Elementary School in the East Penn School District, I continually engaged my students in project-based learning (PBL) experiences. The first few years of this PBL journey, I made plenty of mistakes, and I had many questions. One of these questions was: How do I get grades?

Originally, in my classroom, group projects went hand-in-hand with group grades. At the start of a project, each group received a "rubric" that more or less contained the project's directions regurgitated in list format, with each item on the list weighted according to how valuable I thought it was within the context of the project. At the conclusion of the project, all of the item's scores were added up to for an overall raw score (e.g., 25 out of 30), and then total points earned (25) was divided by total points possible (30) to determine a percentage grade (83%) that was assigned to all group members.

After some trial and error, I made two big shifts. The first shift was rethinking the rubric's content when I realized that I was pretty much grading my students on their ability to follow directions (which promotes compliance). As a result, regurgitated directions were replaced with the learning targets (student-friendly standards) that served as the basis for the project.

The second shift involved completely doing away with group grades during group projects. Generally, there were two ways I made this happen. The first option involved every student still receiving a rubric, as its learning targets were crucial for the facilitation of goal-oriented feedback (teacher, peer, and self-feedback) throughout the project. In other words, the rubric was now used for assessment and feedback, not grades. Then, at the conclusion of the project, each student was formally assessed using another method: test, quiz, essay, video reflection, etc. For group and individual projects, we can also formally assess each student at a few specific points throughout, such as when a project reaches a "hinge point" when there is a clear shift in content.

The second option involved jigsawing (which isn't mutually exclusive from the first option), with each student in a group being held accountable and graded on a specific, unique portion of the group's work. While this approach can help to tidy up and streamline "who does what," for jigsawing to be defensible, we also need to make sure students can't skate by without (a) actually collaborating and (b) having to immerse themselves in and be assessed on valuable aspects of the project.

Policy/Procedure Example

Pewaukee High School
Pewaukee, Wisconsin

GUIDELINE 7: Grades will be a clear depiction of individual student learning.

- Grades must be reflective of an individual's performance; therefore, group grading is not permitted.

(Pewaukee High School, 2015, p. 8)

CHAPTER 3

FIXES FOR LOW-QUALITY OR POORLY ORGANIZED EVIDENCE

Fix 7 Organize and report evidence by standards/learning goals or targets; don't organize by assessment methods or report a single subject grade.

> I slowly implemented adjustments to grow a culture of learning. The biggest change was clear and deliberate standards-focused learning and assessments. As I began to change my language focusing on student learning rather than grades, the students followed suit and asked more intentional questions. As I provided feedback rather than reporting scores on assessments, the conversation switched from earning points to progressing their learning.
>
> *(Moran cited in Budrow & Hillman, 2020, pp. 36-37)*

Grades are broken when evidence of learning from multiple sources is blended into a single grade and the communication fails to show how successful students have been in mastering individual standards/learning goals. The fix is to base grades on published school/district/state/national standards (e.g., learning outcomes/goals, essential learnings, expectations, strands) and to report them for each standard to create a more complete profile of individual student strengths and weaknesses. Evidence also may be summarized into a subject grade if required, but the communication must also, and always, report achievement by standard or by some categories derived from the standards. This requires curriculum, instruction, assessment, grading, and reporting all to be based on standards. Many schools have successfully done so with curriculum and instruction and, increasingly, assessment has become aligned as well. However, while many schools/districts have embraced standards-based grading and reporting at the elementary level, there still remains much work to be done, especially in middle and high schools. Schools focused on standards only for curriculum, instruction, and assessment are standards referenced, not standards-based.

Traditionally, teachers have organized their evidence of student achievement for all learning goals simply in categories based on the type of assessments, such as tests, projects, and homework assignments in the order collected over time. For each collection, they distill the individual scores into a single summary grade and report that grade. What is not recorded and therefore not reported is vital information revealing how well each student has mastered each learning goal. In other words, although each student's performance can be summarized with a single symbol/grade, this approach provides no basis for reporting direct evidence of student performance on each learning goal unless accompanied by a narrative report that describes learning in relation to the written curriculum. To be standards-based in grading, teachers plan each assessment to provide direct evidence of student proficiency on specific learning outcomes/goals and then record this evidence by learning goal, dedicating columns or blocks of space in their gradebook to each learning goal. Figure 7.1 shows a sample of such a gradebook using standards for Physical and Health Education. The standards are the basis for organizing assessments and collecting evidence from tests and performance assessments ("PA" in the figure) to determine a grade for each standard and an overall subject grade (if required).

Achievement Evidence								
Strands	Assessments							Grade
	10/1 PA	10/15 PA	11/7 Test	11/18 PA	12/8 PA	12/17 PA	Strengths, Areas for Improvement/ Observations	
Movement	3	3	3 (15/20)		3	3		3
Fitness Management				1				NA
Physical Activity Safety	2		4 (19/20)	2	2	2		2
Personal Safety	4	4	1 (12/20)		4	4		4
Personal/ Social Management	3	2	3 (12/20)	2	3	3		3
Healthy Lifestyle		1	2	3	4	4		4

Figure 7.1. Standards-Based Gradebook for Physical and Health Education

In this example the test was not just 10 questions worth 2 points each with a single score recorded and reported as X out of 20; the test elicited information on five of the six standards shown, and our example student received a level score on one standard and scores out of 20 on four standards that were converted to levels. The performance assessments (PA) provided level scores for four or five standards. By the end of the grading period, there are at least five scores for each standard, which is sufficient evidence to make summary judgments for that standard. All performance scores/marks must be recorded using a common scale, so the teacher uses cut scores based on four levels of proficiency to determine and record the scores on the test (see Fix 8 for an explanation of cut scores for points to levels). Grades for the six standards are then determined based on the most consistent level of achievement on each standard with emphasis on more recent achievement (see Fix 11 for a more detailed explanation of how the grade for each standard is determined). This gradebook format enables teachers and students (and parents) to see a profile of student performance that clearly identifies areas of strength and areas for improvement. In this example, the student excels on Personal Safety and Healthy Lifestyle, is proficient on Movement and Personal/

Social Management, is approaching proficiency on Physical Activity Safely, and there isn't enough evidence to determine a grade for the Fitness Management standard.

This gradebook example shows a page for one student because I believe this is the best way to illustrate this fix and is also the best way to collect evidence of student achievement. However, most teachers would find this method burdensome, so the practical ways to record scores from standards-based grading are to use a spreadsheet or computer grading software. Many computer grading programs can now be used for standards-based grading because these programs rely on "bins," or categories. Teachers have generally made those bins tests, projects, homework assignments, and so on, but they may just as easily be standards or strands. The only limitation is the number of bins or categories allowed by the program. So, wherever teachers are on the technological continuum—from a hardcopy paper gradebook through spreadsheets to computer grading programs— they can put this fix in place. There is a lot of work involved at first to organize, record scores, and determine grades in this way. However, in a relatively short timeframe, teachers then find that assessment and grading are easier to organize, as they are "working smarter, not harder," using the same organizing structure right through the process and not using one structure for curriculum, instruction, and assessment and a different structure for grading and reporting.

How Many Standards?

Guskey and Bailey (2010) made the helpful distinction between "curriculum standards" and "grading and reporting standards" (p. 43). *Curriculum standards* are whatever is in the national, state, or provincial curriculums that a school/district decides or is required to use. Usually, these standards are many and detailed and are frequently expressed in educator language. For example, the Wisconsin standards for Computer Science are organized into five content areas with a total of nineteen standards, and the Ontario Grade Nine Issues in Canadian Geography course has five strands, fourteen overall expectations, and fifty-three specific expectations.

Grading and Reporting are summarizing strategies that are used to communicate student achievement. Generally, the number and complexity of curriculum standards are too large and have to be translated into a manageable number of *grading and reporting standards* that are few and broader and expressed in student and parent friendly language. There are different opinions on the appropriate number, but I recommend between four and ten for each subject so that grading and reporting are feasible for teachers, and report cards aren't overwhelming for parents.

It is worth noting that, more recently, Guskey has separated grading and reporting standards and suggests that schools/districts should utilize the work of the professional organizations of educators in each academic discipline and use four to six reporting strands for each subject (links to the U.S. National Standards in 7 subjects can be found at Education World, 2022). He suggests if parents and families want more detail on student achievement on the specific standards addressed in a strand during a grading period, they should be directed to the gradebook. He says this is now practical because of the improved capability of computer grading programs to display data on multiple standards and because of widespread access to parent portals. The Rocky View School Division in Alberta is utilizing this approach and has even taken it one step further by eliminating report cards except for an end-of-year report card. They call it Real-Time Reporting (detailed information can be found at Rocky View School Division, 2022).

What Standards

Guskey (2021) states that

> "The fundamental premise of all standards-based initiatives is clarity and transparency in all elements of the teaching and learning process: curriculum, instruction, assessment, and grading and reporting" and that "Transparent curriculum means all teachers articulate precisely what they want students to learn and be able to do, and then share those expectations with students and their families. In other words, the learning goals are well-known and clear to everyone involved." (p. 193)

More detailed information on the learning goals must be accessible for parents but the most frequent, and possibly the main way, in which stakeholders identify what the learning goals are for each grade level and subject is through the information that is provided on report cards. This reinforces the importance of deciding what grading and reporting standards are chosen. Schools/districts have to make choices about the level of specificity of the standards, type of learning goals, and the words used. There is a range of choices from very specific to general and generic, and I will move through that range in describing the alternatives.

Level of Specificity

The highest level of specificity is provided by target-based grading. According to Hierck and Larson (2018), "target-based assessment grading, and reporting requires teachers to assess, grade, and report against specific learning targets, and not the standard as a whole" (p. 3). This means that teachers have to break the national, state, or provincial standards that have been chosen by the school/ district into specific learning targets. Further, the authors stated that "Units of instruction are (then) designed to help students meet specific learning targets, rather than the general standard" (Hierck & Larson, 2018, p. 3). A process for doing this as well as many examples of standards and learning targets can be found in Hierck and Larson's book. Below is an example of the standards and learning targets for high school Art Survey courses in Winneconne, WI.

Art Survey Standards and Learning Targets

(Updated May 27th 2021)

Art Survey Learning Standards are organized in four strands and 17 targets:

Create

ASCr1. Inspiration or Theme: Students will be able to develop original ideas while working with themes and prompts
ASCr2. Ideas: Students will develop original thoughts through brainstorming.
ASCr3. Research: Students will be able to articulate, What do I know and what will I need to know to complete this work.
ASCr4. Create Concepts: Students will be able to develop ideas through thumbnail sketches, and practice.
ASCr5. Art Making: Students will be able to create and finish artistic works that demonstrate growth in artistic thought and skill.

Perform:

ASPr1. Craftsmanship: Students will be able to create well-crafted works that show appropriate level of craftsmanship.
ASPr2. Skills: Students will develop skills appropriate for age and grade level within a variety of techniques and a variety of media.
ASPr3. Finish Art for Display: Students will be able to mat and display twork in a professional manner within the school or exhibits.
ASpr4. Sketchbook: Students will demonstrate the ability to maintain a sketchbook that shows growth in technique, concept development and solutions to prompts and themes.

Respond/Reflect

ASRCq1.Describe: Students will be able to describe art through appropriate vocabulary.
ASRCq2. Analyze: Students will be able to analyze art works and infer how the work was created..
ASRCq3.Interpret: Students will be able to interpret the meaning or significance of artworks.
ASRCq4. Inquire: Students will be able to formulate questions concerning the merits or meaning of an artwork through discussion.
ASRCq5. Evaluate: Students will be able to evaluate and analyze the quality, craftsmanship and manner in which a work was constructed.

Figure 7.2. High School Art Survey Learning Targets, Winneconne High School (Hierck & Larson, 2018, pp. 62-63)
Permission provided by the Winneconne School District

Using this approach, all the targets for each domain, standard, or unit would appear in the computer gradebook where parents can see feedback and scores on each target.

▾ 5th ELA Period 0 STA[redacted]		
▾ Reading-Literature	3	3
▸ support predictions and draw conclusi...	2	2
▸ summarize a text using important idea...	3	3
▸ determine the theme of a text and sup...	3	3
▸ compare and contrast two or more cha...	3	3
▸ determine the figurative meaning of w...	3	3
▸ explain how a portion of the text fits th...	3	3
▸ identify the narrator's point of view and...	2	2
▸ identify characteristics of a theme, topi...	3	3
▸ compare/contrast how stories of the s...	2	2
▾ Reading-Informational Text		
draw conclusions with evidence from a...		
summarize two or more main ideas an...		

Figure 7.3. Winneconne Elementary Target-Based Gradebook
Permission provided by the Winneconne School District

Report cards are, however at the strand level.

WINNECONNE SCHOOL DISTRICT

Student: [redacted]
6th Grade

WINNECONNE MIDDLE SCHOOL
2020 - 2021
PROGRESS 8/SEMESTER 2

Class : **HEALTH 6-ROTATION CLASS**
Teacher: [redacted]

HEALTH 6 ROTATION

	P5	P6
HEALTH 6 ROTATION		

HOMEWORK

	P5	P6

Class : **LANGUAGE ARTS 6**
Teacher: [redacted]

Attendance
Excused : 1
Unexcused: 0
Tardy : 0

Class Grades

	P1	P2	P3	P4	S1	P5	P6	P7	P8	S2
Class Grades		D	B							

LANGUAGE ARTS 6

	P1	P2	P3	P4	S1	P5	P6	P7	P8	S2
LANGUAGE ARTS 6		D	B	B	B	B	B	B	B	B
RL.1			3	3	3	3	3	3	3	3
RL.4			3	3	3	3	3	3	3	3
RL.7		2	2	2	2	2	2	2	2	2

HOMEWORK

	P1	P2	P3	P4	S1	P5	P6	P7	P8	S2

Class Comments for P1 (09/01/20 - 09/03/20)
PAW: PRACTICE KINDNESS - 3: CONSISTENTLY
PAW: ALWAYS SHOW RESPECT - 3: CONSISTENTLY
PAW: WORK TO DO YOUR BEST - 2: SOMETIMES
Jackson is respectful, works well with others, and is engaged in class discussions. However, he is sometimes missing assignments that should be completed at home.

Class Comments for P2 (09/01/20 - 11/02/20)
PAW: PRACTICE KINDNESS - 3: CONSISTENTLY
PAW: ALWAYS SHOW RESPECT - 3: CONSISTENTLY
PAW: WORK TO DO YOUR BEST - 3: CONSISTENTLY

Class : **MATHEMATICS 6**
Teacher: [redacted]

Attendance
Excused : 0
Unexcused: 0
Tardy : 0

Class Grades

	P1	P2	P3	P4	S1	P5	P6	P7	P8	S2
Class Grades		A	A							

MATHEMATICS 6

	P1	P2	P3	P4	S1	P5	P6	P7	P8	S2
MATHEMATICS 6		A	A	A	A	A	A	A	A	A
6NS1		3	3	3	3	3	3	3	3	3
6NS2			3	3	3	3	3	3	3	3
6NS3			3	3	3	3	3	3	3	3
6G1		3	3	3	3	3	3	3	3	3

MATHEMATICS 6

	P1	P2	P3	P4	S1	P5	P6	P7	P8	S2
6SP1			3	3	3	3	3	3	3	3
6SP2		3	3	3	3	3	3	3	3	3
6SP3			3	3	3	3	3	3	3	3

HOMEWORK

	P1	P2	P3	P4	S1	P5	P6	P7	P8	S2

Class Comments for P1 (09/01/20 - 09/03/20)
PAW: PRACTICE KINDNESS - 3: CONSISTENTLY
PAW: ALWAYS SHOW RESPECT - 3: CONSISTENTLY
PAW: WORK TO DO YOUR BEST - 3: CONSISTENTLY

Class Comments for P2 (09/01/20 - 11/02/20)
PAW: PRACTICE KINDNESS - 3: CONSISTENTLY
PAW: ALWAYS SHOW RESPECT - 3: CONSISTENTLY
PAW: WORK TO DO YOUR BEST - 3: CONSISTENTLY

Class : **PHY ED 6**
Teacher: [redacted]

Attendance
Excused : 0
Unexcused: 0
Tardy : 0

Class Grades

	P1	P2	P3	P4	S1	P5	P6	P7	P8	S2
Class Grades		A	A							

PHYSICAL EDUCATION 6

	P1	P2	P3	P4	S1	P5	P6	P7	P8	S2
PHYSICAL EDUCATION 6		A	A	A	A	A	A	A	A	A
4.1		3	3	3	3	3	3	3	3	3
4.2		3	3	3	3	3	3	3	3	3
4.3		3	3	3	3	3	3	3	3	3
12.1		3	3	3	3	3	3	3	3	3
12.2		3	3	3	3	3	3	3	3	3

HOMEWORK

	P1	P2	P3	P4	S1	P5	P6	P7	P8	S2

Class Comments for P1 (09/01/20 - 09/03/20)
PAW: PRACTICE KINDNESS - 3: CONSISTENTLY
PAW: ALWAYS SHOW RESPECT - 3: CONSISTENTLY
PAW: WORK TO DO YOUR BEST - 3: CONSISTENTLY

Class Comments for P2 (09/01/20 - 11/02/20)
PAW: PRACTICE KINDNESS - 3: CONSISTENTLY
PAW: ALWAYS SHOW RESPECT - 3: CONSISTENTLY
PAW: WORK TO DO YOUR BEST - 3: CONSISTENTLY

Class : **SCIENCE 6**
Teacher: [redacted]

Attendance
Excused : 0
Unexcused: 0
Tardy : 0

Class Grades

	P1	P2	P3	P4	S1	P5	P6	P7	P8	S2
Class Grades		A	A							

Figure 7.4. Winneconne Middle School Standards-Based Report Card
Permission provided by the Winneconne School District

Hierck and Larson (2018) see the advantages of target-based grading as follows:

– Teachers are able to utilize the information from assessments to determine the next best instructional steps to support student learning (p. 3)

- Reassessment becomes a much more manage able task as students are reassessed only on targets with which they struggled (p. 3)
- Greater accuracy of grades leads to a reduction in the number of students having to take remedial course in college (pp. 4-5)
- Improved consistency in the assessment and grading practices of teachers (pp. 6-7)

The next four levels of specificity involve *standards-based grading and reporting based directly on the public, published standards.* The greatest specificity is provided when all of the standards for the curriculum for a subject are recorded in the gradebook and included on the report card. As examples, using this approach for the Wisconsin Computer Science standards mentioned above the nineteen standards would be in a teacher's gradebook and on the report card, and for Grade 5 Common Core Mathematics all twenty-seven standards would receive grades and be included in the report card. The problem with this approach is that there are so many standards that keeping records for teachers is cumbersome, and the often-lengthy report card can be overwhelming for parents.

Somewhat less specificity is provided when grading and reporting are based on the standards for each subject but up to approximately the most important ten standards are selected as the grading and reporting standards. The selection of grading and reporting standards should be done by the experts—the grade level or subject teachers who will base their instruction, assessment, grading, and reporting on the chosen standards.

Another approach that provides less specificity is to use only the domains or strands in the national, state, or provincial standards. Using the Wisconsin Computer Studies and Grade 5 Common Core Mathematics examples, there would be five strands/content areas in teachers' gradebooks and on report cards. A slightly different approach that works well for some teachers and subjects is a blending of the two approaches described above. For example, there are five strands (now called "goal areas") in the ACTFL World-Readiness Standards for Learning Languages: (a) Communication, (b) Cultures, (c) Connections, (d) Comparisons, and

(e) Communities. The Communication goal area has three standards: (a) Interpersonal Communication, (b) Interpretive Communication, and (c) Presentational Communication. There is a distinct likelihood that some students would achieve very differently on each of these. For effective communication and instructional decision making, a foreign language teacher would record information about achievement on each of these standards separately, but for the other goal areas, the teachers collect and report information at that level, which means there would be seven categories in the gradebook and on the report card.

The next level of specificity of content standards is provided by what are often called "Power" or "Priority" or "Essential" Standards. These are usually determined by teams of teachers in schools or districts who decide what are the most important "big ideas" in the national, state, or provincial standards that are the base for the curriculum. Townsley and Wear (2020), drawing on the work of Larry Ainsworth and Douglas Reeves, suggested the following criteria for determining Priority Standards with a "yes" for three or more indicating that it is a priority standard:

1. Teacher Input: Is this standard important to know?
2. Can a student learn the content – the big concept – without having this information.
3. Endurance: Do we really expect our students to retain the knowledge and skills over time, as opposed to merely learning them for a test?
4. Readiness: Is the standard essential for success in the next unit, course, or grade level?
5. Leverage: Will proficiency in this standard help our students in other areas of the curriculum and in other academic disciplines?
6. State or Provincial or National Testing: Is this standard tested (p. 35)

Although not identified specifically as "Priority Standards," in the following Educator Vignette, Tanya De Hoog describes how in the Junior School at Southridge School in Surrey, B.C. they defined three to six standards for each subject, with a focus on ensuring that wording is specific, while also being broad enough to be informed by multiple pieces of assessment evidence during the reporting period. Examples of their reporting standards for Grades 3-5 and 6-7 are shown in

Figure 7.5.

GRADES 3 - 5

English Language Arts
Communicates orally for different purposes (e.g., inform, retell, collaborate, formally present)

Demonstrates comprehension (e.g., vocabulary, retell, describe story/text features, infer) of grade-level texts

Synthesizes (e.g., combine) ideas or information

Writes for different purposes (e.g., inform, persuade, explain, entertain)

Applies grade-level writing conventions (e.g., spelling, grammar, punctuation, sentence structure, paragraph structure) in different contexts

French
Understands gestures, vocabulary, and expressions

Uses vocabulary, expressions, and gestures to communicate orally

Uses vocabulary, expressions (Gr. 3/4/5), and conventions (Gr. 5) when communicating in writing Demonstrates comprehension of text through oral (Gr. 3/4/5)

and written (Gr. 5) responses

Mathematics
Demonstrates mastery of number concepts (e.g. place value, fact fluency, multi-step operations)

Communicates (e.g., use terminology, show work, construct models) thinking and/or understanding of concepts (e.g., measurement, data, geometry)

Applies understanding and/or strategies to solve problems (e.g. interpret terminology, use steps, justify solution)

GRADES 6 - 7

Design
Inquires and analyzes (e.g., explain and justify the need for a solution)

Develops ideas (e.g., present ideas and justify chosen design)

Creates a solution (e.g., create and present prototype based on plan)

Evaluates (e.g., reflect on the overall success of the solution)

Physical and Health Education

Demonstrates activity/sport specific knowledge and understanding

Plans for performance (e.g., set goals, outline plan to improve skills and overall well-being

Applies and performs (e.g., use sport-specific skills/strategies in games and/or performance)

Reflects and improves performance (e.g., accept and use feedback, demonstrate sportsmanship and fair play)

Visual and Performing Arts: Music
Demonstrates knowledge and understanding (e.g., use appropriate/specific terminology in various contexts)

Develops and applies skills and techniques (e.g., vocal, instrumental)

Thinks creatively (e.g., explore ideas, plan, problem solve)

Responds (e.g., make connections, analyze and evaluate music of self and others)

Figure 7.5. Southridge Grading and Reporting Standards
Permission provided by Southridge School

Type of Learning Goals

There is a huge dilemma in education about whether standards should be focused on content or skills. I'm not going to weigh into that discussion here except to note that, in the examples referred to and/or shown above, some have a greater emphasis on content, some have a greater emphasis on skills, and some have a mixture of both. One way that some organizations/jurisdictions have resolved the dilemma is to use broad categories that are the same or similar for all subjects. An example can be found in the categories used for the Achievement Charts in Ontario – Knowledge and Understanding, Thinking, Communication and Application. Another example is the International Baccalaureate (IB) Diploma program that uses the categories of Knowledge and Understanding, Application and Analysis, Synthesis and Evaluation, and Use and Application of Appropriate Skills.

Choice of Words

This is easy—the words used for the standards on report cards must be parent and student friendly, avoiding typical educator jargon. An example of how this can be done comes from Pernille Ripp, an amazing middle school English teacher in Wisconsin

Standard	Official language	Student Language
ELA 1:	Determine/analyze development of central ideas/themes in a text.	Decide or figure out and add your own thoughts as evidence about the main ideas of the text and the theme; summarize a text
ELA 2:	Analyze how story elements interact.	Interpret/analyze and put in your own words how things such as conflict, theme, tough questions, and other things affect the story.
ELA 3:	Write informative texts to convey ideas; select, organize, and analyze content; summarize.	Write informational text to show your ideas/thoughts, select, organize and interpret (put into your words) the information. Summarize.
ELA 4:	Write narratives to share real events, using vivid detail and ordered sequence.	Write stories to share real events, using powerful details and an order of events that makes sense.
ELA 5:	Draw evidence from texts to support written analysis.	Pull out text evidence that supports the thoughts/topic you are writing about.
ELA 6:	Command the conventions of standard English grammar, usage, and vocabulary.	Master punctuation, grammar, spelling, vocabulary and correct formatting of work.
ELA 7:	Present focused claims with support, using eye contact, volume, and elocution	Present focused claims with support, using eye contact,

Figure 7.6. "Official" and Student Language for ELA Standards
Permission provided by Pernille Ripp

Grades for standards with or without subject grades

From K to 12 (and maybe to K to 16), all grading and reporting should be based on standards and provide information about student achievement on standards. But is there also a need for overall grades for each subject? Ideally, in a perfect world, the answer would be "No" because the valuable information is provided by the student's achievement on the standards, not by an overall subject grade. Subject grades don't add to the communication; they actually detract from it because, when they are provided, parents and students inevitably focus on the subject grade, not the grades for standards. It is also important to recognize that determining an accurate grade for subjects can be extremely difficult for teachers, so we need to question why teachers are required to do this extra task when it doesn't enhance communication. There is, however, almost certainly a need for subject grades when credit for certification or for external purposes is required. Thus, the question becomes for what grade levels are subject grades necessary? I see absolutely no need for subject grades for K-8 and dubious need for subject grades for 9-10. Subject grades are commonly needed for grades 11 and 12 for the issuance of diplomas and for external purposes such as admission to post-secondary education. Having said that, I recognize that most high schools will continue to provide subject grades for grades 9 and 10, but I fervently hope that they will be eliminated in middle and elementary schools.

Summary

Grades are broken when they are not directly based on standards and do not give information about achievement of standards. Fixing this requires the use of standards-based curriculum, instruction, assessment, and grading and reporting student achievement by standards. Teachers should collect information about student achievement of individual learning goals and should be able to discuss this information with students and parents. For report card purposes, learning goals may be grouped together to summarize student achievement as shown in Figures 7.4 and 7.7.

> The simple truth is that a single number describing a student's performance in school is just as ineffectual and difficult to interpret as a single number describing someone's physical health.
>
> *(Guskey, 2020, p. 41)*

Educator Vignette

Tanya de Hoog
Junior School Principal,
Southridge School,
Surrey, British Columbia

Sometimes the assessment culture of a school becomes too focused on achievement as the defining feature of successful learning. When this happens, it's easy to lose sight of sound assessment practices. When I arrived at Southridge Junior School in September 2016, the long-held grading practices were aggregate grades for each subject in the form of a 5-point achievement scale in Kindergarten through Grade 3 and by-subject percentage grades in Grades 5-7. A student's behavior was often the differentiating factor for percentage-based grade boundaries or between achievement scale levels. Furthermore, these methods contributed to a competitive achievement culture in the school. Our grading system was not helping learners understand how they could progress and grow, nor was it serving the needs of teachers. We felt stuck. So, we set out to explore the beautiful question: *How might we implement a balanced K-7 feedback and reporting system that supports enhanced academics, a culture of learning, and personalized growth while also providing accurate, meaningful, and specific feedback, marks, and grades based on developmentally appropriate learning standards and expectations?*

Enter standards-based assessment and reporting. After a two-year adaptive design process involving surveys and empathy interviews with teachers, parents, and students, we were ready to begin recalibrating assessment and reporting practices at our school. The data we collected from surveys and empathy interviews were instrumental in determining the most critical shifts and areas for improvement. We learned that teachers dreaded writing report cards because they undermined teaching and learning. Teachers also felt frustrated that aggregated numbers and percentages often overshadowed the comments they spent so much time writing. Parents expressed frustration about Edu-jargon and the role of behavior in determining grades. Many also shared that it wasn't clear what aggregated grades and percentages communicated, so they compared their child's standing to other children to get a sense of where their child was. We also found that parents did not know about standard-based assessment, which opened opportunities for parent education. We were surprised to learn that students perceived anything less than 80% as a failure. It was time to begin shaping a new narrative around assessment and reporting at our school.

Focusing on standards-based assessment and grading helped us begin a complete recalibration of our assessment and grading philosophy and practices. We started by separating behavior from achievement by defining essential skills (e.g., self-management and social-emotional behaviors) that all learners should consistently demonstrate to succeed at school. We then developed a unified Kindergarten to Grade 7 progress and final achievement scale with symbols and explicit descriptors for each of the four performance levels. Finally, we defined three to six standards for each subject with a focus on ensuring that wording is specific but also broad enough to be informed by multiple pieces of assessment evidence during the reporting period. Although collaboratively defining the standards took the most time and effort, the process led to rich discussion and clarification about age-appropriate expectations for each subject. To ensure clarity of language for the standards and the descriptors for the performance scale, we conducted focus groups with teachers and parents throughout the redesign process to get their feedback. Ken O'Connor also came to our school early on to work with our teachers, provide parent education, and support our leadership team in leading and implementing the changes. After two years of learning, iterating, and planning, we successfully launched the first iteration of a standards-based report card. Even now, we continue to collect feedback to enhance the clarity of language for teachers, parents, and students to ensure that the standards and performance scale descriptors are explicit.

The shift to standards-based assessment and reporting enabled us to clearly define subject-specific learning goals against which to measure students' progress and final achievement. Making the change to standards-based assessment and reporting helped us make the monumental shift from an achievement culture to a learning and feedback culture. Approaching assessment and reporting as a communication of learning *system* opened new possibilities for improvement as we sought to deepen and refine standard-based classroom assessment and reporting practices across all grades. It also inspired us to redefine a communication of learning system that seamlessly connects all aspects of learning across the school year. Once our system was in place, we created a *K-7 Communication of Learning Guidebook*. The guidebook defines our standards-based assessment philosophy and practices, provides purpose statements for each communication of learning event, includes annotated report cards to teach parents how to read them (see below), and a glossary of essential assessment terms.

With clearly defined subject-specific standards in place, our written feedback became more meaningful because the standards make the learning goals for each subject clear. Well-articulated subject standards are now the foundation for framing students' progress, strengths, areas for improvement, next steps, and final achievement. We have a saying now at our school: "once your assessment house is in order, everything else falls into place." Making such a profound shift takes time, but it's worth it. Resources, support systems, and transparent procedures are essential for the recalibration process and implementation to succeed. Standards-based grading and reporting were the catalysts for opening an ongoing dialogue about learning as a continuous process instead of a series of reporting stops and starts. Learning is the foundation, progress and growth are the focus, and student success and achievement are the outcomes.

Sample annotated second page from a Grade 3-5 (PYP) Learning Semester 1 Progress Report:

English Language Arts

Strengths:

Area(s) for Improvement & Next Steps:

Defined Standards:	S1	S2	Final
Communicates orally for different purposes (e.g. inform, retell, collaborate, formally present)			
Demonstrates comprehension (e.g. vocabulary, retell, describe story/text features, infer) of grade-level texts			
Synthesizes (e.g. combine) ideas or information			
Writes for different purposes (e.g. inform, persuade, explain, entertain)			
Applies grade-level writing conventions (e.g. spelling, grammar, punctuation, sentence structure, paragraph structure) in different contexts			

French

Strengths:

Area(s) for Improvement & Next Steps:

Defined Standards:	S1	S2	Final
Understands gestures, vocabulary, and expressions			
Uses vocabulary, expressions, and gestures to communicate orally			
Uses vocabulary, expressions (Gr. 3/4/5), and conventions (Gr. 5) when communicating in writing			
Demonstrates comprehension of text through oral (Gr. 3/4/5) and written (Gr. 5) responses			

Strengths and Areas for Improvement/Next Steps: for each subject, the subject teacher will highlight strengths and areas for improvement/next steps. **Strengths** are intended to celebrate what a student is doing well/successfully in the context of their subject-specific learning. **Areas for Improvement** are intended to clearly indicate an area that the student needs to focus on to strengthen their subject-specific learning or skills. **Next Steps** are action-oriented and highlight what the student can do next to positively impact their learning. If support is needed from home to help the student with next steps, this will be indicated in the comment for clarity. Otherwise, next steps are supported at school.

The previous Learning Semester's progress indicators are visible in the Learning Semester 2/Final report to help track progress.

Figure 7.7. Southridge School Report Card
Permission provided by Southridge School

Solon School District
Solon, IA

1. Entries in the grade book that count towards the final grade will be limited to course or grade level standards.

   What it means

   - When creating a new entry in the gradebook that counts towards the final grade, it must be a standard such as "Find the area of a regular polygon by applying trigonometric ratios" or "Understands how evolution occurs (natural selcction, mutation, migration, and genetic drift).
   - Assignments or other activities that do not count toward the final grade may still be recorded in the grade book for the purpose of communicating with students and parents; however, it should be clearly noted as such.

   What it doesn't mean

   - Course or grade level standards must be word-for-word from the Iowa/ Common Core essential concepts and skills lists.
   - Entering "Mitosis Project" or "Unit 5 Test" in the grade book.

(Solon Community School District, 2012)

Christel House Academy
Indianapolis, IN

Students at Christel House Academy receive scores on standards rather than assignments or tests. This helps teachers communicate the students' true academic achievement and focus in on knowledge, reasoning and skills deficiencies and strengths. It also allows students to focus on their growth and development, while setting specific goals related to their academics, character, and habits of work. For example, rather than earning a "3" on a unit exam, the student receives a grade for each learning target or standard assessed on the unit exam.

(Christel House Academy, 2018, p. 5)

Fix 8 Provide clear descriptions of proficiency levels; don't assign grades using inappropriate or unclear performance standards.

> Performance standards describe levels of achievement in key areas of learning. Performance standards answer the question(s): "How good is good enough?
>
> *British Columbia Ministry of Education, 2020*

Grades are broken when they are determined using poorly defined performance standards, such as letter–number relationships (e.g., A = 90–100, B = 80–89) that have traditionally masqueraded as performance standards. The fix is to develop clear and rich criterion-referenced descriptions of a limited number of levels of achievement. Whatever symbols are used to summarize student achievement (e.g., A B C D F; 4 3 2 1; E M N U), each level must be described clearly, with the level considered "good enough" (i.e., "competent," "proficient," "meeting") precisely identified as the basis for levels above and below.

The judgments made when developing the descriptors and when evaluating student work are always subjective. These are not matters of learning science but are common communication conventions. As long as everyone involved accepts that those who have developed the descriptors and levels are qualified and understands the terms used, we can communicate effectively. That, however, is easy to say and hard to do. I can't emphasize strongly enough that the most common reasons for parent opposition to standards-based grading has been lack of clarity in the description of the performance standards and inconsistency in teacher application of those performance standards, especially for the highest level of performance.

How to Develop Performance Standards

The best performance standard setting uses the collective experience of a number of educators who are knowledgeable and experienced. When teams of teachers address performance standards together, they can develop the basis for communicating achievement continua for each standard in ways that all concerned will understand, including students and their families. In that context, the teams can then also set performance standards at the appropriate level along each continuum. Once developed, the resulting depiction of academic success will be published and public for all—administrators, teachers, students, parents, and others—to see from the beginning of instruction (an excellent protocol for this process can be found in O'Connor, 2018, pp. 70-72). Given that states and provinces tend to specify content standards, the determination of overall performance standards is best done at the state/provincial level, but if it has not been done at that level, it should be done at the district level for public schools and at the school level for private schools. Once the performance standards are in place, teachers need frequent opportunities for moderation—professional dialogue about them so they develop shared understanding and apply them consistently. The New Zealand Ministry of Education identified the following benefits of moderation for teachers:

> - Brings together collective wisdom, resulting in greater consistency of judgment, and focused teaching.
> - Provides greater confidence in teacher judgments and assurance that judgments are consistent with other professionals.
> - Leads to shared expectations of learning and understandings of levels and progression of learning.
> - Develops deeper understandings about content and progressions of learning.
> - Improves quality of assessment.
> - Alignment of expectations and judgments with curriculum expectations or progressions, and hence improved teaching and learning.
> - Assurance to parents and others that interpretations of students' progress and achievement are in line with other professionals.
>
> (New Zealand Ministry of Education, 2021)

This points to the need for districts and schools to put a lot of time (and money) into providing opportunities for moderation at the school and/or district level.

How many levels?

In a pure standards-based system we would only have two levels of performance: proficient and not proficient. Some schools/districts use only these two levels, but this is usually restricted to early elementary. Most commonly, performance continua use four levels: (a) a level above proficient, to recognize (and encourage) excellence; (b) proficient; (c) below proficient, but close; and (d) significantly below proficiency, or insufficient. There is not, however, universal agreement about the use of four levels, especially having a level above proficiency. Thus, for example, the Winneconne Community School District (WI) uses only three levels with Proficiency (Got It!) as the highest level (Hierck & Larson, 2018, p. 10). All I can say is that there isn't an absolutely "right" number of levels, but the right number is between two and seven. The reason for that is that we have to be able to describe the levels so that it is clear how each level is better than the level below and not as good as the level above, and it is difficult to describe precisely more than seven levels. This means that *the use of the percentages should be eliminated* because:

1. We cannot describe the differences between 101 levels.
2. Percentages suggest a precision that simply doesn't exist; no one in any meaningful way can tell the difference between 59% and 60% or between 89% and 90%, but critical decisions about pass/fail and which students receive an A are made on that basis.
3. The more decision points there are, the more inconsistent teacher judgments are.

Brookhart and Guskey (2019) stated,

> Using fewer grade categories means that educators contend with fewer borderline cases. If grades are simply Pass/Fail, only scores near the one cut-off are subject to misclassification. With letter grades, there are four cut-offs with potential for classification errors. As the number of categories increases, so do the number of borderline cases and the possibility of miscommunication.

They also note that "Several studies found that the probable error on the 0-100 scale is plus or minus five to six points or even greater," which means with 90% as the cut-off for an A and 80% as a cut-off for a B, a student could be misclassified as receiving an A, B, or a C.

Percentages on their own have no meaning; 30% is excellent and 40% is virtually unattainable in hitting in Major League Baseball, but 80% is necessary for excellence in free throws in basketball. The difference is that hitting a baseball coming at you at 95 miles per hour is much more difficult than putting the ball in the basket with no one trying to stop you. When assessing student achievement, there is variability in the difficulty of skills and concepts and in the difficulty of assessments (intentional or unintentional) that makes percentages meaningless; 70% on difficult skills or concepts or a difficult assessment may represent proficiency or even excellence, but 70% on easy skills or concepts or on any easy assessment would represent less than proficient. This means that if teachers use points-based assessments, they must set cut scores for the levels of proficiency; for example, for a high level of difficulty, 14/20 may be excellent, while for a low level of difficulty, excellence may require at least 19/20 (for a more detailed example, see O'Connor, 2018, p. 92 and for a definitive explanation of why percentages shouldn't be used see Guskey, 2013).

When we deemphasize the percentage system, both our performance standards and the way we report student achievement will be clearer, more consistent, and richer in specific detail. As an added benefit, their clarity and specificity may make them effective teaching and learning tools, partly because a credit will no longer be defined simply as obtaining a mean of 50 or 60 percent; passing and moving on to the next level of study ideally would require proficiency on all standards. This is basis for competency-based systems (see Stack & Vander Els, 2018).

Another issue that needs to be addressed with regard to the number of levels is the use of .5 levels that are basically undescribed levels between two described levels; for example, "3.5 - All of 3.0 plus some of 4.0." This should be seen as unacceptable; if we nominally have a 4- level scale with 1.5, 2.5 and 3.5, we now have a 7-level scale, and each of the levels should have complete and clear descriptions, not just "all of 3 and some of 4."

It is also worth noting that some schools/districts add a fifth level to the common four level scale to indicate that the student provided minimal or insufficient evidence of learning. The symbol for this level is usually a zero or an I.

Finally, with regard to the number of levels, Schimmer and SYS Education (n.d.) show that the number of levels and how we use them also depends on whether the content standard is binary, simple, or complex, as is illustrated in Figure 8.1

below.

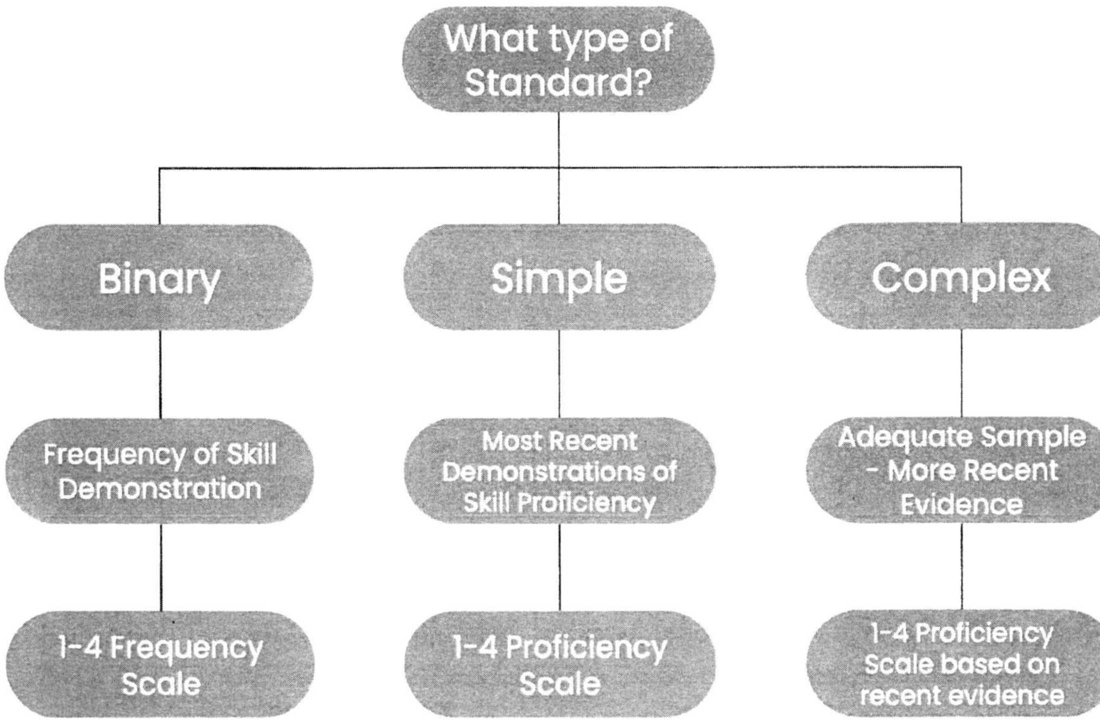

Figure 8.1. How Many Levels *(Developed by Natalie Conway and Tom Schimmer. Permission provided by SYS Education)*

Symbols

As illustrated in Figure 8.2, we commonly identify performance standards with symbols. The symbols are usually letters that are the initial letter or letters of the labels and a numerical designation. It is important that the numerical designation only be used for scoring purposes and that when discussing learning with students or parents, we emphasize words, not numbers.

PERFORMANCE STANDARDS

Symbols	Label	Summary Descriptor	Detailed Descriptor
E	Excellent	Demonstrates an in-depth and/or insightful understanding and application of the learning outcomes.	• Applies concepts in learning situations flexibly. • Reliably transfers understanding to new contexts. • Demonstrates precision and/or creativity in applying skills and strategies between concepts to approach new learning situations.

P	Proficient	Demonstrates a comprehensive and/or thoughtful understanding and application of the learning outcomes.	• Applies concepts in learning situations deliberately • Routinely transfers understanding to new contexts. • Demonstrates flexibility and/or intentionality in applying skills and strategies to approach new learning situations.
A	Approaching Proficiency	Demonstrates a partial understanding and application of the learning outcomes-	• Applies concepts in learning situations predictably. • Occasionally transfers understanding to new contexts • Demonstrates functional and/or straight-forward skills and strategies to approach new learning situations • Application of skills and strategies may be inconsistent and/or predictable.
B	Beginning	Demonstrates an initial understanding and application of the learning outcomes.	• Applies concepts in learning situations minimally • Rarely transfers understanding to new contexts, • Demonstrates limited skills and strategies to approach new learning situations; • Application of skills and strategies with uncertainty and/or difficulty

Figure 8.2. Performance Standards – Symbols, Labels and Descriptors

Adapted from Edmonton Catholic Schools Levels of Achievement (LOA) for Grades 1-12 https://www.ecsd.net/page/17856/understanding-the-codes-in-grades-and-attendance

Labels

For ease of communication, as illustrated in Figure 8.2, we attach labels to each level of performance. The labels are extremely important because, although the real meaning of the levels comes from the descriptors, the most common identification and use of the performance levels is by the labels; often, parents and students think only in terms of the labels. It is therefore very important that the labels be chosen carefully so that the initial impact is positive and that the labels don't cause misunderstanding. A wide range of labels, serious and not so serious, (see Figure 8.3) are used (the numbers and letters are included only as reference points). The labels in Figure 8.3 have varying degrees of acceptability, but there is one label that is often used that should *never* be used and that is *exceeds*. Exceeds is unacceptable for the following reasons:

1. Exceeds suggests that, to obtain the highest level, a student would need to perform above the grade level expectation, but students should be able to obtain the highest level by excelling at grade level;
2. It is very difficult to describe "exceeds" in ways that students and parents can understand; and
3. "As soon as you make the task more difficult or move the learning expectation to a higher and more advanced level you have changed to standard and altered the goal"

(Guskey, 2014).

Beginning	Approaching	Proficient	Excels
Novice	Apprentice	Practitioner	Expert
Emerging	Developing	Meeting	Extending
Minimal	Limited	Skilled	Exemplary
Well Below	Below	Meeting	Advanced
Basic	Acceptable	Competent	Distinguished
Youngling	Padawan	Jedi	Jedi Master
Rookie	Professional	All Star	Hall of Fame
Moving toward the water	Boarding the canoe	Raising your paddle	Journeying into deeper waters
Not Yet	Almost there	Got it	Wow
1	2	3	4
D	C	B	A

Figure 8.3. Labels for Proficiency Levels

Descriptors

After we agree on the number of levels, we then have to determine the characteristics of each level and describe them clearly and concisely. An example of summary and detailed descriptors is found in Figure 8.2 (additional examples of descriptors can be seen in Policy/Procedures for this fix and in Figure 11.5 on page 151). It is important to emphasize that this is an example and not a model. I fully accept that some may feel that the focus on applying skills and on transfer is inappropriate, but it was chosen because of the consistency of the wording from level to level that makes the progression between levels clear. Far too often, we see descriptors where the words describing each level are different, so the progression isn't clear. The summary descriptor provides an overview of each level, and the detailed descriptor provides more specific characteristics with two or three sentences or phrases for each level.

The challenge is to create clear descriptors of the overall levels so that we have a delineated achievement continuum with which we can consistently identify levels of proficiency. It must, however, be emphasized that the overall performance standard is only a starting point in the standards-setting process. We need the overall descriptors so that there is a clear and consistent base for the most important performance standards—those used to give students feedback and/or scores on their demonstrations of learning. Thus, when the overall performance levels and descriptors have been described, task and/or grade level rubrics and performance standards must be developed using the language of the standard. Then, these rubrics written in the actual language that describes levels of achievement for the subject and grade level standard need to be supported by exemplars demonstrating levels at, above, and below proficiency. Again, the best classroom performance–standard setting process pools the collective experience of several educators. These teachers—confident, competent masters of the relevant academic discipline who have extensive teaching experience—set standards based on their collective study of samples of student evidence of learning. Here again, teachers using these standards need frequent opportunities for professional dialogue about them, so they develop shared understanding and apply them consistently.

Ideally, rubrics are strength-based and written as much as possible in positive language. Rinkema and Williams (2019) have developed what they call "scales," and the following illustrates the difference between their old rubrics and their new strength-based positive scales (pp. 33-41):

Old Rubric for Evidence

Uh-Oh (0%-69%)	Needs Some Work (70%-79%)	Very Good (80%-89%)	Excellent Work! (90%-100%)
There is little to no evidence in this essay. It's not clear the student has read the novel.	The essay is missing some evidence or the evidence doesn't support the thesis. Evidence is not cited.	Evidence from the novel supports the thesis but isn't the best available. There are at least three pieces of evidence. Evidence is cited.	Evidence from the novel is well chosen and is clearly the best available. There are more than four pieces of evidence. Evidence is cited correctly.

New Scale for Evidence

Output: Use of Evidence	I can support my claim with my own ideas about my purpose.	I can support my claim with evidence that relates to my purpose.	**I can support my claim with multiple, credible pieces of evidence that support my purpose.**	I can support my claim with varied pieces of evidence that work together to help prove my purpose.

Figure 8.4. A traditional ("old") rubric and a scale that describes each level positively (Rinkema & Williams, 2019, p. 3)
Permission provided by Corwin Press

The performance standards, rubrics, and exemplars need to be published and public for all to see from the beginning of instruction. The key to success is to describe levels of achievement in terms of the characteristics of the actual kind of academic achievement (or behaviors) being judged. Obviously, therefore, performance standards for feedback and scoring will be very different for different contexts (i.e., subjects and grade levels). When such descriptions are accompanied by samples of student work depicting each level of proficiency, we lay a solid foundation for effective judgment of and communication about student achievement.

There are a number of other aspects of describing the performance standards that are important.

1. How the level above proficiency is described.

According to Schimmer (2020), "It should *not* mean making the top level of performance opaque, artificially more difficult to achieve, or only accessible to a few." [Emphasis added] The problem is illustrated in this parent complaint:

> "When a student asks a teacher how to achieve a '4,' they are told simply you need 'to go above and beyond.' What does that even mean? How do you translate that into learning or achievement? You can't"
>
> (Fannon, 2019).

This level is not above grade level, and it should not be described as going beyond what was taught; rather, it must be clearly described, taught, and assessed, and it must be attainable by students.

2. Performance, not learning progressions

It is essential that performance standards describe the how well, not the what, but some so-called proficiency scales describe learning progressions, not performance progressions. Consider this example from a deliberately unnamed school district:

> Power Standard: Students will analyze and solve linear equations with one variable, including rational coefficients and using the distributive property and combining like terms.
>
> 4.0 Students will be able to:
>
> 1. Solve single and multi-step equations using the properties
> 2. Transform equations into different forms
> 3. Communicate their reasoning for every skill
>
> 2.0 Students will be able to perform basic processes such as:
>
> 1. Write examples of equations with one variable
> 2. Solve equations using the order of operations
> 3. Use the distributive property to solve and simplify equations

Without making any comment on the quality of the alignment between the power standard and what the students are required to do, the activities in 2.0 are building blocks for what students are required to do in 4.0 (i.e., a learning progression). Also, apart from indicating that for 4.0 there should be "No major errors or omissions from the C (2.0) and A (4.0) content," there is nothing about how well—everything listed in 4.0 and 2.0 could be done anywhere from superbly to poorly, and the proficiency scale provides no indication of what those quality variations are. If this scale actually provided a performance progression it would provide descriptors for four achievement levels for each of the three components of 4.0.

Reibel and Thede (2020) provided this helpful explanation of the difference between learning progressions and proficiency progressions, which they call "proficiency gradations."

> Proficiency gradations maintain the same verb in each level, but the modifying language is changed to communicate the level of mastery expected . . . In contrast, learning progressions use a different verb with each level, (often) ranging from simple application or depth of knowledge to more complex application or depth of knowledge. (p. 31)

To create effective proficiency gradations, Reibel and Thede suggest three rules: Don't be negative, Don't use numbers, and Don't change the verb (p. 33).

Another situation where learning and performance progressions are often confused pertains to Webb's Depth of Knowledge (DOK) levels. Erik Francis, an expert on the use of DOK, stated that the four levels of DOK and the four levels of proficiency commonly used in standards-based grading do not align with each other. He asserted,

> SBG is about proficiency. The four levels serve as scales that measure how successfully students can meet the learning expectation set by an academic standard. . . The levels measure academic success. Webb's DOK levels code the cognitive demand of the learning expectation of the standards. They designate the depth and extent students must demonstrate and communicate their knowledge and thinking – or learning. That is based on the most cognitively demanding performance objective of the standard. (Francis, 2019)

The problem is that if the DOK levels are used as performance levels and the

DOK level required by a standard is, say, level 1, then the score would be a 1 but the student may have been proficient and should receive a 3. Everything at each of the DOK levels can be done well or poorly or anywhere in between so what teachers must do is identify the DOK level of the standard and then identify the performance level achieved by the student. This, and not the DOK level, is what is recorded in the grade book.

3. Descriptors should never include "help" or "support."

Achievement must be assessed based what students can do independently, so it should be seen as a given for all levels (except for students on IEP's). Help and support are instructional variables, not assessment variables.

4. Rubric development

It has generally been accepted practice that rubrics should describe all (four) levels and that development should be the starting point for describing proficiency. Both aspects have been challenged recently with many advocating for single point rubrics (e.g., Ripp, 2019), and Guskey (2017) suggesting very strongly that the starting point should be describing the level above proficiency.

When - at the time of reporting or year-end standards

Most standards are described as the expectation for the end of the year/course, but most schools provide formal report cards two or three or four times a year. Because of this, decisions must be made about whether the performance standards are for what is expected at the end or at the time of the report card part way through the year. Schools/districts must state clearly, preferably on the report card, whether the levels describe performance at the time of the report card or the performance level expected at the end of the year. This choice must be made and communicated clearly to teachers, students, and parents. If the choice is year-end performance levels, everyone involved, especially parents, must be helped to understand that there will be few, if any, proficient grades on report cards until near the end of the year.

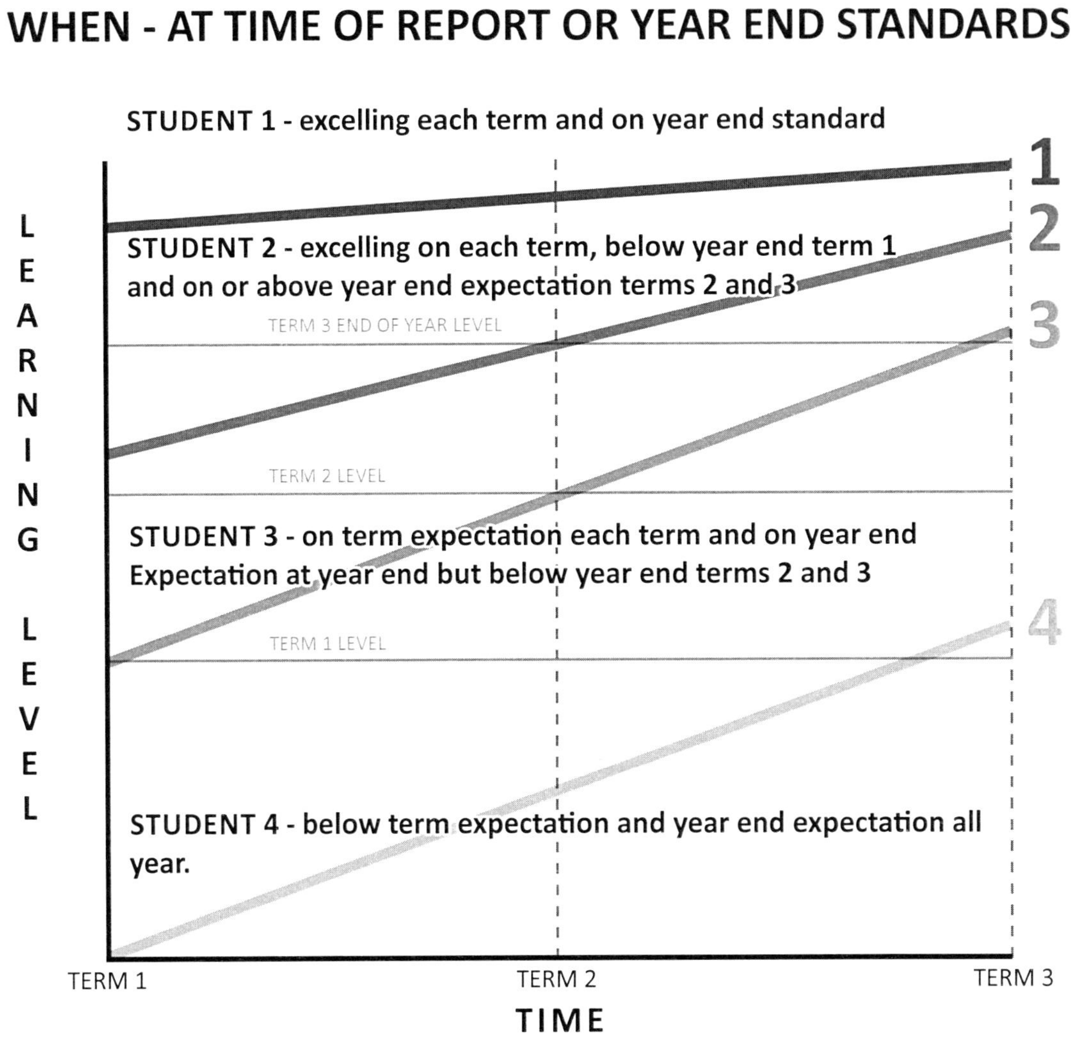

Figure 8.5. When Illustrated

Achievement, growth, or progress

Achievement	"The act of achieving or performing; an obtaining by exertion; successful performance."	Absolute (e.g., "he/she…is 4 feet 6 inches tall" … is reading at Grade 2 level" "**Achievement at**…"
Growth	"The process of growing: increase in size, number, frequency, strength, etc."	Relative achievement measured against where a child was (e.g., "he/she… grew three inches since last measurement" . . . "has moved from Grade 1 level in the last month" "**Growth from**…"

Progress	"Movement, as toward a goal; advance."	Relative achievement measured against a goal, standard, future result, e.g., "he/she . . . is now one inch below average height for age" . . . "is now two grade levels below expected level for age" **"Progress to/ toward. . ."**

Figure 8.6. Definitions and Examples of Achievement, Growth, and Progress

It is also important to recognize that performance standards are about achievement, not about growth or progress. For example, a student could make significant personal growth while making limited progress at a (relatively) low level of achievement (e.g., Student 4 Figure 8.7). Also, a student could make limited growth and progress at a (relatively) high level of achievement (e.g., Student 1 Figure 8.7). Achievement, growth, and progress are closely related but different concepts (Figure 8.6). Achievement is an absolute and is the grading variable (the basic ingredient of grades), while growth and progress are both relative and can be reporting variables (i.e., aspects of student performance that should be communicated about but not included directly in grades). The reference point for growth is the individual—one grows from where they were previously. The reference point for progress is proficiency—one progresses to or toward proficiency. Although it is critical for intrinsic motivation that students have a clear sense of their own growth and progress, grades must be measures of achievement only so that everyone knows what they mean.

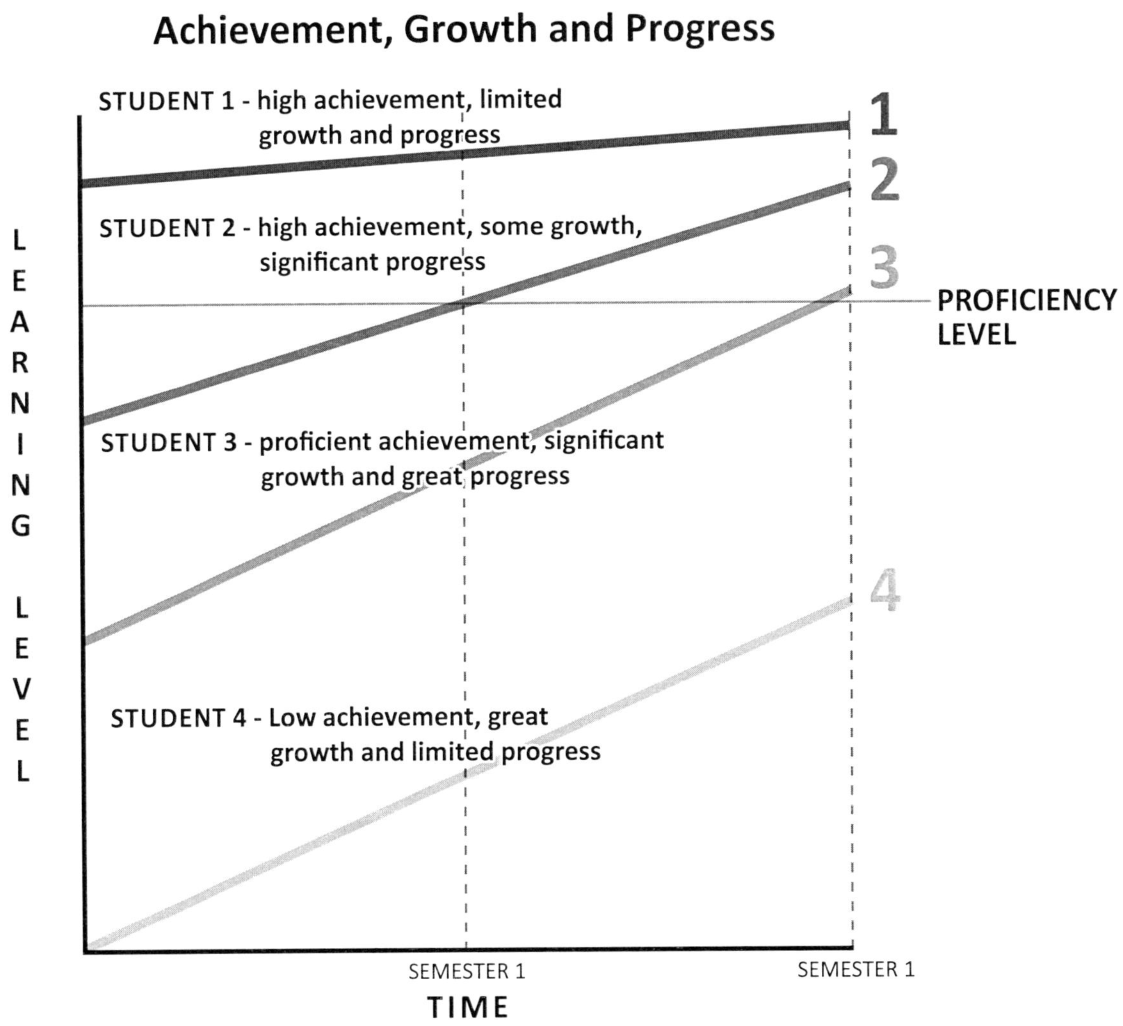

Figure 8.7. Achievement, Growth and Progress Illustrated

Student Involvement

This is a critical area for student involvement. The better students understand the performance standards, both overall and at the task level, the more likely it is that they will achieve at a high level. Students therefore require opportunities to develop and use task-specific scoring tools containing age-appropriate, student-friendly descriptors of the meaning of the relevant summary symbols, so that they can accurately and usefully self-assess and set goals.

Summary

The keys to success are thus as follows:

Use

1. Overall and specific performance standards with a limited number of levels, clearly described in the language of the appropriate achievement continuum.
2. Professional dialogue about performance standards between teachers so a shared understanding may be developed and standards applied consistently.
3. Clear, easily understandable student- and parent-friendly descriptors made available from the beginning of instruction.

Don't use

- Learning progressions that masquerade as performance standards
- Percentage scales
- .5 levels
- Support or Independence as part of the descriptors for levels
- Exceeds
- Progress when you mean achievement and vice versa

> "Performance standards are the other – and often (somewhat) forgotten part of standards. . . . Performance standards are about the "how well" we expect the content standard to be performed. For there to be any possibility that grades will be consistent, every school/district must have clear, well written, public performance standards that are understood by teachers, students, and parents ... One reason that (performance standards) have received less attention is that developing clear and useful performance standards is very difficult; in fact, the development of performance standards is probably the most difficult part of the whole process (of standards-based grading) because it requires very high-quality critical thinking and provides a challenge to our ability to use the English language (or any other language) clearly and precisely."
>
> *(O'Connor, 2013, pp. 47-48)*

Educator Vignette

John W. Stephens
Grade 8 Mathematics Teacher
Stonepark Intermediate School,
Charlottetown, Prince Edward Island

To support students' skill development in math, I use the following learning and achievement progression as a foundation for feedback on formative, summative, and self-assessments. The purpose is to help students understand what they are doing well with respect to the outcome being learned and assessed and also what they need to learn next.

The implementation of this progression occurs in three intentional ways within my classroom:

1. *As Curriculum.* Each outcome is broken down into a set of "I can..." statements organized into three criteria: Concepts, Calculations, and Conventions. The "I can..." statements are constructed through an analysis of the provincially authorized curriculum.

2. *As Instruction.* I consistently refer to the progression throughout units, lessons, and as students are working through problems. For example, students are often assigned (or have the option to select) practice grids which are aligned to specific levels within the outcome we are working on. Practice Grid 1 may be designed to support students at a Constructing stage while Practice Grid 3 may focus more on Refining or Agility.

3. *As Assessment.* Feedback is provided using the progression on all major assignments. Students do not receive a percentage score on tests/assignments. Performance on a given artifact is indicated using the descriptors, feedback is given regarding next steps, and opportunity is provided for reassessment. Students are able to self-assess and track their progress on the "I can ..." statements using the same descriptors and progression on specific tracking sheets and google forms. All of this information is synthesised at the end of a unit in a student conference where a final grade is co-constructed

between the student and the teacher.

Using a consistent learning and assessment tool across all units allows the students to build familiarity with the language and the process. This empowers students to become more self-aware and self-reflective of their work which leads to increased motivation and removes unnecessary competition between students. Students begin to work towards personal bests as opposed to trying to get more points than the next person.

Descriptors	**Learning Progression** *(What the Learner is doing)*	**Achievement Progression** *(How well the Learner is performing)*
Following	*Building Understanding* • Completes tasks and problems focused on the primary concepts and basic calculations related to the outcome. • Uses manipulatives and models to explore key concepts. • Follows step-by-step processes and/or receives guided support from a teacher or peer.	*Beginning Proficiency (not meeting the outcome)* • Requires more consistency when applying concepts to problems and situations to reduce conceptual errors. • Solves basic problems with minor calculation errors. • Requires improved organization and conventions to reduce errors and frustration.
Constructing	*Building Key Skills.* • Independently completes tasks and problems representative of the breadth of the outcome. • Asks questions for clarity. • Uses manipulatives and models to explain concepts. • Corrects calculation and conceptual errors with support and/or corrective instruction.	*Developing Proficiency (working at the outcome level)* • Applies concepts and procedures correctly in most problems and situations. • Solves basic problems with minimal calculation errors. • Solves outcome-level problems with calculation and/or conceptual errors. • Requires more consistent use of conventions and organization methods to help reduce and identify errors.
Refining	*Becoming Precise* • Completes problems representative of the full depth and breadth of the outcome. • Uses manipulatives and/or models to support solutions. • Performs calculations using standard algorithms and procedures. • Identifies errors independently. • Communicates concepts and calculations using proper conventions.	*Proficiency (meeting the outcome)* • Demonstrates precision and accuracy with the concepts, procedures, and algorithms required. • Solves outcome-level problems with minimal error. • Consistently corrects errors in calculations. • Demonstrates proper conventions and solutions are well organized.

Showing Agility	*Building Confidence* • Analyses complex and/or unique problems to determine which algorithm, model, or procedure is most reasonable for the problem. • Explores multiple methods to calculate and verify solutions. • Makes connections between key skills and concepts to support and communicate solutions.	*Strong Proficiency (meeting the outcome)* • Demonstrates confidence, sophistication, and intention with the concepts, procedures, and algorithms required. • Selects appropriate procedures best suited to the problem or situation and accurately performs calculations. • Communicates using well-organized explanations of the concepts and appropriate conventions.
Demonstrating Fluency *Note: Fluency does not exceed the skills required by the outcome.*	*Naturalizing* • Creates contextual examples to support understanding of key concepts. • Calculations and conventions required to communicate solutions to tasks and problems are becoming second nature.	*Exemplary Proficiency (meeting the outcome)* • Seamlessly combines the Refining and Agility levels. • Communicates solutions to any type of problem connected to the outcome with a high degree of accuracy. • Demonstrates fluency through the skillful execution of concepts, calculations, and conventions.

Figure 8.8. Learning and Achievement Progressions

Sample chart used on assessments - this is the last page of a test or major assignment on the outcome.

PR2 - Solving Equations (Algebra) Model and solve problems using linear equations of the form: ;ax=b; x/a=b, a not = 0; ax+b=c; x/a+b=c, a not = 0; a(x+b)=c, concretely, pictorially and symbolically, where a, b and c are integers.		
Criteria	**Performance Standard (I can..)**	**Progression**
Concepts	• I can model a linear equation and solve the equation using algebra tiles.	*Following*
	• I can translate a real-world problem into an algebraic equation.	*Constructing*
	• I can isolate the variable using opposite operations.	*Refining*
	• I can use the substitution method to verify the solution to an algebraic equation.	*Showing Agility*
	• I can use the inspection method to solve one step algebraic equations.	*Demonstrating Fluency*

Calculations	• I can solve one-step algebra equations in the form $a + x = b$ (addition/subtraction) • I can solve one-step algebra equations in the form $ax = b$ (multiplication) • I can solve one-step algebra equations in the form $x/a = b$ (division) • I can solve two-step algebra equations in the form $ax + b = c$ • I can solve two-step algebra equations in the form $x/a + b = c$ • I can solve algebra equations using the distributive property $a(x + b)= c$	*Following* *Constructing* *Refining* *Showing Agility* *Demonstrating Fluency*
Conventions	• I can identify and correct errors in solutions to algebraic equations. • I can identify the variable, constant, and coefficient in a linear algebraic expression. • I can reorganize algebra equations into their standard form. • I can organize my evidence of learning in a logical structure.	*Following* *Constructing* *Refining* *Showing Agility* *Demonstrating Fluency*

Figure 8.9. Sample chart used on assessments

Policy/Procedure Example

El Monte City School District
El Monte, California

REGULATION 5121: Grades/Evaluation Of Student Achievement
Original Adopted Date: 06/26/2018 |
Last Revised Date: 05/20/2019

1. 21st Century Skills

Students must develop essential skills in the areas of critical thinking, creativity, communication, and collaboration for success in today's world. The marks (see chart below) listed in the 21st Century Skills section in each of these categories—self-directed learner, quality producer, collaborative worker, responsible engaged citizen and (for grades 7 & 8) complex thinker—indicate how a student is progressing towards acquiring and demonstrating these essential skills. These skills are not taken in isolation, but rather present an overall picture of the habits students need to develop in order to be successful. 21st Century Skills are reported in homeroom for grades TK-6 and in each content area for grades 7 & 8.

Exemplary	Satisfactory	Needs Improvement	Unsatisfactory
E	S	N	U

Exemplary	Exemplary performance is evidenced by daily demonstration of the skills listed with few exceptions. A student whose 21 century skills are exemplary demonstrates these skills consistently and independently.
Satisfactory	Satisfactory performance is evidenced by daily demonstration of these skills. A student whose 21 century skills ware satisfactory demonstrates these skills with occasional intervention.
Needs Improvement	Performance that needs improvement is evidenced by inconsistent demonstration of the skills listed. A student whose 21 century skills need improvement demonstrates these skills on a limited basis and needs frequent intervention.
Unsatisfactory	Unsatisfactory performance is evidenced by a conscious, consistent, or pervasive failure to demonstrate the skills listed. A student whose 21 century skills are unsatisfactory needs constant intervention. This mark is inappropriate for a student whose qualifying condition prevents demonstration of one or more of these skills.

2. Overall Academic Achievement and Progress

a. The academic achievement grade is an indicator of a student's proficiency in grade-level CA Common Core State Standards and in content standards for areas where no CA Common Core Standards exist. Students demonstrate what they know, understand, and can do as measured through multiple assessments and observations.

b. Students' academic achievement will be measured using the following scale:

Academic Achievement

4	3	2	1
Mastering	Meeting	Partially Meeting	Not Meeting

Achievement Marks	Descriptor
4 - Mastering	Student performance demonstrates a complete and in-depth understanding of grade-level standards. Assessment evidence indicates that the student consistently applies and possibly extends the skills, processes, and key concepts with fluency and ease. A mark of "4" during or at the end of the year indicates that the student has a firm grasp of the learning targets that have been assessed.
3 - Meeting	Student performance demonstrates understanding of grade-level standards. Assessment evidence indicates that the student proficiently applies skills, processes, and key concepts with some errors. A mark of "3" during the year indicates that the student is progressing as expected, and a "3" at the end of the year indicates that the student has met the learning targets for the grade level.
2 - Partially Meeting	Student performance demonstrates a partial and/or inconsistent understanding of grade-level standards. Assessment evidence indicates that the student inconsistently or incompletely applies skills, processes, and key concepts with frequent or significant errors. A mark of "2" during the year may indicate that the student is in the process of learning; however, a "2" at the end of the year indicates that the student has not met learning targets and is below grade level.

1 - Not Meeting	Student performance demonstrates minimal understanding of grade-level standards. Assessment evidence indicates that the student is unable to apply the skills, processes, or key concepts. A mark of "1" at the beginning of the year indicates that significant progress must occur for the student to meet learning targets; however, a "1" at the end of the year indicates that the student has not made sufficient progress towards meeting learning targets and is far below grade level.
Other Marks	
*	Indicates a differentiated academic achievement grade. The student has an IEP, is an English learner who has been in U.S. schools for less than two years, or is working towards standards that are above grade level.

c. For all grade levels, except transitional kindergarten, an overall academic achievement grade will be reported twice per year at the end of second and fourth quarters.

El Monte City School District 2019
https://simbli.eboardsolutions.com/Policy/ViewPolicy.aspx-?S=36030649&revid=ZtnxIFws9UaHFEahekA7XA==&PG=6&st=progress&mt=Exact

The above regulation also states that progress toward proficiency will be reported on each report in various ways each term; for example, for grades K-6 progress towards proficiency will be reported for the first and third quarters for each content area andand and for quarters two and four, progress marks will be reported in sub-categories for reading and math. In this regulation there is no indication of how progress is communicated but in a previous regulation it was communicated as follows:

3. Progress Toward Proficiency

These marks represent the measurement of a student's growth toward and attainment of mastery of each district Power Standard in Reading, Writing and Math. Progress is measured by a variety of evidence, which includes quality standards-aligned assessments, portfolios, and other multiple measures.

√ Meets Standard	^ Adequate Progress	__ Insufficient Progress	X Standard Not Assessed

√ Meets or Exceeds Standard –The student has mastered the entire standard. Unless reassessment indicates otherwise, the √ is repeated in subsequent trimesters.

^ Adequate Progress (Used 1st and 2nd Trimester only) – Based on what has been taught and assessed, the student is on track to master the standard by the end of the year. This symbol is not used third trimester.

__ Insufficient Progress – Based on what has been taught and assessed, the student has not demonstrated that s/he is on track to master the standard by the end of the year. For third trimester, this symbol represents that the student has NOT demonstrated mastery of the standard in its entirety.

X Standard Not Assessed – (Used 1st and 2nd Trimester only) – Standard has not been taught and/or measured to date. This symbol is not used third trimester.

Fix 9 Compare each student's performance to preset standards; don't assign grades based on student comparisons.

> In a normal distribution most of the data will be near the middle, or the mean, with very few figures on the outside of the bell, known as outliers. All things being equal, if test scores were normally distributed, 2.1% of the tested students will receive an A on the test, 13.6% will get a B, 68% get Cs, 13.6% get Ds, and 2.1% of the class gets an F.
>
> *(Roell, 2019)*

Grades are broken when they are used to compare students to each other. The fix is to base grades on pre-set achievement standards (Fix #2) and to be criterion—not norm— referenced. In doing so, we acknowledge that it is possible for all students to receive an A or for all students to receive an F or any other grade. There would be no plan to intentionally distribute grades on a construct such as the bell curve, ensuring a few As, more Bs, even more Cs, some Ds and a few Fs.

You can test the thinking in your school or district by asking this question: "What do you think would happen if you did an outstanding job, all the students in your class did an outstanding job, and all the students received an A or whatever is the highest possible grade?" If the response is that the grades would be questioned with comments such as, "easy teacher," "no or low standards," or "grade inflation," then you are in a norm-referenced setting. If, on the other hand, the grades were questioned but the comments were "great," "that's what we want," or "let's celebrate lots of excellent learning," you are in a criterion-referenced setting.

The rationale often cited for creating a competitive grading environment in schools is that it provides motivation for students and that highly motivated students learn more. In fact, however, the motivational effects are not beneficial for all students. Students who expect to finish very high in the ranking and hope to get high grades may indeed be motivated, but they are motivated by points, not learning. For those not at the very top, motivation wanes. They set lower standards for themselves in order to maintain their personal sense of self-worth and put forth only the effort required to meet those adjusted standards. Competitive grading systems do not help those students who are often "left behind" their peers both in school and beyond.

Another rationale for using the bell curve is that it counters grade inflation but, as Adam Grant pointed out,

> the forced curve suffers from two serious flaws. One: It arbitrarily limits the number of students who can excel. If your forced curve allows for only seven A's, but 10 students have mastered the material, three of them will be unfairly punished (i.e., inaccurately graded)
>
> The more important argument against grade curves is that they create an atmosphere that's toxic by pitting students against one another. At best, it creates a hypercompetitive culture, and at worst, it sends students the message that the world is a zero-sum game: Your success means my failure.
>
> (Grant, 2016)

The final "nail in the coffin" for norm-referencing to determine grades is that, mathematically, the bell curve represents random human variation (in say, height), but teaching and learning are purposeful activities that aim to maximize student success so a bell curve for grades would only happen if teaching was ineffective.

Summary

Grading students by comparing their performance to one another distorts individual achievement. We need clear, criterion-referenced achievement standards—absolute, not relative, standards that describe a limited number of levels: at, below, and above proficiency. Teachers in a noncompetitive grading system assign grades to each student based only on that student's own achievement in relation to the applicable standards.

By setting rigorous criteria, teaching to that criteria, and surrounding students with the necessary support and interventions to get there, teachers send the message that they believe in the potential of each and every one of their students. It is still primarily up to the student to fully invest in their learning and rise to the level of excellence established.

(Schimmer, 2020)

Educator Vignette

Shannon L. Schinkel
Humanities and Drama teacher
Prince George, British Columbia

In my Humanities and Drama classes, at report card time, many of my students receive As. I don't hand them over casually like candy at Halloween; students earn these As because I've embraced a standards-based proficiency sequence approach to teaching and learning. I've always felt that all students can be successful if the path is clear and learning opportunities that purposefully provide challenges and stretches are given. But sometimes I'm told by other educators that I must have "gone easy on them" to hand over so many high grades, right? The opposite is true because I have a criterion-reference mindset, and they have a norm-referenced or bell curve mindset. Students work intently and push themselves to achieve their potential. I am their learning facilitator and guide.

Below is an example of a Social Studies proficiency sequence. Students are evaluated based on how far they progress along the sequence. Each level can be taught to students, so they have the opportunity to show proficiency at the highest level possible. How is this used to assess proficiency? Evidence is gathered through observations, products, and conversations in relation to each standard. A student who shows they can perform the first three levels of the sequence (Need to do → Can do), for example, is evaluated at Developing for this standard. Then, the student and teacher can reflect and goal-set for the next level in the sequence.

Social Studies 8 Curricular competency: CAUSE & CONSEQUENCE

I can determine which causes most influenced particular decisions, actions, or events, and assess their short-and long-term consequences.

First...this is what **I NEED to do**	Then...this is what **I SHOULD DO**	After that...this is what **I CAN do**	Next...this is what **I COULD do**	Finally, this is what I can **TRY to do**
EMERGING	**BEGINNING**	**DEVELOPING**	**APPLYING (PROFICIENT)**	**EXTENDING**
I can determine the short-term influence of a historical decision, action, or event. I can show the immediate, logical impact of a cause and accurately explain how the consequence is a result of the cause. Eg: Flooding from heavy rains Damage to houses / Damage to crops As a result of flooding, the immediate effects I on the village was damage to both houses and crops because water damages wood and water drown plants.	I can determine the long-term influence of a historical decision, action, or event. I can show several logical consequences for a cause that span over an extended period of time. I can accurately explain how the causes and consequences are connected. Eg: **Flooding from heavy rains** Damage to houses / **Damage to crops** **Crops not harvested** **Loss of income** **Bank threatens to foreclose on homes** The long-term effect of flooding was loss of a homes because as a result of damage to crops, crops could not be harvested and sold which provides the revenue to pay a mortgage.	I can determine the comprehensive, long-term influence of a historical decision, action, or event. I can show multiple logical consequences for a cause that span over an extended period of time. I can accurately explain how the causes and consequences are connected and possibly interconnected. Eg: **Flooding from heavy rains** **Damage to houses** / **Damage to crops** **Houses need to be repaired** / **Crops not harvested** **Pay deductible** / **Lose income** **Some families did not have money to pay deductible** / **Bank threatens to foreclose on homes** The long-term effect of flooding was the loss of homes because as a result of damage to crops, crops could not be harvested and sold which provides the revenue to pay a mortgage. Without that revenue, some families did not have enough savings or predictable income to pay the deductible to repair the house.	I can determine which cause most influenced particular decisions, actions, or events by comparing the comprehensive, long-term influences of each. I can justify which cause had the greatest impactful consequences by giving logical reasons as to why it is more impactful over the other(s) based on the evidence given. Eg: Between this historical flood and the earthquake five years prior, this flood had a greater impact because the earthquake damaged the road leading to the town which prevented crops getting to market for one month. The one-month financial setback did not cause long-term hardship with the exception of planned entertainments which had to be put on hold. The flood caused evictions and relocations. The town didn't look the same economically and socially.	I can determine which cause most influenced particular decisions, actions, or events by predicting its broader long-term influence. I can infer several, clear, reasonable consequences to support my predictions that go beyond what is historically presented. Eg: **Forced to relocate** Find new job / Find new land Need training / Prepare & plant I learned that families relocated as a result of the flooding. I can infer that relocating added to the long-term impact of the flooding because the families could have had to start new jobs requiring more training or they could have tried to find new land to grow crops again. Both could be burdens because both involve risk, finding suitable land, and a long period of time before a job or harvest makes a positive financial impact.

Figure 9.1. Social Studies 8 and Curricular Competency (See page 143 for a larger version.)

When a student reaches *Can do*, to prepare them for the next level, I purposefully create a learning opportunity using the wording from *Could do,* or hand over the responsibility to the student and have them generate their own learning opportunity, such as creating an inquiry question (e.g., *Of all the reforms Charlemagne implemented in the Early Middle Ages, which one had the greatest impact and why? Which Renaissance advancement had the greatest impact on their society and why?*). The language of the learning opportunity presents a formula for success and is within reach.

Come report card time, I consider how far individual students achieve on the proficiency sequence and I evaluate them based on their most recent or relevant evidence. It might take one student multiple learning opportunities to reach Applying (Proficient) while it takes another just once, but they are both ultimately evaluated at Applying. They both met the same criteria goals but in different ways and at different times.

I don't measure my students' success by comparing them to each other. Instead, I lay out this proficiency sequence framework, give students chances to practice without penalty, and provide detailed supports for all students to grasp each level. When students are stalled at one level or need challenge to stretch to the next, I personalize their learning goals. This individualized approach to learning makes students feel like winners because it is focused on meeting students where they currently are and providing them with learning opportunities to reach success. Students have told me that learning in my classroom feels possible because the only person they are competing with is themselves. When students want to reach the next level, that's the essence of a growth mindset.

Policy/Procedure Example

Hong Kong International School

HKIS high school teachers will:

Measure achievement against clear assessment criteria linked with established HKIS standards and learning targets (criterion referenced), not against the performance of other students (norm referenced).

RATIONALE: Grading students by comparing their performance to one another distorts individual achievement. Grading on a curve makes learning a highly competitive activity in which students compete against one another for the few scarce rewards (high grades) given out by the teacher. (Hong Kong International School, 2018, p. 2)

Fix 10 Use evidence from high quality assessments; don't use evidence from low quality assessments.

> The primary purpose of classroom assessment is to inform teaching and improve learning. . . This principle suggests that assessment be viewed as an ongoing process instead of a single event at the conclusion of an instructional segment. . . assessment results provide more than just data for grading students; assessments provide feedback as the fuel for improving teaching and learning.
>
> *(McTighe & Ferrara, 2021, pp. 1 - 2)*

Grades are broken when the evidence used comes from poor quality assessment and thus misrepresents student achievement. This is the classic "garbage in, garbage out" syndrome. The fix is to have clear standards of assessment quality and to apply these standards to each and every assessment.

Figure 10.1 provides a framework for ensuring high-quality assessment. Quality assessment requires that we have accurate assessment that is effectively used. Accurate assessment, the focus of this fix, requires that we pay attention to five questions: Why are we assessing? (Key 1), What are we assessing? (Key 2), How will we assess it? (Key 3), How will use the results? (Key 4), and How will we communicate the results? (Key 5).

Key 1 requires that the purpose of each assessment must be clear. This is addressed in Fix 13. Key 2 requires that the learning goals to be assessed are those public, published standards on which students should achieve proficiency, specifying both what is expected and how well students must perform to earn each grade. The "what" of the learning is addressed in Fix 7 and the "how well" is addressed in Fixes 8 and 9. Key 4 regarding the use of assessment results, especially formative usefulness, are addressed primarily in Fixes 13 and 15. The questions in Key 5 about the effective communication of assessment results are also addressed in Fixes 13 and 15 and in Fixes 1 and 11. This means that although all of the five keys are essential for quality assessment, the primary focus of Fix 10 is on Key 3— the sound design of assessments. Sound design has five primary considerations: the right method, quality and clarity of assessment prompts, tasks and scoring tools, appropriate sampling, and the control of bias.

FIGURE 1.4 Five Keys to Classroom Assessment Quality

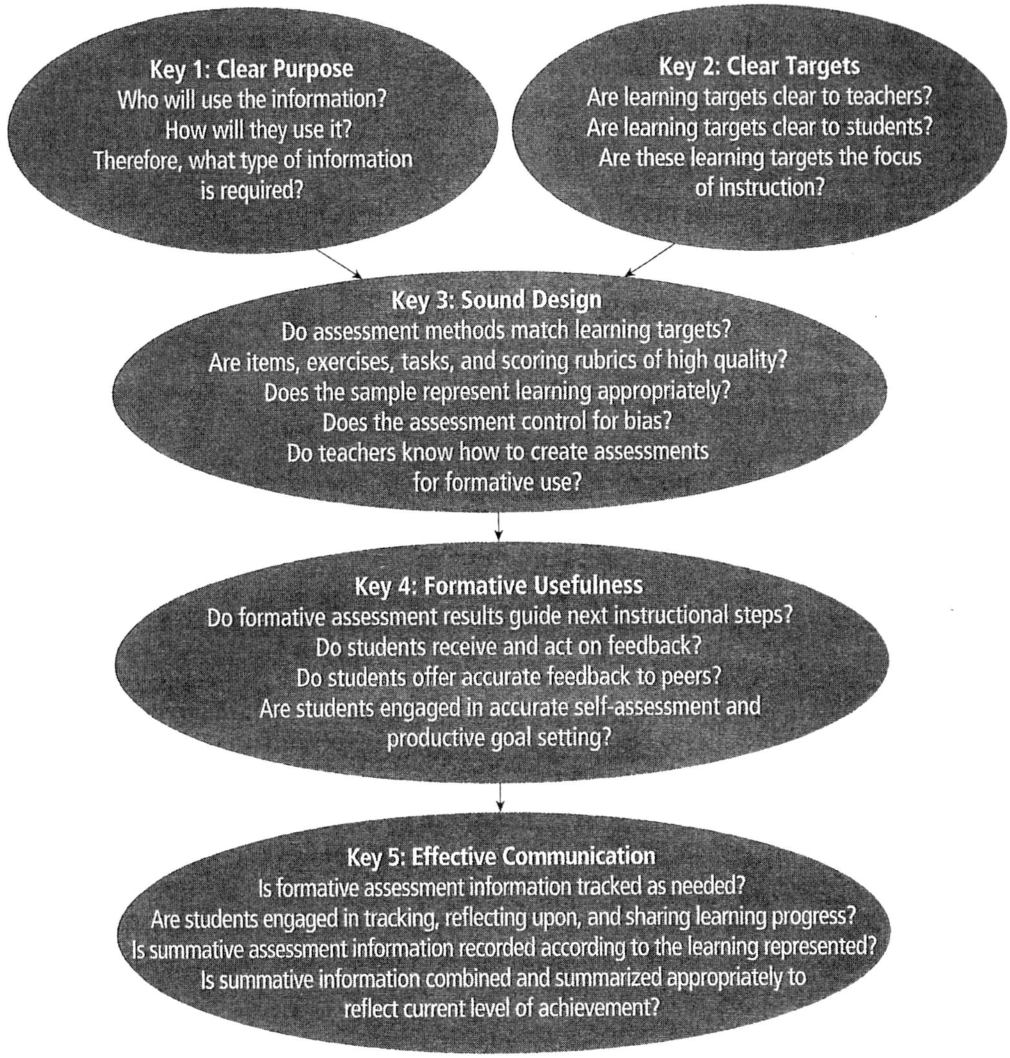

Figure 10.1. Five Keys to Quality Classroom Assessment
(Chappuis & Stiggins, 2020, p. 23)

The sound design considerations are as follows:

1. *The Right Method.* This means target-method match which requires that the most effective and efficient method is used for gathering the needed evidence of student achievement. There are four basic categories of assessment methods: Selected Response, Written Response (short or extended), Performance Assessment, and Personal Communication. The right match depends on the nature of the learning goals that can be categorized as

Knowledge, Reasoning, Performance Skill, and Product. So, for example, to assess knowledge, we can appropriately use selected or written response, but to assess performance skills or the ability to create products, we must use performance assessment (a chart illustrating target-method match in detail can be found in Chappuis & Stiggins, 2020, p. 106)

2. *Quality and clarity of assessment prompts, tasks and scoring tools.* This requires that these components of assessments are well written, clear and unambiguous, at the right reading level, and meet technical requirements.

3. *Appropriate sampling.* Assessment is a sampling procedure; that is, teachers need to gather enough evidence to make accurate judgments of student achievement.

Sampling is partly about *quantity*—we know we have enough evidence when we can confidently say that, if we gathered one more item, it would simply confirm what we know now. There is a base or minimum amount of evidence needed from every student, but that amount will not be the same for each student. The more consistent a student is, the less evidence is needed; the more inconsistent, the more evidence is needed. Teachers have tended to over sample rather than under sampling, and a good rule-of-thumb is that we need a minimum of three pieces of evidence on each standard. The first may be luck, chance, or measurement error in one direction, the second may be luck, chance or measurement error in the other direction, but a third will tend to confirm the first or the second.

Sampling is also about *variety*—we can collect evidence of achievement from products, from observation, and from conversation. If we only have one type of evidence, it may not provide an accurate indication of what each student knows, understands, and can do, so as much as possible, we should collect evidence from all three sources. This allows for the triangulation of evidence that will provide greater confidence in the accuracy of our judgment of student achievement.

4. *Control for bias.* We need to control bias that can distort results. There can be problems with the student, the assessment setting, the assessor, and/or with the assessment itself that can cause the result to misrepresent student achievement. Problems that can occur with the student include

lack of reading skill, emotional upset, poor health, lack of test-wise-ness, and evaluation anxiety. Problems within the setting that can distract students include heat, noise, and lack of light. Problems with the assessor include implicit bias and lack of assessment literacy. Problems with the assessment itself are the other sound design issues including one that I would like to emphasize: insufficient time for all students to complete formal assessments (i.e., tests and exams). If a student only completes 70% of an exam and gets 90% on what they do, but the exam is scored as if they completed it, their score would be a very inaccurate 63%. If speed and pressure are conditions of quality, like in air traffic control, then strict time limits are necessary; if, however, speed isn't a condition of quality, tests and exams should have flex time not fixed time. For flex time, the teacher identifies the base time that most students need and then they should add one-third of the base time to allow for individual differences in such things as handwriting or keyboarding speed and thinking/processing speed (not quality). As Jo Boaler (2016) notes in her wonderful book *Mathematical Mindsets,* "For about one-third of students, the onset of time testing is the beginning of math anxiety" (p. 38). Regarding one of her norms, she further states, "I don't value students working quickly; I value (them) working in depth" (p. 172).

The explanation of this fix here is far from an in-depth treatment of the issues involved in the development of high-quality assessment; for readers who want more depth, I highly recommend McTighe and Ferrara (2021), Chappuis and Stiggins (2020), and especially Cooper (2022), who says *Rebooting Assessment* is his "attempt to nudge student assessment into the modern era through a technology-supported and balanced approach that includes conversations and performances as key components in a teacher's toolkit" (p. 4). I also highly recommend the Michigan Assessment Literacy Standards for Teachers (Michigan Assessment Consortium [MAC], 2020. pp. 8-9).

Summary

Grades are broken when they arise from poor-quality assessment because the evidence is not accurate. The fix is to check every assessment for quality—clear purpose, clear learning goals, sound design, the effective use of results, and communication of results. Assessments that do not meet these five keys of quality will mismeasure student achievement and thus will lead to inaccurate grades.

> **Assessment can give us powerful information when framed to help students, their teachers and teams understand strengths and identify next steps in achieving essential grade level standards and critical competencies.**
>
> *(Dimich, 2021)*

Educator Vignette

Katie White
Coordinator of Learning,
North East School Division
Melfort, Saskatchewan

When I began teaching senior English language arts in an asynchronous, online context during the pandemic, I was aware of the need to enhance my assessment tools and processes to support students who would not benefit from face-to-face explanations and time to ask questions in the moment. I really started to think about how to make sure my assessment decisions reflected careful consideration of quality, clarity, and alignment to my learning outcomes.

The first thing I thought about was how to make the learning goals (outcomes) really clear to students. I wanted them to understand what kind of action they needed to take to demonstrate proficiency. I decided to make these goals very obvious, often placing them in a text box at the beginning of an assessment tool (assignment). I supplemented these goals with very specific success criteria, which described the quality of the products or performances the students were about to undertake. I wanted to be sure that if I was assessing a particular skill, students were very clear about this ahead of time. I wanted them to allocate effort to the most important things.

Next, I tried to predict what might act as a barrier to students accessing their best thinking and skill demonstration during the assessment process. I thought about things like bias and interest, and often offered choices to students so they could more easily place themselves in the context of the assessment. I also tried to add audio or video files to assignments so students could both read and hear the directions. Lastly, I made sure that students had a way to ask me questions before and during the assessment, so any challenges could be addressed immediately. I was careful to address their clarifying questions without over-scaffolding their processes. Making sure that the rigor of the assessment was not compromised was a priority. However, in many instances, the problem was in my directions; I often assumed students understood vocabulary or processes that were actually unclear to them. In these cases, I was careful to enhance my directions for everyone and was grateful that students felt comfortable pointing out the confusing elements of my assessment so I could make it better and ensure what I was receiving from the students reflected their best thinking and skills.

Lastly, I made sure that for every outcome I graded, I provided students multiple opportunities for practice, mistake-making, risk-taking, recovery, and feedback. I knew that my summative assessment would not be considered quality if it was disconnected from what we did every day as we engaged in learning.

Trying to design assessment in an online context was a challenge but it made me increasingly clear about what makes the difference between a quality and a not-so-quality assessment. Ensuring I was not the difference between students performing well or not was a challenge I took very seriously. When I communicated student strengths and needs, I wanted to be sure my communication was as accurate as possible. Attending to the quality of my assessment design was really important.

As schools transitioned back to face-to-face contexts, I soon realized that the careful thinking I had done around designing quality assessment for my online courses was just as important in face-to-face contexts. In fact, striving for assessment clarity by articulating learning goals and success criteria, predicting needs and barriers and being proactive in preventing as many barriers as possible, and engaging students in the best kinds of iterative assessment processes are always important, no matter the context. Assessment design always needs to be aligned to learning goals, intentional in accurately capturing evidence of student learning, and informative in directing next steps.

Policy/Procedure Example

Langley School District
Langley, British Columbia

These Guiding Principles of Classroom Assessment were co-created by a group of classroom teachers, district teachers and administrators K-12 in partnership with the Langley Teachers' Association. This highly collaborative process was a powerful process that produced buy-in to the principles throughout the District.

EFFECTIVE ASSESSMENT

- ✓ Standards-Based

  Effective assessment reflects what a student understands, knows and can do in relation to the Learning Standards (competencies and the content). Evidence of learning and professional judgement determines proficiency.

- ✓ Explicit, Accessible and Transparent

  Effective assessment requires clear learning intentions and communicates success criteria so that learning is accessible for all students.

- ✓ Relational

  Effective assessment fosters hope, efficacy, and a culture of learning.

- ✓ Reflective and Responsive

  Effective assessment includes ongoing descriptive feedback to promote student reflections and inform next steps.

- ✓ Student-Centered

  Effective assessment empowers students through voice and choice.

- ✓ Student-Agency

  Effective assessment guides students in understanding and articulating their learning. (Langley School District, 2021, p. 3)

EVIDENCE OF LEARNING

Evidence of authentic learning should be attained from a variety of sources

- Provide different opportunities for students to demonstrate their learning.
- Consider quality over quantity.

- Involve students in the process.

Assessment needs to be competency-based

- It reflects where the student's skill level is in relation to the curricular competencies.

Assessment needs to be based on clear criteria

- It is aligned to the Learning Standards.
- Criteria is shared or co-created with students.

Evaluation is based on a student's current understanding and progress.

- It is a snapshot in the moment rather than averaging across the term.

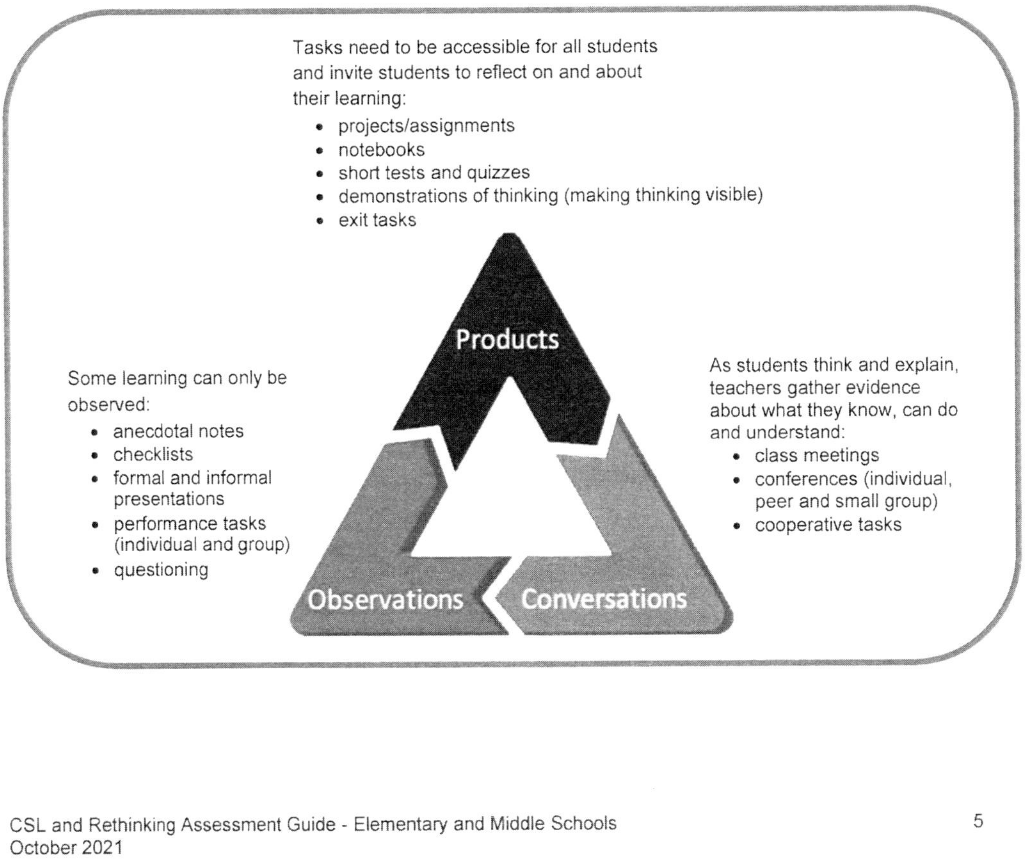

Figure 10.2. Effective Assessment
Permission provided by the Langley School District
(Langley School District, 2021, p. 5)

Social Studies 8 Curricular competency: CAUSE & CONSEQUENCE

I can determine which causes most influenced particular decisions, actions, or events, and assess their short-and long-term consequences.

First...this is what **I NEED to do**	Then...this is what **I SHOULD DO**	After that...this is what **I CAN do**	Next...this is what **I COULD do**	Finally, this is what I can **TRY to do**
EMERGING	**BEGINNING**	**DEVELOPING**	**APPLYING (PROFICIENT)**	**EXTENDING**
I can determine the short-term influence of a historical decision, action, or event. I can show the immediate, logical impact of a cause and accurately explain how the consequence is a result of the cause.	I can determine the long-term influence of a historical decision, action, or event. I can show several logical consequences for a cause that span over an extended period of time. I can accurately explain how the causes and consequences are connected.	I can determine the comprehensive, long-term influence of a historical decision, action, or event. I can show multiple logical consequences for a cause that span over an extended period of time. I can accurately explain how the causes and consequences are connected and possibly interconnected.	I can determine which cause most influenced particular decisions, actions, or events by comparing the comprehensive, long-term influences of each. I can justify which cause had the greatest impactful consequences by giving logical reasons as to why it is more impactful over the other(s) based on the evidence given.	I can determine which cause most influenced particular decisions, actions, or events by predicting its broader long-term influence. I can infer several, clear, reasonable consequences to support my predictions that go beyond what is historically presented.
Eg: Flooding from heavy rains → Damage to houses; Damage to crops	Eg: **Flooding from heavy rains** → Damage to houses; **Damage to crops** → **Crops not harvested** → **Loss of income** → **Bank threatens to foreclose on homes**	Eg: **Flooding from heavy rains** → **Damage to houses** → **Houses need to be repaired** → **Pay deductible** → **Some families did not have money to pay deductible**; **Flooding from heavy rains** → **Damage to crops** → **Crops not harvested** → **Lose income** → **Bank threatens to foreclose on homes**; **Lose income** → **Some families did not have money to pay deductible**	Eg: Between this historical flood and the earthquake five years prior, this flood had a greater impact because the earthquake damaged the road leading to the town which prevented crops getting to market for one month. The one-month financial setback did not cause long-term hardship with the exception of planned entertainments which had to be put on hold. The flood caused evictions and relocations. The town didn't look the same economically and socially.	Eg: **Forced to relocate** → Find new job → Need training; **Forced to relocate** → Find new land → Prepare & plant
As a result of flooding, the immediate effects I on the village was damage to both houses and crops because water damages wood and water drown plants.	The long-term effect of flooding was loss of a homes because as a result of damage to crops, crops could not be harvested and sold which provides the revenue to pay a mortgage.	The long-term effect of flooding was the loss of homes because as a result of damage to crops, crops could not be harvested and sold which provides the revenue to pay a mortgage. Without that revenue, some families did not have enough savings or predictable income to pay the deductible to repair the house.		I learned that families relocated as a result of the flooding. I can infer that relocating added to the long-term impact of the flooding because the families could have had to start new jobs requiring more training or they could have tried to find new land to grow crops again. Both could be burdens because both involve risk, finding suitable land, and a long period of time before a job or harvest makes a positive financial impact.

Figure 9.1. Social Studies 8 and Curricular Competency

CHAPTER 4

FIXES FOR INAPPROPRIATE GRADE DETERMINATION

Fix 11 Consider several measures of central tendency and use professional judgment; don't rely on the mean.

> For too long and from too many teachers students have received false reports of their performance against standards. The practice that creates these false reports is so entrenched in our profession, it has won general fiat and seems irreproachable. Yet its continued use thwarts students' learning and casts doubt on our instructional decisions.
>
> Let's right the wrong. It's time to stop averaging grades.
>
> *(Wormeli, 2018, p. 186)*

Grades are broken when the summary they provide of student achievement is inaccurate because faulty procedures have been used to arrive at the grade. For example, grades may mislead when they are based on simply calculating the mean (average) of a series of scores, due to the effect of outlier scores. The fix for grades broken in this way is to not use the mean as "the measure" by considering other measures of central tendency and to recognize that grading should not be merely a numerical, mechanical exercise; it should be an exercise in professional judgment.

The mean is very well named—it is truly "mean" to students because it overemphasizes outlier scores, which are most often low outliers. As we see in the following case, the calculation of the mean can distort the final grade. Ten assessments have been converted to percentage scores to calculate a final grade:

91, 91, 91, 91, 91, 91, 91, 70, 91, 91

Total = 889, Mean = 88.9, Final grade = B

This student performed at an A level 9 times out of 10, and the 70 is clearly an anomaly. But the grade as calculated in most schools would be a B. This example raises both a general issue—How should evidence be summarized? And specifically should evidence be summarized by strict mathematical calculation?

Somewhat ironically, in most states and provinces, usually in Grade 5, students are taught in Math class about three methods of calculating central tendency—mean, median, and mode. They are taught that each measure of central tendency has both strengths and weaknesses, and that, depending on the distribution of scores and your purpose, you should carefully choose the appropriate measure for every situation. Somehow, though, teachers frequently ignore this in managing their own gradebooks. If students are very consistent, each measure will produce the same result and the mean can suffice. But the more inconsistent a student's performance, the less effective any of the measures of central tendency are in accurately summarizing student achievement. Guskey (1996), addressing the issue of summarizing when the record includes extreme scores, noted,

> Averaging falls far short of providing an accurate description of what students have learned. . . If the purpose of grading and reporting is to provide an accurate description of what students have learned, then *averaging must be considered inadequate and inappropriate.* (p. 21, emphasis added)

So, if the mean is "inadequate and inappropriate," what number crunching should be done? The median (middle score by rank) or the mode (the most frequently occurring score) are generally more appropriate than the mean when confronted with extreme scores. In the previous example, if the median or the mode is used, the student would get their deserved A. It is necessary then for teachers to consider all measures of central tendency when determining grades.

At this point, we have to ask, should grades in fact be determined by mathematical computation only? Given the limitations of measures of central tendency to deal effectively with all score distributions and the many factors affecting student performance, I conclude that we have to see grading not as simply a numerical, mechanical exercise, but primarily as an exercise in professional judgment. It calls for teachers to demonstrate two key aspects of professional behavior—the application of craft knowledge of sound assessment practice and the willingness and ability to make and be ready to defend one's professional judgment. As teachers, we must ask the question, "Based on all the evidence of achievement a student has produced, which summary symbol most accurately represents that achievement?" That is why I always talk about "determining," not "calculating" grades—number crunching may be necessary, but ultimately, grading requires professional judgment. Each teacher must be prepared to specify: "These were the learning goals (both what and how well), here is the evidence of each student's level of achievement on them. Using the following summary process, here is the grade I determined for each student . . ."

Teachers at all levels should be determining grades for standards and some will be required to determine grades for subjects. Thus, they need clear guidance on how to accurately determine grades for standards and for subjects. Grades for standards should be determined by the most consistent level of achievement with emphasis on more recent evidence. This isn't just calculation—it also requires professional judgment. Determining grades for standards is illustrated in Figure 11.1 and can be summarized as the following:

Mode + More Recent + Professional Judgment

Physical/Health Education

Student: ______________________________

ACHIEVEMENT EVIDENCE								
Strands	Assessments							Grade
	10/1 PA	10/15 PA	11/7 Test	11/18 PA	12/8 PA	12/17 PA	Strengths, Areas for Improvement/ Observations	
Movement	3	3	3 (15/20)		3	3	Completely consistent	**3**
Fitness Management				1			Not enough evidence	**NA**
Physical Activity Safety	2		4 (19/20	2	2	2	Consistently 2, 4 is an anomaly	**2**
Personal safety	4	4	1 (12/20)		4	4	Consistently 4, 1 is an anomaly	**4**
Personal/social management	3	2	3 (12/20)	2	3	3	Inconsistent but 3 is mode and more recent	**3**
Healthy lifestyle		1	2	3	4	4	Steady improvement, 4 is mode and more recent	**4**

Figure 11.1. PHE Grades for Standards

The explanation for the grade determination for each standard is indicated in the second last column in Figure 11.1. Level scores have been recorded for each assessment. For the performance assessments, the scores were determined using rubrics, but the tests were points-based, so the level score was based on the difficulty of the skill or concept and/or the difficulty of the prompt/question (see

Fix 8, p. 106).

If grades for subjects are required (hopefully only for high school), it is important to recognize that

> "from a measurement perspective, scales with fewer levels (for example 0-4) simply *cannot* be accurately or validly converted to a scale with more levels. In essence any conversion to percentages is inadequate, inappropriate, and invalid."
>
> (Guskey, 2020, p. 92)

For that reason, the preferred method of determining subject grades is to use a logic rule like the one in Figure 11.2

Fosterville High School Letter Grade Logic Rule		
At least 3 on all standards, 2 or more are 4, no 2s or 1s	=	**A**
At least 3 on all standards, 1 is 4, no 2s or 1s	=	**A-**
3 on all standards	=	**B+**
4s, 3s, and 2s on all standards, more 3s and 4s than 2s	=	**B**
3 and 2 on all standards, equal 3s and 2s	=	**B-**
3 and 2 on all standards, more 2s than 3s	=	**C+**
2s on all standards	=	**C**
1 on any standard	=	**E**

Figure 11.2. Logic Rule for Converting Standards Grades to Letter Grades
(Developed by and permission provided by Aric Foster, Armada High School, MI. Fosterville High School is not a real school)

An example of a logic rule for a high school in Oregon that only uses A, B, C and NP (Not Proficient) as letter grades can be found in *How to Grade for Learning* (O'Connor, 2018, p. 192).

Sadly, Ministries of Education in all provinces in Canada, many international schools, and many districts and schools in America require that teachers determine percentage grades for high school students and sometimes also for some or all of the grades below high school. In these situations, teachers have to able to convert grades for standards to percentage grades. This can be done with conversion scales like the following examples (not models):

Standards Average	Letter Grade	%
3.9 – 4.0	A+	100
3.7 – 3.8	A	96
3.5 – 3.6	A-	92
3.3 – 3.5	B+	89
3.0 – 3.2	B	86
2.7 – 2.9	B-	82
2.4 – 2-6	C+	79
2.0 – 2.3	C	75
1.7 – 1.9	C-	70
1.4 – 1.6	D+	67
1.2 – 1.3	D	63
1.0 – 1.1	D-	60
0.0 – 0.9	F	55
Incomplete	I	50

Figure 11.3. Conversion Chart for Converting Standards Grades to Letter or % Grades

# Reporting Standards	Max	A+	A	A-	B	C	D	F
3	12	12	11	10	9	8	6	5 and below
4	16	16	15	14	12	10	9	7 and below
5	20	19+	18	17	15	12	10	9 and below
6	24	22+	21	19	17	14	11	10 and below

Figure 11.4. Conversion Chart for Converting Standards Grades to Letter Grades Based on the Number of Reporting Standards

(Max = Maximum possible total)
Adapted from a conversion scale from a European International School

This could be extended up to the number of reporting standards for each subject, so, for example, 9 reporting standards would be as follows:

#Standards	Max	A+	A	A-	B	C	D	F
9	36	33+	30	29	24	20	15	13 and below

For Teachers: Yukon Education Grade Conversion Guide (Grades 10-12)

This guide will assist with converting standards-based grades on learning standards to a final percentage grade **for a course**. It uses a four-point standards-based grading system, a student's more recent evidence, and the logic rule below. **The process is meant to be led by teacher professional judgement**.

Proficiency Scale	Logic Rule	Percentage Grade Range	Percentage Grade Reported [3]	Yukon Letter Grade
Extending (4) The student demonstrates a sophisticated understanding of the concepts and competencies relevant to the expected learning.	All 4s	86-100	100	A
	Almost all 4s and the occasional 3		96	
	Mostly 4s, some 3s		92	
Proficient (3) The student demonstrates a complete understanding of the concepts and competencies relevant to the expected learning.	Mostly 3s, some 4s	73-85	85	B
	Almost all 3s and the occasional 4		81	
	Mostly 3s, one/two 2s and no 1s		77	
Developing (2) The student demonstrates a partial understanding of the concepts and competencies relevant to the expected learning.	A mix of 2s and 3s, mostly 2s	50-72	72	C+
	Mostly 2s, no 1s		66	C
	Mostly 2s, some 1s		59	C-
Emerging (1) The student demonstrates an initial understanding of the concepts and competencies relevant to the expected learning.	Mostly 1s, and the occasional 2	40-49	45	F

Figure 11.5. Conversion Chart for Converting Standards Grades to Letter Grades or % Grades from a Logic Rule (Yukon Education, n.d.)
Permission provided by Curriculum and Assessment, Yukon Education

Figure 11.5 is based on the unique grading scale used in Yukon (and British Columbia), but it could be easily converted to a more common grading scale. In Figures 11.3, 11.4 and 11.5, the number of letter grade categories ranges from six to fourteen, but each example could be adjusted for a different number of letter grade categories.

It has become somewhat common to blame computer grading programs for all the evils of calculation, but most computer grading programs can currently do everything described above except for logic rules. For example, for any set of standards scores in PowerSchool, the software automatically calculates and displays mean, weighted mean, median, mode, highest and more recent that clearly shows there isn't one right answer Additionally, PowerSchool displays a professional judgment indicator for the more recent calculation (the default is the most recent three scores) if there is a discrepancy between the summary grade and the most recent score. This alerts teachers to pay special attention and use professional judgment, not just rely on the calculation.

In explaining this fix, I have focused on the calculation issues with measures of central tendency, not the issue that measures of central tendency may misrepresent a student's current level of achievement because they include historical data that is no longer relevant. The issue of emphasizing more recent evidence is addressed in Fix 14, but it is worth noting that if Fix 14 is implemented, much of Fix 11 is no longer applicable.

Summary

Grades are frequently broken (inaccurate) when they result only from the calculation of the mean in contexts where extreme scores distort; they can be repaired by considering other measures of central tendency and using professional judgment. Thus, we should think and talk about not the calculation, but the determination of grades.

> The "jaggedness principle" holds that we cannot apply one-dimensional thinking (the average) to understand something that is complex and "jagged." What precisely is "jaggedness? A quality is jagged if it meets two criteria. First, it must consist of multiple dimensions. Second, these dimensions must be weakly related to one another. . . . . Almost every human characteristic that we care about – include talent, intelligence, character, creativity and so on (achievement), – is jagged.
>
> *(Rose, 2016, p. 82 quoted in Dueck, 2021, p. 104)*

Educator Vignette

Phil Stringer
Department Head of Mathematics,
Crofton House School,
Vancouver, British Columbia

AP Statistics - Mean, Median and Mode

As we neared the end of the year, students had completed the AP examination and were interested in the final project. I had given them many options, including researching vaccination statistics (at the onset of the Covid-19 vaccination distribution in Canada) and providing a statistical analysis of the way their grades were determined using our department's approach to standards-based grading (SBG). Ultimately, almost the entire class was working on the SBG problem: which method of determination of their grades best fit the evidence.

Groups of students began comparing means, medians, and modes. Two students quickly recognized that the mean, as they had learned in their AP course, could easily be distorted by very high or very low marks. For instance, they were upset that a student who scored 40, 40, 80, 90, and 100 throughout the course on a single standard did not get an A (86%) or even a B (73%). They also recognized that a student could learn slowly and that valuing their growth over time should be included in their final standing. Another group noted that the mode was generally not a great indicator. They built off the argument for the above student (40, 40, 80, 90, 100) and also noted that the mode of 40 did not seem to represent this student's overall abilities.

Their attention then turned to median and to recency. Looking at the more recent evidence (say, the most recent 3-4 items), they tried mean, median, and mode. The results felt better to them. And, of these, the median was the one that they were most comfortable agreeing was the best. However, their final conclusion was that the teacher should, as many teachers in my school do, sit down with each student and have a conversation about the grading; allow professional judgement and dialogue to be at the forefront.

Mathematics 8 – Professional Judgment

Instead of focusing on units of instruction, the students in my Mathematics 8 classes spiral through the curriculum slowly building on prior knowledge. As the focus at the beginning of the school year is on building these basic skills, student confidence, and classroom routines, the assessment is entirely formative. As they are learning the tools needed to progress in the course as well as fill in any gaps from previous learning, students are given opportunities daily to see where they are at through small check-in quizzes, group work and discussions at the vertical whiteboards, and through journaling.

I remember the students asking about their grades quite early in the year. They were used to, especially in mathematics, having quizzes and tests out of a certain number of points and they felt unsure about getting feedback and descriptive levels of accomplishment. I engaged the class in many discussions about this assessment process and remember students having two main viewpoints. Some students still felt apprehensive. They understood grades as a currency, and they explicitly commented that the grades helped define who they were as mathematics students! The bulk of the students commented that they enjoyed not having a focus on their grades as well as being able to simply learn and enjoy the classes.

Throughout the year, we continued to build our knowledge and expand into mixed problem-solving and applications of the content. All the while, students were formatively assessed daily both individually (check-ins, quizzes) and collectively (board work, class discussions). Every few weeks, I would give the students a pre-quiz which would include about three questions. They would attempt the quiz and receive feedback. About one week later, they would take another quiz on the same topics. This process allowed them to focus on improving any misunderstandings before the assessment counted. It also provided me with feedback regarding what teaching and learning opportunities I needed to adjust to in preparing future class. These students never wrote a 70-minute unit test, only a series of these smaller assessments (I never called them quizzes or tests). Anxiety was low, students felt they were confident with the material or confident that they could improve, and there were no surprises. The largest improvement was with the students needing additional support. As the assessments were clear and reasonably short, those students requiring additional time were not over-burdened with giving up their recess, lunch, or missing another class.

The students' final few assessments were cumulative and very rigorous. These students did not write a final examination, and I did not feel that I needed them to, as I had collected enough data throughout the year to clearly understand their level of performance in the course. They left the course confident, able, and with a mindset that they can do math.

Policy/Procedure Example

Lambton Kent District School Board
Chatham, Ontario

REPORTING: DETERMINING A REPORT CARD GRADE

Teachers will take various considerations into account before deciding upon the grade to be entered on the report card.

When determining a final grade, multiple sources of evidence including conversation, observation, and product should be considered to provide students with opportunities to demonstrate what they know in ways that are equitable and accurate. Determining a final grade will involve teachers' professional judgement, and interpretation of evidence should reflect the student's most consistent level of achievement. Recent evidence gathered during periods of learning throughout the term that demonstrates growth in a students' knowledge/skills should be given more consideration than earlier demonstrations of learning that may represent early and emerging understanding of curriculum expectations.

It is expected that both professional judgement and mathematical calculations will inform the determination of percentage grades

(Lambton Kent District School Board, 2021, p. 11).

N.B.

1. In the original the word "mark" was used instead of "grade" because that is the common terminology in Ontario.

2. Provincial policy in Ontario (sadly) requires percentage grades for grades 7 to 12.

Fix 12 Use Incomplete or Insufficient Evidence and provide support when evidence is missing; don't include zeros in grade determination.

> If you do not get all the evidence you deem essential, you should not determine a student's overall proficiency. It is your professional duty not to do so. In the case that teachers do not get enough of the right evidence to judge a student accurately,the grade of incomplete . . . is most appropriate.
>
> *(Reibel & Thede, 2020. p. 104)*

Grades are broken when zeros are entered into a student's academic record for missing evidence or as punishment for transgressions. When combined with other evidence, the resulting grade does not accurately reflect student achievement. There are several fixes for the use of zeros in grades. By far the best is the use of "I" as a final grade, indicating Incomplete or Insufficient Evidence, but as transitional approaches or in situations where calculation "rules," acceptable alternatives are the use of equal difference scales or the use of a "floor" score that makes a percentage scale an equal difference scale.

Zeros most commonly are found in teachers' gradebooks when students fail to submit required assessment evidence, such as turning in assignments or being absent for tests. They are also sometimes used for serious behavioral infractions such as academic dishonesty. There are three fundamental problems with zeros:

- Zeros give a numerical value to something that has never been assessed and therefore has no basis in reality.
- They have counterproductive effects on student motivation.
- They involve inappropriate and incorrect mathematics.

But the most important issue is that zeros in the record render grades ineffective as communication because the resulting grade is an inaccurate representation of the student's achievement. The mathematical problem with zeros is that they are the ultimate outlier, and their effect on the grade is always exaggerated. As we have established, this is not acceptable. Thus, *the compelling reason* for not using zeros is the mathematics. If teachers use a percentage scale with 60 points for an F and 10 or 11 points for each of an A to D, a zero is a K, not an F, and I doubt that anyone would really advocate for the use of Ks.

Alexis Tamony, a high school mathematics teacher, makes the case against zeros brilliantly in an Edutopia article (2021a) and a YouTube video (2021b). She explains it this way:

> I'm a math teacher and I *love* number lines. So, what does this have to do with grades? Let's envision a number line with the traditional 0–100 grade scale on it. Way over on the right would be the A grade band (90–100). The B band would be from 80 to 90, a C from 70 to 80, and a D from 60 to 70. When a student receives an F, that grade band doesn't continue with that nice equal 10-point interval from 50 to 60. When we give students a zero, that zero is in grade purgatory! If we continued the equal-interval spacing of 10 points per letter, a zero would actually be a K. I think *K stands for "Kill Grade."* (Emphasis added)
>
> Let me explain. Think about a student who does consistent B (85) 'work.' Their first two assignments are solid 85s, so the average is an 85. If this student doesn't turn in the third assignment and receives a zero, their grade drops to an F (57). Because of that one zero, it will take that student 14 more 85s just to get their grade back to an 80. (2021a)

Regarding motivation, as soon as students have more than one zero, they have little chance of recovery, increasing the likelihood that they will give up. In high school, for some students, this can happen as early as the end of the first month of the school year, effectively rendering the remainder of the year a waste of time, at least from a learning perspective. One potential side effect is that students who have given up often have discipline problems. The other motivational problem is that students who are not concerned about grades are willing to "take a zero" and are thus not held accountable for their learning. We are faced with the irony that a policy that may be grounded in the belief of holding students accountable (giving zeros) actually allows students to escape accountability for providing evidence of learning.

The best alternative to the use of zeros is an "I" for Incomplete or Insufficient

Evidence. When desired evidence of student achievement is missing, teachers enter an "M" (missing) or "NS" (Not Submitted) in their grade book and, when it is time to determine a report card grade, they decide whether they have sufficient evidence to determine a grade; if the student has provided sufficient (not necessarily all) evidence, the grade is determined, but if they do not provide sufficient evidence, the teacher assigns an "I". "I" clearly places the responsibility where it should be—with the student. It is the student's responsibility to produce sufficient (but not necessarily all) evidence required so the teacher can make a valid summary judgment. It is extremely important that schools/districts have this option available to teachers on each report of student achievement, including the final report card. The "I" has the same impact as an F (in high school = no credit), but it accurately communicates what the problem is. Another benefit is that while zeros can doom students to failure very early in the school year, with support and time, an Incomplete can most often be made complete (sufficient). Schools/districts need to have clear procedures and timelines for students to move from an "I" to a grade that accurately represents their achievement. This is the positive, supportive approach that is likely to be much more effective in promoting further learning than is the negative and punitive impact of zeros.

According to Hill and Hillman (2018), "The consequence for not turning in an assignment is that the student still has to complete the assignment on *their time*" (p. 13), so schools need to establish support times like those described for late submission in Fix #2 for missing assignments (i.e., the difference between late and missing is just the amount of time passed). Those support times may be before school, at lunchtime or after school, or at a planned time in the daily schedule. If missing assignments are a chronic problem, schools may want to consider the approach called "Power of ICU" that was developed by two Tennessee middle school principals (Hill, 2021). Power of ICU (Intensive Care Unit) is an approach that provides highly structured and persistent support to ensure that students submit required assignments (detailed descriptions of the application of this approach are provided in O'Connor, 2018, pp. 181-184).

For consistency across each school, the specific procedure adopted should be developed at the school/district level. Teachers may then apply the procedure in the manner best fitting their classrooms. Given that some schools/districts are still in transition to a full standards-based approach and many still have grading procedures that require calculation (often including the use of percentage scales), we also must consider alternatives to zeros in those situations.

Zeros are generally used in grading scales which include unequal differences between points on the scale so that an included zero has a disproportionate effect. The most commonly used grading scale has 11 points for an A, 10 for each of B, C, and D, and 60 points for an F. The problem with using this scale, and three possible solutions, are illustrated in Figure 12.1. This student was supposed to do five assessments but does only four; his scores are A, B, C, and D (represented by midpoint percentage scores in Column 1) on the four assessments and a zero for the assessment he does not submit. The mean for the four assessments he did is 80 percent—a B—but the zero lowers the mean to 64 percent, or a grade of D, a drastic reduction caused by the range for an F being approximately six times greater than the range for the other grades (Column 2). Alternatives appear in Columns 3 and 4 (Equal Difference Scales) and in the bottom row (Median). Using the 5-point scale in Column 3 results in a summary grade of C, which is still lower than the mean of this student's scores but is a more reasonable summary of his achievement. Column 4 turns the percentage scale into an equal difference scale by having (almost) the same number of points for each grade level, using a floor of 50 percent. Instead of recording a zero for missing evidence, the teacher would record a score of 50 percent. This symbolic percentage is chosen to equalize the points per A, B, C, D, and F grades; it does not mean that students have mastered 50 percent of what is expected. It means that if students actually attempt an assessment and receive a failing percentage grade, it should be recorded as a percentage between 50 and 59. As Wormeli (2018) pointed out "Once a student has entered into "failure," delineating degrees of failure doesn't help anyone, and it lessens the usefulness of the grade" (p. 204). The third alternative appears in the bottom row—use the median instead of the mean. Note that each alternative results in a grade of C (for further information about alternatives to zeros see O'Connor, 2018, pp. 177-186).

Figure 12.1.

Alternatives to Zeros

Scores		*101 Point Scale*	Equal Difference Scales *5-point scale*	*50-point scale*
	95	90-100 (A)	4	95
	85	80-89 (B)	3	85
	75	70-79 (C)	2	75
	65	60-69 (D)	1	65
	0	0-59 (F)	0	50
Mean	64 (D)		2 (C)	74 (C)
Median	75 (C)		2 (C)	75 (C)

Figure 12.2 illustrates the need for more than simply numerical alternatives to the use of zeros. In this example, none of the measures of central tendency provide sufficient accuracy. Students were expected to submit 10 assessments on the same set of standards. This student submitted only 3, receiving scores of 95, 95, and 100 percent. A zero was assigned for each of her missing assignments. If the traditional percentage scale is used, she would receive a failing grade. But the 3 assessments that were submitted clearly indicate that she had an excellent understanding of the standards assessed. If an equal difference scale such as the 5-point scale in Table 8.2 is used, she receives a passing grade, but it is unlikely that she provided sufficient evidence if she only did 3 of 10 required assessments. Also, such an approach would support the undesirable idea that students can pick which assessments they do and choose to take a zero on other assessments. Thus, there is a problem with both scales, and the median is clearly not helpful in this situation because it would be zero. This student's appropriate grade would be an "I" for Incomplete or Insufficient Evidence because it most clearly communicates the problem without distorting her actual achievement.

If you want more on the issues of zeros and incomplete, in-depth treatment can be found in Freedman (2020, pp. 75-90) and Wormeli (2018, pp. 204-208) as well as the classic articles by Reeves (2004) and Guskey (2005).

Figure 12.2.

The Impact of Zeros

	101-Point Scale	*5-Point Scale*
	95	4
	0	0
	0	0
	0	0
	95	4
	0	0
	0	0
	0	0
	0	0
	100	4
Total	290	12
Mean	29	1.2
Median	0	0
Letter Grade	**F**	**I**

Hopefully it is clear that the simplest and best solution to the issue of zeros is to use an equal difference scale with a limited number of levels but, whichever scale is used, if the student hasn't produced sufficient evidence, the grade must be an "I."

Student Involvement

When students understand the impact of not submitting required assessment evidence and know what alternatives are in place in their school, they are better able to decide about submitting needed academic evidence and/or making up an Incomplete. Support sessions should be available in which they can participate. Students also can be involved in determining the consequences for failure to submit required assessment evidence. For example, they may agree to a contract that requires them to meet certain timelines and/or to attend specific support sessions. Student-led conferences also may help students recognize their responsibilities by helping them identify both their strengths and areas needing improvement.

Summary

Grades are broken when zeros are used for missing evidence of learning; zeros are mathematically incorrect, distort the actual achievement record, and can decrease student motivation to learn. The best fix is to use an "I" grade when there is insufficient evidence of learning and provide support for students.

> A teacher using this approach (zeros for missing assessments) might be advised to announce to students and parents at the beginning of each term that, although the course is titled Algebra 1, for example, the grading methods employed expose the fact that is really a work-ethic course – missing work counts much more than work turned in demonstrating mastery of course content and skills. "We do a little Algebra in here, but this course is mostly about work-ethic."
>
> *(Westerberg, 2016, p. 11)*

Educator Vignette

Tom Schimmer
Author/Consultant
Vancouver, British Columbia

The single biggest lie educators tell themselves about assigning zeros to students who have failed to submit their assignments is that the students are *being held accountable* and being *taught responsibility*; a zero does neither of those things. It's mathematically invalid, it's disproportionately punitive, and it actually allows students to leverage early success to opt out of what they were initially told was required. It's one thing to philosophically believe that students deserve a penalty when they have not followed through on their responsibility, but couching this response as something noble and necessary is disingenuous and needs to stop.

During my time as a high school vice-principal, one conversation I had with a teacher about the assigning of zeros stands out as an encapsulation of the first point in need of reconciliation. This teacher, who by all metrics was an excellent teacher who built great relationships with his students, came into my office to further discuss the topic of zeros, which we had discussed extensively as a full faculty at our monthly meeting the prior afternoon. He came into my office and expressed that he was on board with almost everything we were talking about within our assessment and grading reform effort but that he was still struggling both conceptually and practically with the elimination of zeros. He said to me, *"I get where you're coming from Tom, but I just think students need to be held accountable."* My response caught him off-guard: *"I totally agree with you, students do need to be held accountable."* He looked confused and, after a slight pause, he said, *"Oh, ok, I guess we're more on the same page than I thought we were after yesterday's meeting."* I looked him square in the eyes and replied, *"No we're not. You and I have a different working definition of the word accountability."*

For some, the word *accountability* is synonymous with *punishment;* for others it's about being *accountable* to the *learning.* Those two ideas are incongruent; it really comes down to the response pathways we choose. What is most interesting is how readily some accept this cross application in one direction but think the other is seen as absurd. While many accept the traditional paradigm that a *behavioral* misstep (e.g., failure to submit an assignment) results in an *academic penalty* (e.g., zero in the gradebook) leading to a lower academic grade, rare is the teacher who would support that an *academic misstep* (e.g., can't add fractions) result in a *behavioral penalty* (e.g., suspension).

As the conversation between the teacher and I unfolded, the above *argument of convenience*—how one side of the assertion is an accepted mindset while the reverse is absurd—came up. To be fair, the teacher wasn't aggressive or argumentative in his hesitation; he was genuinely reflective. However, once he came to see the hypocrisy of the *argument of convenience,* he realized that using the gradebook to address irresponsibility is misguided; once he was able to shift from a *punishment* paradigm to a *learning* paradigm, he saw that students could be *held accountable* independent of their academic achievement grade. He, like so many I've had conversations with over the years, mistakenly believed that I believed that deadlines didn't matter and that students could submit assignments whenever they felt like it. That's where our conversation went next; we went back to how we define accountability.

The gist of our conversation centered around two things. First, we talked about how we disprove the theory of needing to impact the achievement grade for the behavioral misstep of missing assignments. I reminded him that we never respond this way when the behavioral misstep is *disrespect*; that our school expected students to be respectful, would *hold them accountable* for any disrespectful actions, and was quite successful in redirecting students to more respectful responses. We did all of that without ever impacting the students' achievement grades, so the assertion that we need to use our gradebooks to hold students accountable for *irresponsibility* is not credible; we disprove that theory every day.

The second part of our conversation centered on *redefining accountability*; we needed to shift to *accountable for the learning* and handle the behavioral misstep outside the achievement grade. We talked about how a student could absorb a zero and still have a 4.0 GPA; that's not accountability. We also talked about how zeros allow students to opt out of what was initially deemed mandatory. A student could absorb a zero, see their grade drop, but remain satisfied with their standing and choose to never submit the assignment as there would be no further impact on their grade; that's not accountability, either. If the evidence of learning is essential, I explained, then it should remain essential, and the student should be expected to complete it in short order through a schoolwide system; that schoolwide system of accountability was something we initially discussed at the faculty meeting the previous day. I spent the few minutes we had left previewing what we (the administration) thought the schoolwide system could look like and that it was something we were going to discuss extensively at next month's meeting. By the end of the meeting, he had a paradigm shift and realized that his assumption that students would be held *less accountable* was inaccurate.

My experience guided me through this conversation because I was in exactly the same place this teacher was just a few years earlier. When I first started teaching as a high school history teacher, I was the zero guy; I was the epitome of the punitive grader. For over a decade, I felt philosophically righteous in my stance and felt students deserved what they got. The evolution of my own assessment literacy and my personal professional growth brought me to the conclusion that my use of these punitive practices did nothing but distort my students' achievement levels, undermine the relationships I had with my students, and create an adversarial dynamic within my classroom. I knew I had to be patient and methodical in that conversation with that teacher because someone had done that for me; someone had taken the time to guide me through my own paradigm shift.

Zeros are a choice; there are other options. Hiding behind tradition or the misguided practice at some post-secondary institutions is a copout. The impact that zeros have, especially in a percentage-based system, is egregious and has to stop. As educators, we can talk all we want about relationships, social-emotional learning, and creating supportive learning environments, but the real test comes when students fall short. Tell me how you handle missing work and I'll know everything there is to know about what you value and the nature of your relationships with your students.

Policy/Procedure Example

Urbana City Schools
Urbana, Ohio

DETERMINING STUDENT GRADES

- The teacher will not allow outliers (extremes in scoring) to skew the true picture of student achievement.
- If a grade of "I" (Incomplete) is assigned, a student has two weeks to submit the missing assignments
- Teachers will not use zeros in grades as punishment (e.g., for academic dishonesty) or when evidence is missing. Instead, the teacher will reassess to determine the true level of achievement or record an "I" for INCOMPLETE.
- If there is insufficient evidence for grade determination, the student will receive a grade of "I."
- The process for a student to recover from a grade of "I' will be clearly defined by the district.
- Zeros don't allow the classroom teacher to measure the learning that has taken place.

(Urbana City Schools, 2015, pp. 5-6)

CHAPTER 5

FIXES TO MAKE LEARNING THE FOCUS

Fix 13 Use evidence primarily from summative assessments to determine grades; don't use evidence from formative assessments.

> Learning is iterative—it's less a process of learning and more one of re-learning from mistakes and experimentation. You wouldn't grade an artist in the midst of creating a masterpiece ("Looks like a block of marble to me, Michelangelo"), but that is, in effect, what we do when we grade learning at every step along the way.
>
> *(Goodwin, 2021)*

Grades are broken if scores for everything students do find their way into report card grades. The fix is to determine grades primarily only on evidence from those assessments intended to document learning—that is, summative assessments designed to serve as assessments *of* learning.

The primary purpose of grades is to communicate a summary of student achievement at a particular point in time, i.e., what students know, understand, and can do as a result of their learning. It is important that teachers, students, and parents recognize that learning is a process in which learners increase their knowledge, understanding, and skills as a result of instruction, engagement in learning, feedback from teachers and peers, and self-assessment and adjustment. For this process to work well, learners must believe that it is important and worthwhile to engage in learning and that it is not only acceptable but desirable that they take risks and make mistakes; it is not necessary to always "get it" the first time.

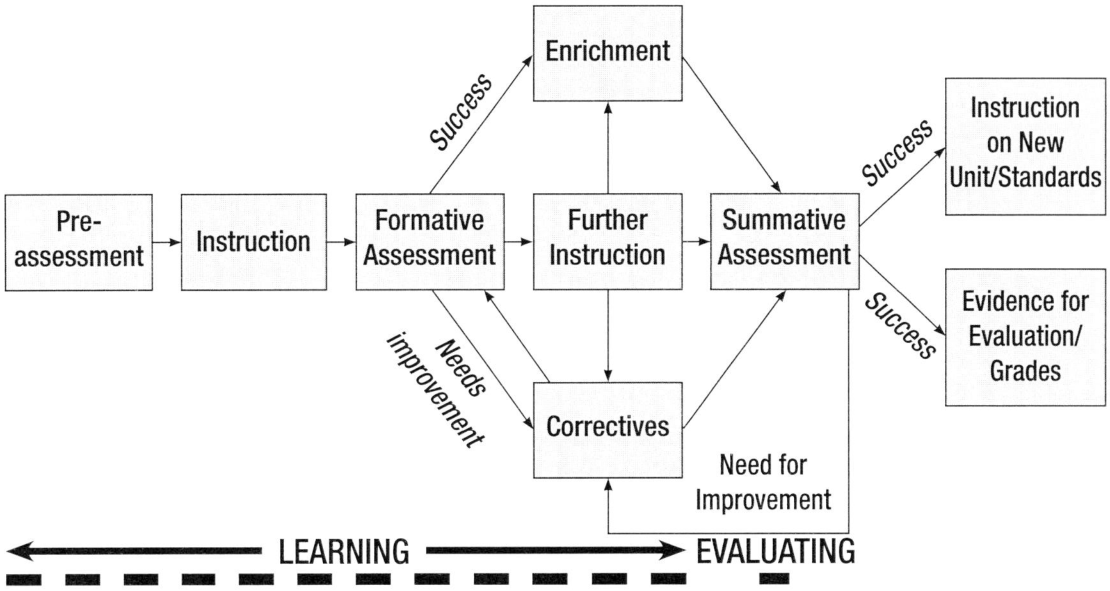

Figure 13.1. The Teaching/Learning/Assessment Cycle
(O'Connor, 2018, p. 130)
Permission provided by Corwin Press

This process is clearly illustrated in the Figure 13.1 However, it is not recognized when teachers include in grades evidence generated during practice (i.e., learning) activities. Unfortunately, this happens daily in many classrooms, when teachers score everything students do, put a number on it, and use every piece of evidence to determine grades.

Standards-based teachers distinguish clearly between teaching/learning activities (which include diagnostic and formative assessment) through which students learn and practice, and summative assessments, when students "perform" and show what they know, understand, and can do. Figure 13.1 may be the most important graphic in the book because it illustrates the teaching/learning cycle that is at the heart of creating a culture of learning in place of a culture of point accumulation. The graphic clearly shows that:

1. Most of the time is spent on teaching and learning (i.e., instruction, formative assessment, further instruction, correctives, and enrichment) before there is any summative assessment,
2. It is a cyclical process in which students and teachers use

information from assessments to adjust teaching and learning, and

3. Student achievement is dependent on teachers carrying out this cycle with fidelity and not short changing the front end in a rush to obtain summative assessment scores for the gradebook. This is illustrated further in Figure 13.6 that starts with analyzing formative assessments so that students are well prepared for success on summative assessments, but it mainly illustrates how the results of summative assessments can be used as an additional part of the teaching/learning/assessment cycle by showing what can— and should— happen after summative assessments have been administered and scored.

Diagnostic—assessment that takes place prior to instruction; designed to determine a student's attitude, skills or knowledge in order to identify student needs.

Formative—assessment designed to provide information for improvement and/or adjustment for individual students or for a whole class, e.g., observation, quizzes, homework (usually), instructional questions, initial drafts/attempts.
*(Assessments **FOR** learning)*

Summative—assessment designed to provide information to be used in making judgments about a student's achievement at the end of a sequence of instruction, e.g., final drafts/attempts, tests, exams, assignments, projects, performances.
*(Assessments **OF** learning)*

Figure 13.2. The Purposes of Assessment

It is critical that both teachers and students recognize when assessment is primarily *for* learning (formative) and when it is primarily *of* learning (summative). Students understand this in band and sports when practice is clearly identified and separate from an actual performance or game. But often this is not clear in the classroom. If we did in hockey or any other sport what we frequently do in the classroom, the game would not start 0–0, but each team would start with a score based on an assessment of the quality of their practices in the days leading up to the game. Obviously, this doesn't happen and would be absurd—and it is equally so in the classroom.

Since "Inside the Black Box," the classic paper by Black and Wiliam (1998), a large and growing body of research supports this distinction. Black and Wiliam pointed out,

> Firm evidence shows that formative assessment is an essential component of classroom work and that its development can raise standards of achievement, Indeed, they know of no other way of raising standards for which such a strong prima facie case can be made.
>
> (editor's introduction to Black & Wiliam, 1998, p. 139).

Their research and the work of others have shown that improving formative assessment and using assessment *for* learning raises the achievement of all students, but also that it has the most significant impact on low achievers. Learning gains made through using assessment *for* learning are similar to those achieved through one-on-one coaching.

The key components of assessment *for* learning are as follows:

1. Sharing the learning target(s) with students from the beginning of the learning,
2. making adjustments in teaching as a result of formative assessment,
3. providing descriptive feedback to students from informal and formal formative assessment, and
4. providing opportunities for students to self- and peer-assess so that they understand their strengths and what they need to do to improve.

As identified in number 3 above, formative assessment can be both formal (e.g., quizzes, drafts, practice) and informal (e.g., usually oral, second-to-second, minute-to-minute, hour-to-hour and every day in the classroom) and in fact most formative assessment is informal. Shirley Clarke (2021) pointed out,

> 'In the moment' feedback has more impact than written feedback after the lesson. . . The number of words said face-to-face to a child in a 2-minute conversation during the independent stage of the lesson would take up several pages of written comments in the child's book, and has the advantage of relationship advancement. (p. 68)

This is obviously very different from the primary summative use of assessment, or putting a score or number on what students do and including it when determining grades. Students should be assessed regularly; everything (or almost everything) they do can be assessed and/or checked, but everything does not need a score and every score need not be included in the grade. Some student learning activities must be for practice only and on which they receive the kind of feedback that will help them do better the next time.

The Council of Chief State School Officers defines formative assessment as

> "a planned, ongoing process used by all students and teachers during learning and teaching to elicit and use evidence of student learning to improve student understanding of intended disciplinary learning outcomes and support students to become self-directed learners"
>
> (CCSSO, 2018, p. 2).

The CCSSO also noted that

> "Effective use of the formative assessment process requires students and teachers to . . . (use) evidence and feedback to move learning forward by adjusting learning strategies, goals, or next instructional steps"
>
> (CCSSO, 2018, pp. 2-3).

To appropriately modify learning, feedback has to be effective; it has to be timely, describe features of the evidence relating directly to learning goals and/or standards of quality, be strength—not deficit—based (White, 2017, p. 104), be actionable and low stakes (i.e., allow for adjustments by the student before it "counts"). Examples of the types of feedback prompts that meet these conditions are provided by McDowell (2021, p. 37).

Surface	Deep	Transfer
I noticed that....	What are the key similarities and differences between...	What do you notice about....
I wondered about...	Why did you use_____ suggestion?	What are your key wonderings....
I was confused by...	What was your reasoning for....	What are you confused by...
I suggest that....	Why did you select this option as opposed to....	What do you suggest....
Have you thought about....		What thoughts have emerged for you....
You might consider....		What might you consider....

Figure 13.3. Powerful Feedback Prompts
Permission provided by First Educational Resources

Teachers often struggle with providing strength-based feedback. These lists from the Langley School District (2021) are helpful:

What does it look like?

- Is learning to
- Seeks opportunities to
- Can continue to start
- Practice, review, read and improve
- Will continue to develop
- Works on developing
- Will be reminded to
- Is beginning to demonstrate
- Uses strategies for
- Extend [NAME's] participation by
- Can re-examine
- Evaluate
- Utilize supports or resources
- Can participate
- Applies...to...
- Is clearly committed to

What does it sound like?

- Completely
- Consistently
- Effectively
- Masterfully
- Precisely
- Thoroughly
- Successfully
- Models collaboration by
    - — Thoroughly understands

— Has developed
- Demonstrates
- Continues to
- Uniquely

Figure 13.4. Strength-based Feedback Language
(Langley School District, 2021, p. 14)

To be effective, feedback has to be descriptive, not evaluative. A 7/10 or a 3 (from a rubric) going into a gradebook is high stakes, provides no useful information about the learning goals, and contributes nothing that will improve learning. One of the important implications of this is that teachers need to identify clearly and record evidence derived from formative assessment separately from that of summative assessment. This can be done using separate pages for each in the gradebook, by color-coding entries, and/or by giving a zero weight to formative assessments in a computerized gradebook or spreadsheet.

A critical issue with regard to feedback and the recording of evidence from formative assessments is whether they should be scored or be comment only. As noted above, a score contributes nothing that will improve learning. It is the descriptive feedback that can make a difference and many educators, including myself, believe that when students receive a score and descriptive feedback, most students ignore the descriptive feedback, meaning that it is a waste of teachers' time to provide both. According to Guskey (2019), "the research on this issue is far more complicated and more highly nuanced than most writers acknowledge." He says that there appears to be a large number of contextual factors that influence the effects of scores versus comments including the nature of the assessments, the subject area, the age or grade level of the students, the background and previous experiences of the students, individual students' beliefs about success or failure and their sense of self-efficacy, and the nature of the grades and comments and what each communicates. He concluded,

> (scores) help students identify where they are in their journey to mastery of important learning goals. But, just like assessments, (scores) alone don't help students improve. Comments that identify what students did well, what improvements they need to make, and how to make those improvements provided with sensitivity to important contextual elements, can guide students on their

> pathways to learning success and ensure that all learn excellently.

Having acknowledged that research, Dylan Wiliam's December 2018 tweet on the issue of scores vs comments is worth considering:

> I think the crucial point is that it's very hard to get students to pay attention to the comments if there's a score. So, my advice is either tell students how to get better, or tell them how good they are, but don't try to do both at the same time.

This may also be an area where teachers can work smarter, not harder, because as Zerwin (2020) pointed out,

> choosing numbers to evaluate student 'work' may take more time and energy than it does to provide descriptive statements about student 'work.' If I'm describing instead of evaluating, I can actually work faster because I don't have to expend brain energy deciding where my student's 'work' falls on a predetermined scale and then justify the decisions I make. (p. 107)

As a practical solution to the scores vs comments issue, Jung (2020) made this suggestion:

> So, what do we do? Do we add a score or only provide feedback? Really, to score or not to score is not the question. The questions are: (1) For what understandings and skills would it be helpful to reduce information to a number or letter, and (2) Do I need to show these numbers or letters to a student? Reducing data to a symbol may help us organize and make decisions, but we do not always have to display these judgments to students. In this way, we can have the best of both worlds: efficiency of reduced data and detailed, descriptive feedback with no grade for students. (p. 37)

One of the most common practices in North American education has been requiring lots of homework and scoring and including all homework as a significant part of grades. This has been done in the belief that it promotes responsibility in students, but in fact, it often has the opposite effect. Careful consideration has to be given to the amount and purpose(s) of homework. Sometimes homework requires students to show what they know by extending or integrating their knowledge and understanding through projects or assignments done partially or completely outside the classroom. This is clearly summative assessment and is legitimately part of grades as long as there is careful monitoring that it is the student's own evidence of learning and that they have the resources and situation to be able to complete it outside the classroom. Both of these caveats are difficult to ensure, so it is best if all summative assessment is done under the teacher's eyes. Mary Davenport, a high school English teacher at an international school in Sao Paulo, wrote the following:

> teachers at the school agree that the best option is for students to complete all (learning activities) during class. The next best option is for students to finish uncompleted class (learning) at home as a homework assignment of less than 30 minutes. The last option – the one we try to avoid as much as possible – is for students to be assigned and complete new (learning) at home. (Davenport, 2020)

(Note that the words in parentheses replace "work" in the original.)

Another purpose for homework is preparation—introducing knowledge, understanding, and skills intended to help students to be ready for subsequent lessons. As this happens before instruction, any assessment would be diagnostic, which obviously has no place in grades. Most often, however, homework is practice of whatever was learned in class that day, and any assessment of this should be regarded as formative. Practice is valuable only to those students who can have some degree of success on their own without teacher support. It is of little or no value to students who don't need to practice, and it can actually be damaging to students who don't understand because they may embed misunderstandings that will be difficult to correct.

Putting a score on evidence of learning done for practice renders it effectively summative, not formative. When homework assigned as practice is scored and included in grades, what becomes most important to students is that it be done because it "counts," not because of any learning that might occur. It becomes an issue of compliance and thus it really doesn't matter who does the homework—the student, a parent, a sibling, or a friend. If we want homework to be about learning, we need students to understand that it is for practice if they need it, not compliance or grading, because then the person who benefits from the homework is the learner.

One major concern that is often expressed about not including practice homework in grades is that "Students won't do their homework if I don't grade it!" We have done an absolutely superb job of training students into this perspective by putting a number on everything they do and making every number part of their grade. But as we have trained them into it, we can train them out of it. The motivation for practicing and doing homework should come from each student's clear understanding that it will contribute to their learning. We want them to feel a sense of satisfaction from knowing, understanding, or being able to do something better today than yesterday. We want them to come to understand, "If I had done my homework, I would have done better on the test." We can tell them this day after day with no effect, but when they see the assessment evidence speak for itself and understand that practice really does help, they will come to this realization themselves.

As stated previously, including practice homework in grades can be damaging to struggling students because they may develop misunderstandings that will be difficult to correct. It is also damaging to these students because it reduces their willingness to try. If they know that they are going to get a low score, then to avoid yet another failure, one defense mechanism is not to do it. It is better to keep the stakes low and have students understand, "It is okay to try because if I try, I am going to get feedback on what I did well and what needs improvement."

Finally, including in grades practice and/or learning activities can harm students who initially have little understanding but are taught well and learn effectively and consistently improve. Consider the high school Mathematics class with three formative quizzes and one summative test over a three-week period. Jeremy receives scores of 20, 40, and 60 percent on the quizzes and 95 percent on the test. He has almost certainly mastered whatever was taught over that unit. But if the quizzes count for 20% of the grade and the test for 80% of the grade—which is common—he would receive a grade of 83 percent, which in some high schools would be a C instead of the A he deserves.

The fix for all these broken grades is to not include scores from learning activities, including practice homework, in grades. One of the best ways to ensure this happens and to make the process clear to students is to develop assessment plans and (age appropriately) make them known to students.

An assessment plan should start with the desired results—the learning goals derived from the standards. The summative assessments that are going to be used to determine whether the student "knows and can do" (i.e., the only assessments that will be used to determine grades) follow. Next are the diagnostic assessment(s) that are going to help determine the "what" and the "how" for teaching and learning. Finally come the formal formative assessments that are going to help students achieve the learning goals and through which the teacher will adjust teaching and learning activities, such as the homework and quizzes that help students to be successful on tests, the practices that lead to performances, and the series of drafts that help students to produce high-quality products of such a plan.

Assessment Plan for a unit including three standards

Formal Formative Assessment

TASK	METHOD(S)	STRATEGY(IES)	SCORING TOOL	ASSESSOR
ROLE PLAY Practice(s)	Performance Ass't	Performance	Rubric	self/peer
QUIZ(ZES)	Paper and Pencil	Selected Response	Marking Scheme	Teacher
BROCHURE Draft	Performance Ass't	Product	Rubric	peer
BROCHURE Near Final	Performance Ass't	Product	Rubric	self/peer

Summative Assessment for "Unit 1"on 3 standards

TASK	METHOD(S)	STRATEGY(IES)	SCORING TOOL	ASSESSOR
ROLE PLAY	Performance Ass't	Performance assessment	Rubric	Teacher
TEST(S)	Paper and Pencil	Selected & Constructed Reponse	Marking Scheme	Teacher
BROCHURE	Performance Ass't	Product	Rubric	Teacher

Figure 13.5. An Assessment Plan for a Unit with Three Standards
This is from the second edition of the Repair Kit

Note that in this plan there is a clear link between the formative and summative assessments: one or more practices of the role play with descriptive feedback will help students to perform high-quality role plays, one or more quizzes followed by analysis of strengths and weaknesses and appropriate reteaching will help students to be successful on the test(s), and the draft and near final versions of the product with descriptive feedback will lead to high-quality brochures. When a plan such as this is in place and students—and parents—are familiar with it, it is obvious to all that the focus is on the learning, not simply on the accumulation of points.

As a final idea in this Fix, I would like to note that the statement made in the first paragraph of this fix ("primarily only (include) evidence from those assessments intended to document learning") states the principle very strongly. However, once teachers have become clear about the appropriate uses for formative and summative assessment and abandoned the practice of including everything in grades, especially homework, it is acceptable secondarily to consider formative assessment evidence when determining grades. This, of course, also requires that teachers are determining, not simply calculating, grades (see Fix 11). I acknowledge that I overstate when I say summative "only" but, given traditional grading practices and the persistence of schools, especially high schools, in maintaining an 80/20 summative/formative grade calculation, it seems to me that we have to establish this "strong" position. When teachers have developed a deeper understanding of grading issues, they can take a more holistic view of the evidence of achievement that each student has produced and perhaps even embrace these ideas from that Lee Ann Jung posted on Twitter on September 30th, 2021: "'Summative' doesn't imply a single, high-stakes test. Summative is a point in time at which we consider ALL evidence, formal and informal."

As we move forward and attempt to help students to focus on learning rather than the accumulation of points and "does this count," consideration needs to be given to this somewhat different characterization of formative and summative provided by Jung (2021):

> Using data summatively—that is, to summarize learning—should only happen when we need to report learning, typically at the end of reporting periods. Those grades should only become "fixed" at the end of the academic year. With this mindset, we don't really have to have formative tasks and summative tasks. We can have a formative period of time and summative points in time. The formative period happens over the entire school year, with only a small portion of the year, mostly at the end of terms, spent on summative assessment. The implications for this shift mean that every test, activity, check-

> in, paper, and project is, in fact, used formatively until the end of the year (even if we pause to use some of this evidence summatively at reporting periods). And every bit of information, formal or informal, is considered an important data point that we can use to summarize learning at the end. This gets us out of the game of categorizing what "counts," because it *all* counts.

Student Involvement

This is the most critical area for student involvement because students have often been "trained" in classrooms where no distinction has been made between practice and performance and where there is little feedback or opportunities to make adjustments in learning (or teaching) based on formative assessment. Students who are actively involved in every aspect of assessment are more able to distinguish for themselves between practice and performance and to know what and when they have to practice and deepen their understanding and skills.

Details on how students can be involved in self-assessment and self-adjustment through assessment for learning will be provided in Fix 15.

Summary

Grades are broken when they are merely about accumulating points. To make it obvious that they are about learning, the fix is to distinguish between formative and summative assessment and to include primarily only results from the latter directly in grades.

> The standards movement . . . precipitated a new interest in what might be the most favorable course of action to prepare students to meet the expected standards. . . . What emerged was an almost unified belief that formative assessment practices were the most effective and efficient way to increase student achievement.
>
> *(Schimmer, 2016, p. 10)*

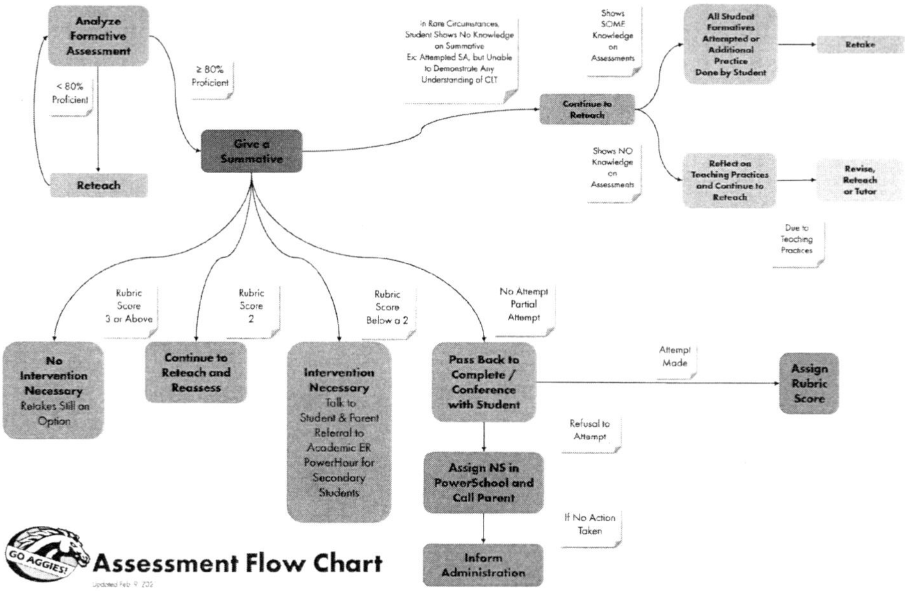

Figure 13.6. Dansville Schools (MI) Assessment Flow Chart
Used with permission from Dansville Schools. (See page 208 for larger version.)

Amy Hodgson

Superintendent
Dansville Schools, Michigan

At Dansville Schools, our teachers use an assessment flow chart to ensure consistency and to determine next steps with the goal of helping students achieve mastery. While the formative assessment section of the chart seems small, it is truly the area in which the most time is spent by students and teachers in the classroom. We know students may need many rounds of practice before they can demonstrate proficiency, which means our teachers spend the bulk of their time providing practice opportunities, observing student responses, offering feedback, and facilitating student self-reflection. While our teachers and students may discuss how practice work would score on the rubric scale to help students gauge their progress, it is a district procedure that none of those scores become a part of a student's grade. Instead, those scores help both our teachers and students determine next steps for learning—need additional practice? Ready for a summative? Reflection is key.

Even after a summative assessment (and a rubric score) is given, the reflective work continues for our teachers and students. Some students may need additional practice in class or after school, and our teachers evaluate how many of their students are proficient on each Clear Learning Target and reflect on their methods of delivery accordingly. The summative score is just one small part of the learning journey.

Leah Braman
Teacher
Dansville Schools, Michigan

I use the flowchart to determine when my students are ready for summative assessment and what steps to take after summative assessments are scored. The formative assessment section of the chart appears small, but it is truly where most of my time is spent. Some clear learning targets are review from previous years and may need little practice, while others are brand new or add layers of complexity that require multiple practice opportunities. I spend the majority of my time facilitating practice, observing student responses, offering feedback, and facilitating student self-reflection. I discuss with students how each formative assessment might be scored, but I don't enter it in the gradebook; instead, those scores help my students and me determine next steps. Only when the majority of the class has shown proficiency during practice do I provide the summative assessment.

When summative assessment is complete, scores go into the gradebook, but that doesn't mean the learning is finished. Some students may still need additional practice, and I provide that practice in the classroom as it feeds into new learning. Other students may need to attend after school intervention for more instruction and practice or to approach the learning target from a new angle. These students practice until they reach proficiency and then retake the assessment on the target. The flow chart helps me and my students reflect on the learning, and the reflection is critical to the success of all.

Policy/Procedure Examples

International Schools Group – Jubail
Jubail, Saudi Arabia

SUMMATIVE AND FORMATIVE ASSESSMENT

ISG Jubail teachers embed both types of assessment into their course structures. The following provides a general description of these two assessment types:

- Formative assessment allows teachers to monitor student learning and provide ongoing feedback regarding the learning process. This is non-graded evidence of student learning. Teachers utilize formative assessment to inform their classroom practices, differentiate instruction, and check where students are in their understanding of content and skills. Students use formative assessment to improve their learning and identify strengths and limitations in the process. Formative assessment allows for:
    - Practice for mastery
    - Continuous feedback
    - Un-graded or no-count grades in Skyward (the computer grading program). A numerical score can be given (although descriptive feedback is encouraged in lieu of numerical scores) but it will not count toward the final student grade
- Summative Assessment evaluates student learning. These typically complete units of study, or come at the end of a learning sequence, to determine the final grade. Summative assessments measure student learning of content standards with clearly described performance standards.
    - The culmination of student learning: graded content in Skyward, takes place at the end of a sequence of learning
    - Accompanied by clearly published guidelines, expectations, and rubrics for students (and exemplars if available; (ISG Jubail, 2019, pp. 2-3)

Winneconne School District
Winneconne, Wisconsin

HOMEWORK

The Winneconne Community School District defines "homework" as practice in the learning progression toward proficiency on identified learning targets. Homework should be looked at as a "tool" in the learning process and not an instrument to measure and report a student's understanding of academic learning targets. When viewed as a tool to help with learning, homework is then not an assessment of the student's understanding of learning targets/content, but rather a step toward learning it (Winneconne School District, 2022)

Fix 14 Emphasize more recent achievement; don't just summarize evidence accumulated over time.

> "With traditional grading practices, teachers often combine what a student knows (now) with what he or she used to not know (typically via mean averaging) to calculate a grade, . . . Giving students full credit for what they know (now), regardless of how slowly they got there, is fundamental to developing a standards-based mindset."
>
> *(Schimmer, 2016, p. 59)*

Grades are broken when learning is developmental (i.e., likely to improve over time with practice and repeated opportunities) and the final grade does not recognize the student's final level of proficiency. The fix for this type of broken grade is that for any learning that grows over time, we must emphasize the more recent evidence and allow new evidence to replace, not simply be added to, old evidence. When we are standards-based (Fix #7), all learning is developmental; thus, this fix applies universally to the determination of grades for standards (Fix #11). It also requires that students have multiple opportunities to demonstrate their level of learning on each standard; these multiple opportunities may occur through the spiraling of assessments or through reassessment.

Two very important issues emerge as we think about determining grades for developmental learning. First, by emphasizing the more recent information, we acknowledge learning as a process and we can give students the message, "It is never over until it is really over!" One of the most unfortunate effects of the common practice of simply adding up all the scores and calculating the mean is that many students will never be able to overcome the impact of early failures/very low scores. This is a terrible situation for both students and teacher because students who have no hope of success give up—and, as noted previously, frequently become at risk for discipline problems. If, however, our message to students is that we will acknowledge their learning whenever it occurs, then they have no reason to give up. In fact, this approach is a powerful motivator for students achieving at any level, because every student will know that improved achievement will receive full recognition.

The second issue concerns averaging. With developmental learning, more recent information should not be simply averaged with outdated evidence when determining grades. Only the more recent data should be used. Fix 11 is relevant to this context. In it, I proposed that we see grading as an exercise in professional judgment, not just as a numerical, mechanical activity. The practical implication of this is that an established practice in many schools, especially in middle and high schools, must be abandoned—that of determining final grades by adding the grade for each grading period and dividing by the number of grading periods. Attempts have been made to devise a "power formula" or weighting to be applied when calculating grades that would emphasize more recent achievement while still allowing teachers to calculate grades, but none of these is as good as teacher judgment.

DON'T DO THIS

Each student starts each quarter fresh. Therefore, each quarter grade is separate.

- Semester grades are calculated as follows:
- Quarter 1 grade x 2
- Quarter 2 grade x 2
- Semester exam grade x 1
- ______________________
- TOTAL divided by 5 = Semester average

DO THIS

- Grades are cumulative over a whole course/year and are determined by
- Mode + More Recent + Professional Judgment
- Quarters/terms/semesters are only administrative and communication conveniences

---

Figure 14.1. Grading Periods Don'ts and Do's

By emphasizing more recent evidence we acknowledge the impact of good teaching on student success. Consider the learning achievement curves of the four students in the graph shown in Figure 5.3 for one standard.

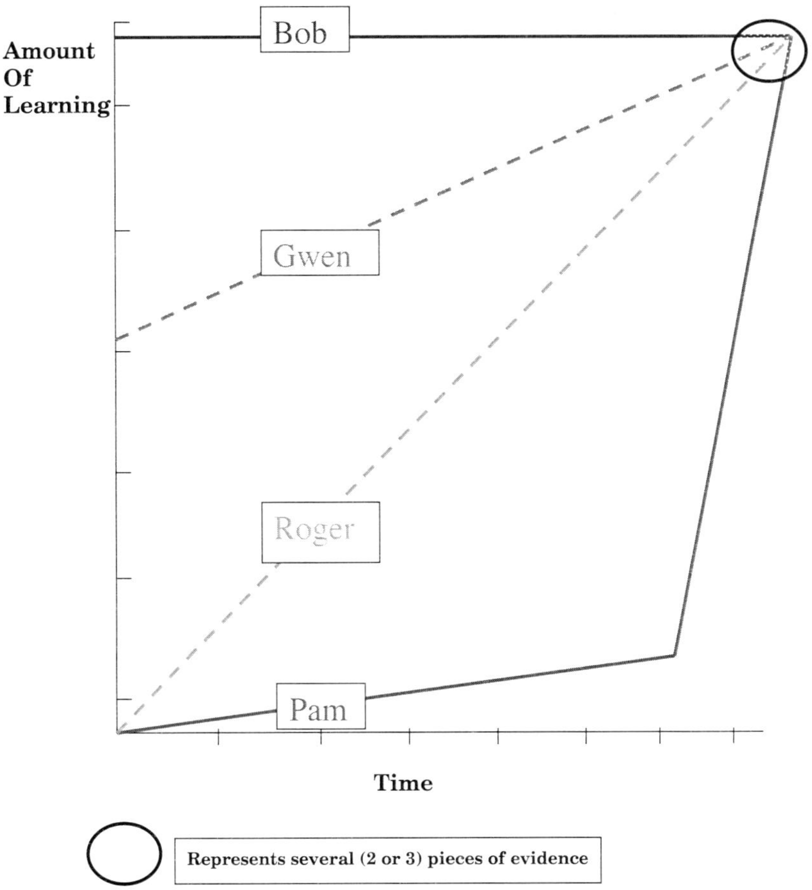

Figure 14.2. Levels of Achievement Over Time for a Standard

Bob is basically the student who almost doesn't need a teacher; Gwen is a fairly typical successful student, while Roger and Pam need time to develop understanding/skill. If all four of these students receive the same grade, it will acknowledge their equally high achievement at the end. If Roger and Pam get lower grades, as they would traditionally, their achievement is misrepresented, which is academically unjustifiable. Also, almost certainly, Roger and Pam reached the high level of achievement because they received high quality instruction, so if teachers really help students to meet standards and students then do so, the contribution of teachers to that achievement needs to be recognized.

Figure 14.2 shows that the students had multiple opportunities to demonstrate their achievement on a standard, so we have to consider how those multiple opportunities occur. Most commonly, they occur by allowing students to take formal reassessments/redos/retakes. It is essential that these opportunities are available but there are many problems associated with reassessment. First and foremost is the issue of feasibility for teachers in terms of time—time to develop, time to administer, and timc to scorc. Equally important arc thc conditions of reassessment for students so that the message that they receive isn't you don't have to prepare well/try the first time because there will be an automatic retake opportunity.

There are two ways to alleviate the problems with formal reassessment. The first and best way is to avoid the need for them by spiraling assessments so reassessment occurs on an ongoing basis. In a standards-based system, instruction and learning opportunities should be planned so that each standard is revisited and reassessed on a regular basis throughout a year or course, thus eliminating the need for formal reassessment. As Kristin Rivera stated,

> Spiral assessments will ensure that a student's grade reflects their current understanding. If a student fails a test on fractions and we never give them another opportunity to demonstrate their understanding as they learn and grow, is that test grade a true refection reflection of their ability level? No.
>
> (Rivera, 2021)

It is also important that teachers understand that reassessment isn't necessary for formative assessments because they are just-in-time assessments that aren't included in grades.

If assessments aren't spiraled and it is necessary to provide formal reassessments, then it is essential that students understand that they will receive full credit for the reassessment (i.e., two or more attempts won't be averaged, the more recent score will be used) and that "correctives" will be required before they are allowed to take a reassessment. The correctives may involve completing the relevant (but not necessarily all the) formal formative assessments that proceeded the summative assessment and/or participating in other relearning opportunities. Formal reassessments may occur during class time, but they may also occur outside of class time when students would prefer to be doing something else like socializing with their friends. This is called opportunity cost—what a person loses when they choose one option over another. The combination of correctives and opportunity cost should send the message to students that it is in their best interest to do well the first time and not rely on a reassessment. David Cutler puts that message to students clearly with this advice for students:

> Aim to perform well the first time around on all assignments and assessments. Otherwise, you create more work and stress for yourself by having to keep up with new work in this and other courses while you prepare for the retake.
>
> (Cutler, 2019)

Dwyer and Hiscock (2019) put it this way:

> Nothing is less productive than allowing reassessment without some kind of extra 'effort' (learning) being put in by the student to demonstrate they have learned what they needed to know. Students must give their best effort on the first attempt, and then show new evidence of learning before being reassessed. (p. 129)

The issues involved with reassessment and how to overcome them are clearly illustrated in the following educator vignette for this fix by Becky Peppler. Also, if you want additional resources on reassessment, look at the books, articles, and videos by Rick Wormeli (2019, 2016, and 2010) listed in the References. And for a somewhat different perspective, read Schimmer (2018).

Summary

When learning is cumulative and developmental and results from a process that unfolds over time so that student achievement increases with practice and multiple opportunities, the more recent evidence should "count" for the student's grade; old, outmoded evidence should be discarded. Grades are broken when this is not done. The fix is to emphasize more recent achievement, with more recent evidence replacing previous evidence.

Learning became less and less about the grade and more about the learning goals. The question "What can I do to boost my grade? became, for instance, "Ms. Vanhala, I still don't understand mole ratios. Can we meet after school to go over my mistakes on this assessment? And then I'll review and schedule a retake for next week."

(Vanhala, 2020)

Educator Vignette

Becky Peppler
Former High School Science Teacher & Instructional Coach
Director of The STAGR Center with FIRST Educational Resources
Winneconne, Wisconsin

I remember when I first heard of the idea of reassessment in my classroom; I just brushed the idea aside and did not spend much time thinking about it. When I started to hear more discussions around the idea, I dug my heels in and graciously resisted. I could not wrap my head around WHY reassessing students would be a good idea. As their teacher, I was supposed to not only be teaching them about chemistry, but also teaching them responsibility and the value of due dates. I originally felt that if I allowed retakes, I wouldn't be doing any of the aforementioned things. I remember thinking "This is the way it has always been done, why on earth should we make any changes?"

Fast forward: it took some time and research to convince me that there was definitely a place for reassessment in the classroom and that it most certainly belonged there. I came to realize that I could get behind the theory on why we needed reassessment and began to understand the value reassessment would have on student learning. But where I was having trouble was implementing the practice. As I started to allow students to be reassessed, I eventually found myself feeling like a top that was spinning faster and faster out of control. I was struggling to keep up with the reassessments. I was teaching 6 classes, 150 students a day, and in every class, students had an opportunity to reassess their summative assessments. I had students coming into my classroom while I was teaching other classes, before school, after school, during my lunch, and prep periods. I always thought of myself as an organized person, but I felt more unorganized than ever. I had papers stacked everywhere and I could not keep up with the feedback and grading of the reassessments. I also had students who would walk into class, before they even took the initial assessment, asking when they could reassess! It did not take me long to realize I was struggling big time with the management behind the reassessment, and it was slowly making me wonder if reassessment was really worth it.

After some reflection, I came to realize that I was not against reassessment, but that I needed to find a way to implement practices that worked for me and my students, still held my students accountable, and required evidence of additional learning to take place prior to the reassessment taking place. I knew that it would be difficult to do alone and that I would need some backing from my administrators and school. It was through a combined effort, between me and the school, to develop and foster an environment conducive to reassessment. So, how did we do it?

Our school had developed a list of non-negotiables around reassessment, which were as follows:

- Reassessments are allowed on all summative assessments that are reflected in what is reported out to parents on our report cards.
- In order for a student to qualify for a reassessment, the student must demonstrate new evidence of learning since taking the initial assessment. The requirements for new evidence of learning "should support learning rather than simply deterring student access to retests" (Dueck, 2014).
- Depending on the number of students reassessing, this may occur during a normal class period. Students not participating in a reassessment may engage in homework/practice from other courses, read, or enjoy extension activities within that content area.
- If a student scores lower on the reassessment than on the original assessment, the assessment that will be reflected for grading and reporting purposes will be the most recent evidence.
- Reassessing can occur in multiple forms, such as another assessment similar to the first, oral discussion with the teacher, or another method that is mutually agreeable between the teacher and student
- Students do not have to retake an entire assessment. If the student struggled on a particular concept or skill, the student is allowed to reassess in solely that area to replace the score assigned to that particular standard.

From there, each department could craft their own policy, keeping the non-negotiables in the forefront (see attached policy). Finally, after three years of updating, we had a policy that did what it was intended to do: it held students accountable while improving student learning. The positive outcomes were plentiful. Our students were being reassessed and acquiring lifelong skills that were usable well beyond their time in our buildings. Some of the outcomes were:

- Improved student learning
- Opened the door to more meaningful dialogue with students regarding their learning.
- Gave students more ownership and responsibility in their learning, which resulted in closing gaps.
- Students learned how to reflect on their own learning and make improvement plans based on their results.

While these were all great outcomes, the question still stands, "How did reassessment become a reality?" If I can leave you with a few pieces of advice, they would be the following:

- Realize it may take a few years to work out the kinks of your policy, and that's okay.
- Develop a set of school-wide reassessment non-negotiables to keep everyone on the same page to allow for consistency where necessary.
- Allow departments to further develop how they want to carry out those non-negotiables. How a student reassesses a lab-based science learning target will look very different than how a student reassesses an ELA target in an essay.
- Communicate and be transparent with the students, the staff, and the community about all of the expectations. The more people that know and understand the policy, the easier it is to carry out.

How do I (the teacher) manage this day to day?

- So simple, but super helpful: all of our retake tickets were printed on purple paper and nothing else was ever on purple paper. This made it really easy for me and the students. We all know what the purple paper meant, so it was easy to find.

- Give a reasonable window of time for students to be reassessed. Give feedback on ALL of the reassessments, for that learning target or standard, after the window has closed (if possible). This will save you time, as a teacher, because you can sit down and give feedback on all of them at the same time.

Looking back, I'm thankful I had to work through the struggles, with myself and my students, because it has allowed me time to see and understand the value of allowing students the opportunity of reassessment. As a result, I saw a dramatic increase in student growth and achievement in my classroom.

Policy/Procedure Examples

Shattuck St. Mary's Forest City International School
Forest City, Malaysia

GRADING BASED ON MOST RECENT EVIDENCE

Accurate grades are based on the more recent and most consistent evidence. When determining a final grade, we will look at the pattern of achievement and rely more on the more recent scores, and not compute the average of all the scores.

MULTIPLE ASSESSMENT OPPORTUNITIES AND REASSESSMENT

An important piece of standards-based grading includes multiple assessment opportunities for each content standard taught in the classroom. When students do not meet standards, they may need opportunities to reassess in order to show growth in their learning over time. All teachers will allow some form of reassessment opportunity for each reporting standard. This occurs most appropriately by spiraling assessments but at times it may be necessary to provide formal reassessment opportunities. Teachers will use their discretion to determine the exact nature of the retake opportunity, the timing of the retake opportunity, and the range of standards needing to be re-assessed.

(Shattuck St. Mary's Forest City International School, 2021, p. 2)

International School of Kazan
Kazan, Russia

FURTHER ASSESSMENTS

In some cases, students extend their learning after completing what the teacher planned as the summative assessment in that area. In these cases, the student should be permitted to do a further assessment in order to demonstrate their new level of achievement. This may be in the form of any task which assesses the needed objective(s) in a fresh context. (Teachers are discouraged from re-administering tasks which the student has already completed, as this is more likely to show direct knowledge of the specific task, rather than transferable knowledge and skills.) Either the teacher or the student may suggest/request such an opportunity. Details of the assessment should be discussed between the student and teacher to ensure there is clarity on expectations and timelines.

(International School of Kazan, 2021, p. 8)

Fix 15 Involve students; don't leave students out of the assessment and grading process.

> In virtual and hybrid classrooms (during pandemic schooling in 2020 and 2021), those who were most likely to succeed were students with higher self-regulation skills, whereas those most dependent on the teacher - or those who had teachers who over-orchestrated their classes – struggled the most. Teachers who talked a lot in class, asked questions that required less-than-three-word responses, and focused myopically on the facts and content had trouble engaging learners remotely. However, teachers who had taught their students skills in self-regulation, engaged in gradual release of teacher responsibility, and focused on both content and deep learning had better outcomes.
>
> *(Hattie, 2021, p. 14)*

> If every aspect of their learning has been explicitly spelled out for them, why are we surprised that when teachers are no longer in direct proximity to students, many of the students are clueless about what to do next.
>
> *(Silver, 2021)*

Grades—and assessment—are broken if teachers simply "run the show." Students must be involved in all stages of the assessment process and should understand (age appropriately) from the outset how grades will be determined. Students can learn how to monitor their own progress and how to communicate that progress to others. In so doing, they understand more deeply their own strengths and areas needing improvement, and can use that understanding to guide specific, meaningful goal setting about what they can learn/do next. Ideas about student involvement have appeared in all of this book's Fixes. Fix 15 is a summary and restatement of the key ideas with some expansion.

Grades should communicate achievement status, and both assessment and grading need to help students achieve at higher levels and develop positive attitudes about learning. This is more likely to happen when students are involved as active participants in ongoing assessment and grading so that they see the entire process as something that is done *with* them, not *to* them. This is most likely to be accomplished when we give students voice and choice (White, 2020).

Students also benefit when teachers share with students from the start of each year/course how they will determine grades, and to this end, Pernille Ripp illustrated the necessity of discussing what the grading symbols mean with this example from her classroom:

> So, on Monday I asked them, "What does a "1" mean to you?" as a way to get our conversation started. I was surprised, to say the least, at their answers...
> "It means that I have failed..."
> "It means I am bad..."
> "It means they didn't try..."
>
> Receiving a "1" on standard score did not mean they were at the beginning of their learning. That they had not yet mastered something. That they had some knowledge but still had a way to go. No, it meant failure, no effort, that they were stupid. Even in our classroom where students self-assess all of the time. Where we have actively tried to change the conversation from a score to feedback. Where I have tried to put students in control of their learning. They still think that if they get a "1" they are bad kids.
>
> So rather than move into the definition of letter grades (they did this after) we stopped for a moment and discussed what each standard score really means. What they need to do when they give themselves a "1" or a "2." How a "1" does not mean they didn't try but that they do not understand yet. That a "2" does not mean they are bad at English but that they still have teaching to be a part of. That those scores certainly can have something to do with effort but must of the time it does not. That those scores do not determine how smart they are but are really just an indication of what they have shown me so far.
>
> (Ripp, 2017, pp. 2-3)

It is also important that students and parents receive clear statements about grading policy/procedures. Figure 15-1 shows an example of such a statement:

2020-2021 Science Grading Process

During this school year Mr. Mattingly will be using a grading process designed to give students more directed feedback about specific learning objectives. Students will know the areas that they have performed well in and areas that need improvement. The following will outline how this grading system operates and what students can expect.

1. For each unit students receive a list of learning targets written in student friendly language. These targets specify what students need to know, be able to do with what they know, and demonstrate. Lessons focus on these learning targets and students know the learning target that the activity/lesson addresses. Students are assessed throughout the unit to see how they are doing on their targets. This information provides feedback to the teacher and student on progress made and where to go next.

2. At the end of each unit, students are assessed on their understanding of the learning targets. Each unit assessment will be planned out so that each target is assessed an appropriate amount and in an appropriate way. The assessment is scored and students will receive a report that indicates their performance on each of the targets (see accompanying Performance Level Descriptor page). The student's grade is determined by the Summary Judgement to Letter Grade Conversion chart that is attached.

3. After receiving feedback on their performance, students will have an opportunity (about a week later) to take a second assessment. This second opportunity will allow students to show if they have improved in their understanding of individual learning targets they initially had trouble with. If students show an improvement on their learning target performance, their grade will go up accordingly. If they don't show improvement, their grade remains the same. There is no penalty for taking longer to demonstrate competency of a learning target.

4. A student who still does not demonstrate acceptable understanding can request help with the learning target from the teacher. They are allowed to check their current understanding at any point during the school year, and they may choose to take another assessment to show understanding. Students can show comprehension of a learning target at any time after the initial unit assessment. Even if it takes them 5 months to grasp the learning target, they can do that and improve their performance if they show the teacher they've mastered it. Whenever this occurs the students score on that target will be changed to reflect this new understanding and their grade will improve accordingly.

This grading process allows students to have ownership of their grades. They have the opportunity to know what they need to improve on and how to improve it. Students also discover that it's never too late to learn.

Thanks,
Ken Mattingly

(a recently retired Kentucky Middle School Science Teacher)

Figure 15.1. Ken Mattingly's Grading Practices for Parents

We must be mindful of the fact that students are users of the information that comes from assessments, so the purpose of each assessment must be clear to them. We must also be sure that students understand the targets; there are many strategies that can be used to help them with this, but one of the most powerful is to involve them in the co-construction of the rubrics we use to provide feedback and/or scores. Probably the most important aspect of student involvement is having them understand their progress and achievement and then communicate about their learning with other students, teachers, and significant adults in their life. One way to do this is to use assessment plans, such as the one shown in Figure 13.5 (p. 190). It is the teacher's responsibility to evaluate the summative assessments, but students should be involved in peer and self-assessment of formative assessments. This allows them to practice the skills of self-assessment and to deepen their understanding of the conditions of quality. Students need to be able to answer what have come to be known as "the learning questions":

> Where am I going?
>
> Where am I now?
>
> What can I do to get better?

Chappuis (2015) provided the strategies listed in Figure 15.2 for teachers to use to enable students to answer these critical questions:

Where Am I Going?

Strategy 1: Provide students with a clear and understandable vision of the learning target. (Fixes 7 and 8)

Strategy 2: Use examples and models of strong and weak "work" (evidence of learning).

Where Am I Now?

Strategy 3: Offer regular descriptive feedback during the learning. (Fix 13)

Strategy 4: Teach students to self-assess and set goals for next steps.

How Can I Close the Gap (or Get Better)?

Strategy 5: Use evidence of student learning needs to determine next steps in teaching

Strategy 6: Design focused instruction, followed by practice with feedback.

Strategy 7: Provide students with opportunities to track, reflect on, and share their learning progress.

Figure 15.2. Seven Strategies of Assessment for Learning
(Chappuis, 2015. p. 11)
Permission provided by Pearson Education

To be able to answer the learning questions, students have to be able to self-assess, but it is a learned skill; thus, Strategy 4 acknowledges that students have to be taught how to self-assess and set goals.

When students become self-assessors who are reflective learners, they can then communicate with parents or significant adults about their strengths, areas for improvement, and next steps in their learning. This means that schools/districts need to set up their communication system to include student-involved or student-led conferences from kindergarten through high school. This type of conference has been found to have a significant impact on students taking responsibility for their own learning and to result in better parent attendance at conferences (comprehensive information about student-led conferencing can be found at https://eleducation.org/resources/chapter-5-student-led-conferences).

It is critical to students' becoming lifelong learners and being successful beyond K-12 in whatever they decide to do that they have become self-directed, reflective learners, which leads to the importance of Chappuis' Strategy 7. The Ministry of Education in British Columbia significantly assists this development by requiring students in K-9 to complete a self-assessment on the Core Competencies (Communication, Thinking, and Personal and Social) at the end of the school year and by directing teachers to use frequent opportunities for students to consider and reflect on the Core Competencies. Students in grades 10-12 continue to reflect and self-assess on the Core Competencies and apply this to their capstone project as part of their graduation requirements. It is important to note that the Core Competencies aren't just 'nice ideas:'

> By design, the Core Competencies are the foundation for the Big Ideas, Curricular Competencies, and Content of the curriculum. This ensures that students are always mindful of their growth in the Core Competencies through awareness and self-reflection, self-assessment, and evidence of growth.

> (B.C. Ministry of Education, n.d.)

Starr Sackstein asserted that "the difference between reflection and just thinking about something . . . is intention" (p. 4). She also stated,

> "Teachers who incorporate student reflection effectively
>
> - Explicitly teach students what reflection is and allow them to practice during class time;
> - Teach students to question everything;
> - Avoid treating reflection as an add-on;
> - Make reflection more about actual learning than about how much students liked the content or the learning activity;
> - Differentiate how students reflect;
> - Ask students to share their reflections with others; and Model reflection."
>
> (Sackstein, 2015, pp. 4-5)

The Comox Valley School District in British Columbia views it this way:

> As students are increasingly involved in classroom assessment and evaluation, it is a natural extension for their own reflections and insights to become a part of reporting. Teachers are explicitly teaching children how to reflect, think about their 'work' (learning) as it corresponds to shared learning intentions or performance rubrics. 'Ownership of learning becomes that much more authentic when a child's voice becomes part of communicating with parents.
>
> (Comox Valley School District, 2015, p. 10)

They also provide a useful taxonomy of reflection as seen in Figure 15.3:

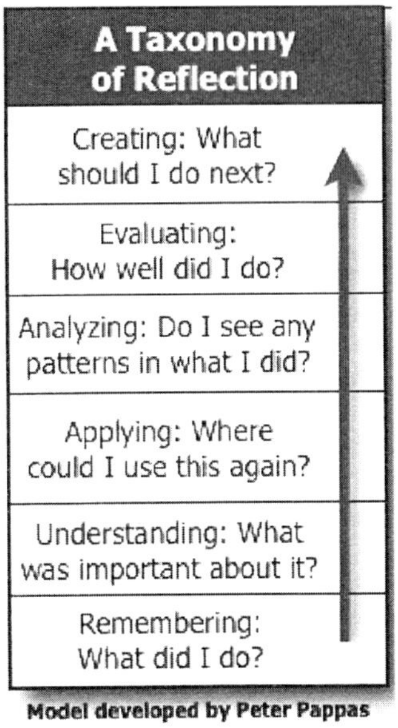

Figure 15.3. A Taxonomy of Reflection
(Comox Valley School District, 2015, p. 10).
Permission provided by Peter Pappas

This fix is about developing what is now often referred to as "assessment capable learners;" I don't know where the term originated, but I think it captures what this fix is about: "learners who know where they are heading, have the resources to get there, and continuously monitor their progress" (Greenstein, 2018,). The information provided here is a start, but it doesn't have sufficient depth or detail for teachers to develop the skills they need to develop assessment capable learners; for that, more comprehensive books on the topic are required. Thus, I highly recommend these two books (in author alphabetical order, not preference or priority): Myron Dueck's *Giving Students a Say* (2021) and Katie White's *Student Self-Assessment* (2022). There is also excellent information in the March 2020 (The Empowered Student) and December 2021/January 2022 (Engage and Motivate) editions of *Educational Leadership.*

Summary

Grades are broken when students do not understand how their grades have been determined and when they have been excluded from assessment, record keeping, and communication. The fix is to ensure that age-appropriately students understand how grades have been determined and to involve them as much as possible in all phases of learning and assessment so that they leave K-12 as confident, self-directed, reflective learners.

Instead of a closing quote for this fix, I'm using a graphic from the Alberta Assessment Consortium developed with the University of Lethbridge and the Livingstone Range School Division. The original is in a variety of colors and states that "Successful learners take ownership for and are engaged in their learning."

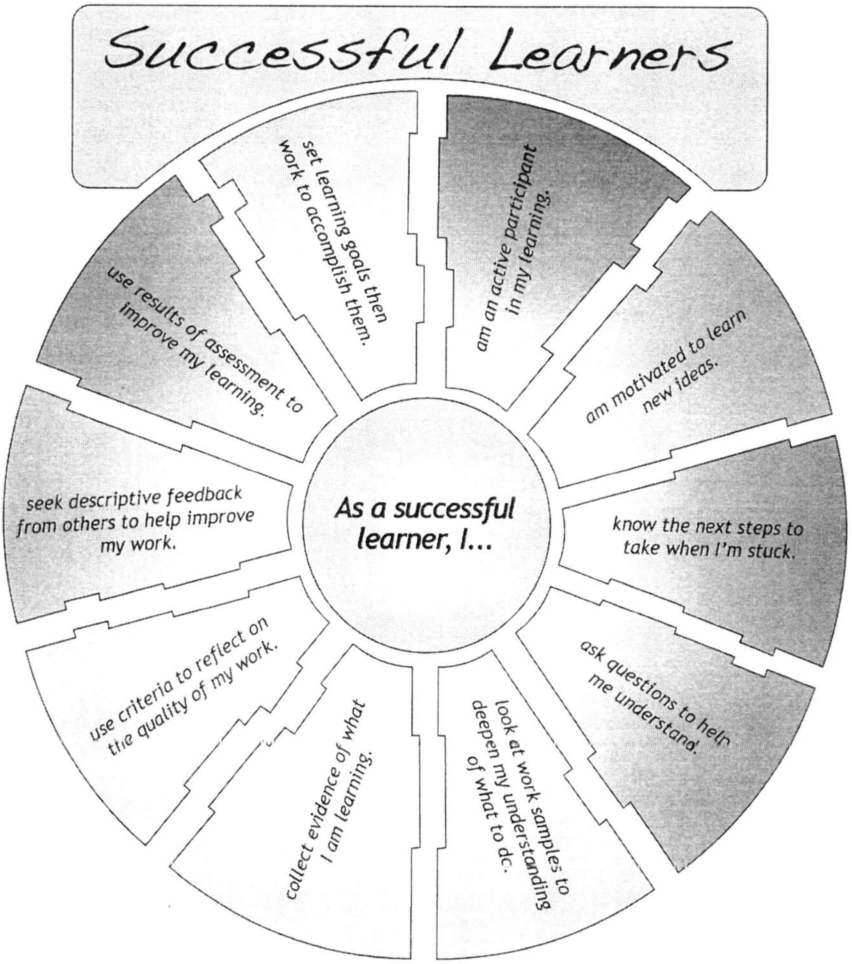

Figure 15.4. Successful Learners . . .
(Alberta Assessment Consortium, 2008)
Permission provided by the Alberta Assessment Consortium

Educator Vignettes

Dr. Erin Beard
Educator and Professional Learning Designer
Medford, Oregon

I was nervous to involve my middle and high school students in assessment and grading processes. Secondary students aren't necessarily known for their willingness to be active in learning processes. Was this change possible? Would it be worth the time and energy to make the shift? The answer was and still is a resounding YES!

First and foremost, I had to work with my students to nurture the culture and conditions for a high-functioning learning team, otherwise there wasn't a foundation of trust and purpose necessary for meaningful partnership in assessment and grading processes. This looked like regular discussions with students where we translated the learning goal (e.g., content standard) into language that made sense to them and reasons for the goal that were connected to their interests and aspirations. Instead of questions from students such as, "Why do we have to learn this?? I'm never going to use this!!" I would spark discussion with, "It's true. Some of you might not ever need to literally analyze literature after high school, but we all need to exercise our brain so that we're ready for the opportunities that are going to come our way. What kind of brain exercise do we gain from analyzing literature? How does the brain exercise support you to be ready for the opportunities that interest and inspire you?" Or when students declared something such as, "I'm terrible at this!" I would respond, "It would be a waste of your time if you already knew what we are learning. We're all here to grow! That's the point of school! You are in the right spot, with the right people, and we're all improving together. How exciting!"

Meanwhile, I also embedded opportunities for self-assessment throughout an instructional unit, not just at the end. For example, I would embed a one-sentence self-assessment prompt in practice (formative) exercises (e.g., *On a scale of 1–5, my claim sentence is currently a ___ because ___*). The students and I would use their self-assessment answers to plan next steps, which sometimes looked like adjusting the lesson plan for the next day for more practice or making mixed groups for the next formative exercise. Students readily engaged in the self-assessment practice because they saw how the information that they provided was immediately used to meaningfully adjust the learning journey. We would also use these frames for peer and teacher feedback processes during the learning journey. Rather than spending hours marking up summative tasks with feedback that the students did not read or use, I reinvested time and energy into student-involved feedback processes that occurred before the summative tasks. This reinvestment ultimately paid dividends— an increase in student success and self-efficacy while preserving teacher time, energy, and sanity.

For the summative task(s), I got into the habit of making sure to include a self-assessment prompt as the last part of the experience. Example: *Use the provided rubric to 1. Circle your levels of achievement, 2. Justify your achievement level circles with examples from your work.* Next, instead of jumping into grading, I would read students work and their self-assessment. More often than not, I would agree with the students' self-assessment and simply put "Agree!" on the assessment, which saved me hours of grading time. When I disagreed with a student's self-assessment, it was usually because they assessed themselves too hard. I would make a note of that on their self-assessment. In the rare occasion that the student's self-assessment was too lenient, I would conference with the student to learn more about their thinking and evaluate the work together. All students received their summative and self-assessment back with my notes. This could happen very fast— sometimes the next day or within the week—because the students did the heavy lifting of meaningful summative self-assessment. This process minimized the number of grade confusion conversations with students or caregivers. What a relief!!

Kristy Dolha
English Teacher
Barriere Secondary School
Barriere, British Columbia

Truth be told, I hate report cards; and I don't think I'm alone in the sentiment. The bleary eyes of my colleagues over morning coffee cups on the day reports are due tell me that, although most of us feel lucky in our vocation day to day, reporting on student learning does not add a lot of joy to the mix. Fix #15— involve students in the assessment and grading process— has made the task of student reporting more rewarding and certainly more meaningful for everyone involved.

When I first decided to tackle Fix 15, it seemed like a lot of time to invest. I put the curricular competency up on the board and challenged my students to break it down and put it into language that actually made sense. On the first go, they struggled. The individual words could be defined easily enough, but put it all together and what does it really mean? It wasn't a slam dunk on the first try, but I persisted.

On my next attempt, I asked them to go a step further and figure out what were the individual skills necessary to demonstrate the competency. As I persevered through elongated silences and wrinkled eyebrows, the students identified the skills. I pushed them on to the next step: take the competency and skills and scaffold them on our proficiency scale with a specific assignment in mind. This is the point where I became a firm believer in Fix 15. Finally, my students seemed to buy into the practice of working through all of the building blocks of a project before getting to the final product; finally, they were engaging in and trusting the process before racing to the finish line. As rewarding as this was, the real dividends for me came with reporting time.

This time, in preparation for report writing, I decided that I would throw it back to the kids. I gave them the competency, skills, and scaffolding on the proficiency scale they had come up with, and I asked them to reflect on their progress so far. I asked three simple questions: What are you learning? How is it going? Where to next? I was floored with their responses. Across the board, students pegged themselves *exactly* where I felt they were on the proficiency scale. There was no judgement. Rather, it was an indication of what they learned, and exactly what they needed to do to push their learning forward. Not only were their reflections spot on, but they were thoughtful and inspired. And I proudly *and simply* passed them on to their parents.

When I commended my students on their mature and honest responses, I asked them what it was about understanding the curricular competencies and assessment process that allowed them to be so reflective. Their responses were what sealed the deal on Fix 15 for me.

Becky was the first to articulate the value in the time invested, "It's not about just looking at the competency and going through the process once, but it needs to be done a lot to really understand it."

Spencer jumped in quickly, "Knowing the curricular competency and how it works on the proficiency scale makes it easier for me to know where I'm at and where I need to go."

And to finish things off, Ruben described it simply as "a tool."

James Mattiace

Principal and teacher,
Panama, Morocco, Oregon and more

After a few years of teaching the IB, I discovered the Grade Descriptors, which are subject based, detailed descriptors of what a numeric 1-7 score looks like in terms of student skills and abilities. At the Diploma Program level, the IB is a two-year program, and teachers are required to give a predicted score for each student. At our school, we were required to give that predicted score in June of Year 1 and again in October of Year 2, and then finally in April of Year 3. Providing a predicted score so early can sometimes overly inflate or deflate a student's sense of academic success.

Sometimes a student can struggle in the first year and then blossom in the second when pieces fall into place. The inverse is also true: a student may do well on introductory material but not be able to do the intellectual heavy lifting when it comes to more critical thinking pieces later in the course.

I decided the fairest and potentially forward moving thing to do would be to give every student a copy of the grade descriptors and ask them to gather evidence, portfolio style, of where they stood. I then had individual conferences with each student to review the evidence and set a predicted score. These conversations were amazingly productive. Students were very aware of the ultimate expectations of them at the end of the course and could measure themselves with the available evidence. I found myself having many conversations with students where I had internally predicted them at a level 4 only to be convinced by their evidence that a 5 was a more apt description. Because it was low-stakes in June (predicted scores stayed in-house and were not sent on to universities), the conversations were very honest. What was most intriguing was the visible learning that happened. It demystified what it meant to be top scholar in the IB program, and students began to see links between the assessments and the course goals. It gave them the key to unlocking their own learning once we laid it out in the open.

Policy/Procedure Examples

Seoul Foreign School
Seoul, South Korea

3.4 INVOLVEMENT OF STUDENTS

Involve students in the assessment process by

- training students in the use of rubrics
- discussing achievement targets and assessment practices with them on an ongoing basis
- ensuring that students have a range of opportunities to demonstrate their learning by using multiple assessment tasks
- giving students a variety of exemplars to help them understand what quality looks like and what is required to achieve the expected learning outcomes
- providing timely, descriptive feedback on what each student knows and is able to do in relation to the expected learning outcomes, and how the student can improve in relation to those outcomes
- providing opportunities for students to give descriptive feedback to each other.

Rocky View Schools
Airdrie, Alberta

ADMINISTRATIVE PROCEDURE 360: ASSESSMENT AND COMMUNICATION OF STUDENT LEARNING

2.2. Teachers and principals will:

2.2.1. Strive to communicate in ways that encourage students to understand themselves as learners, to understand where they are in the progression of their learning and to understand the direction they need to take their learning or what they need to do differently in order to be more successful.

2.2.2. Provide frequent opportunities within their instructional routines, for students to discuss their learning with others using a wide variety of strategies such as effective use of conferencing and portfolios, the collaborative identification of assessment criteria and the corresponding indicators of quality work, and the routine use of self-reflection and peer coaching to enable students to internalize the attributes of quality work and performance. (Rocky View School Division, 2021, p. 3)

River East Transcona School Division
Winnipeg, Manitoba

River East Transcona School Division (2018) recognizes that quality assessment promotes learning and achievement. Students, parent/legal guardian, teachers, and the system all have a role to play to ensure that assessment is valid, fair, inclusive, informative and transparent.

1.) Students

Students obtain and use information about progress towards learning goals through quality assessment.

Students:

- actively participate in assessment and evaluation.
- engage in self-assessment to become more reflective and can set goals for improvement.
- learn to take responsibility for their work and become life-long learners.
- engage in the assessment process to promote accountability and excellence.
- access and utilize feedback to guide their learning.
- build self-awareness and meta-cognition throughout the assessment process.

(River East Transcona School Division, 2018, p. 1)

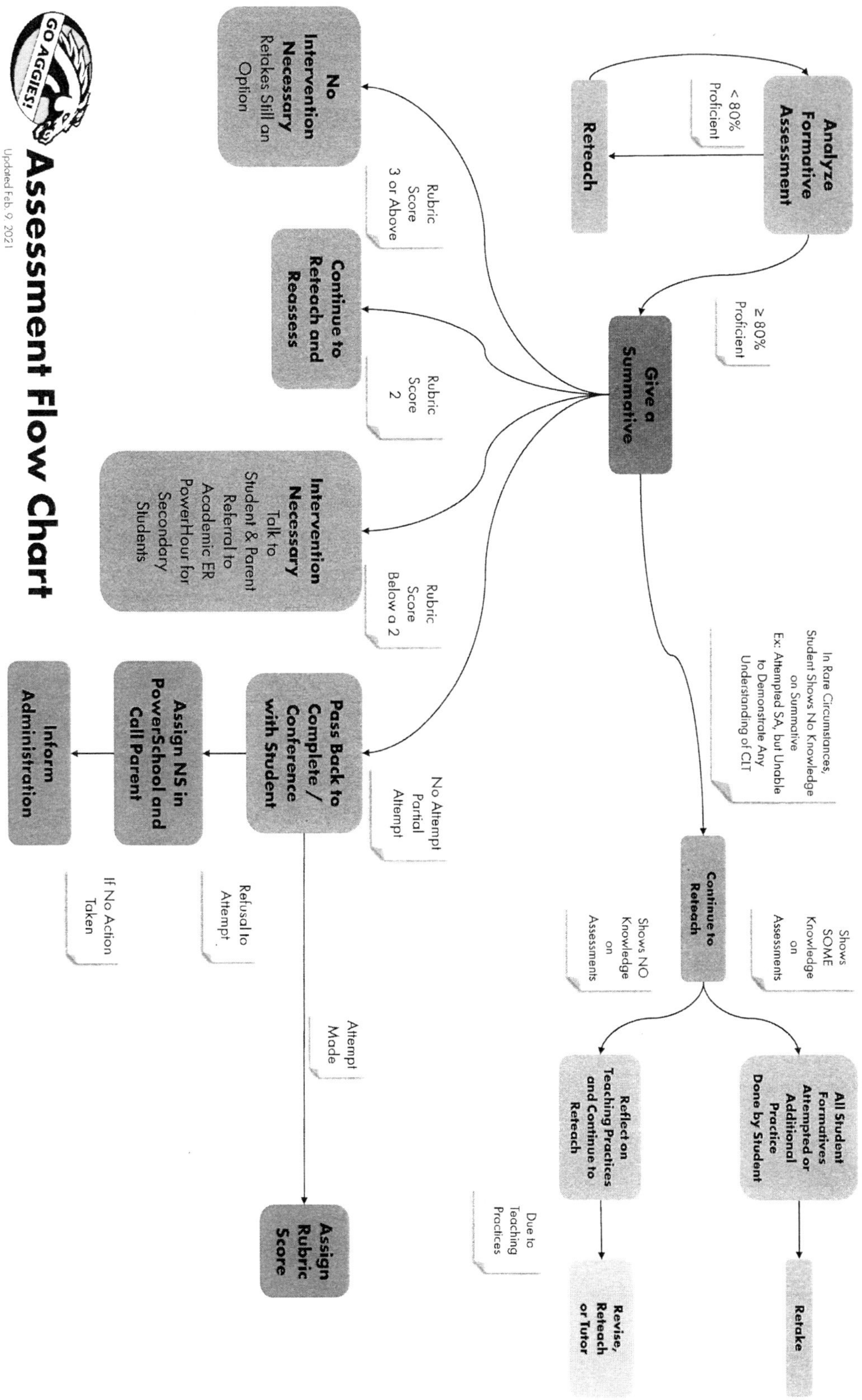

Figure 13.6. Dansville Schools (MI) Assessment Flow Chart
Used with permission from Dansville Schools.

CHAPTER 6

SYNTHESIS AND MOVING FORWARD

The concept of standards-based grading is not easily enacted by teachers, nor is it easily understood by parents. Rather the change is a work in progress which requires educators and parents to work together to relearn what we have been taught in the past about grades.

(Lisa Westman in DeWitt, 2017)

Grades are summary symbols that should communicate only about student achievement at a point in time. To be effective, they must be consistent, accurate, and learning focused and meaningful. Unfortunately, because grading has often been an unexamined and private practice, grades have frequently not met these standards and, as a result, are very often broken. In this book, I have described 15 Fixes for broken grades—fixes for ingredients that distort achievement, low-quality or poorly organized evidence, inappropriate grade calculation, and lack of support for learning.

Linking the Fixes to the CALM criteria for effectiveness described in detail in Chapter 1, for Consistency Fix 8 needs to be in place; for Accuracy, Fixes 1 to 6 and 9 to 12 need to be used; for Learning-focused, Fixes 13, 14, and 15 need to be implemented, and for grades to be Meaningful, Fix 7 needs to be used.

Fifteen fixes make a long list, and implementing the Fixes is not necessarily easy, as the quote above indicates. Achievement in standards-based systems means proficiency on the standards. Required content standards (the what) and performance standards (the how well) must be clear and must be the focus of curriculum, instruction, assessment, grading, and reporting. Assessment must be accurate and the process of learning emphasized by involving students in assessment, record keeping, and communication.

Practically, any one (or more) of the Fixes can be used as a starting point. But effective grading in standards-based systems really flows from Fix 7 because as soon as one is truly standards-based in assessment and grading, the other Fixes become logical extensions. When grading is only about achievement of standards, it quickly becomes obvious that it is inappropriate to include factors other than achievement (1–6), that it is necessary to have quality evidence (8–10) that accurately summarizes student achievement (11, 12), and that the emphasis needs to be on the learning process. I now believe that there are eight "musts" that can be questioned with regard to details and implementation but not with regard to the basic principle involved:

- Standards-based curriculum, instruction, assessment, AND grading and reporting with no single subject grades except for grades 11 and 12; (Fix 7)
- Performance standards with clear criterion-referenced descriptions of a limited number of levels with no use of percentages; (Fixes 8 & 9)
- All assessments must be of high quality (Fix 10), and
- Students must be involved in the assessment process. (Fix 15)
- Achievement separated from behaviors with no mark penalties for late work, academic dishonesty or attendance; (Fixes 1-6)
- Summative assessments providing (almost) all the evidence for determining grades with no mark, comment only formative assessment; (Fix 13)
- More recent evidence emphasized in the determination of grades when learning is cumulative and developmental; (Fix 14) and
- Careful and limited number crunching with no zeros and use of professional judgment and the use of median and mode in addition to or in place of the mean. (Fixes 11 & 12)

Implementing the fixes generally has a range of relative philosophical and organizational difficulty; some fixes are—or should be—philosophically relatively easy to get agreement, while others are more difficult. The same is true organizationally because some are easy to implement once the philosophy has been decided while others require much more work to implement effectively. My version of relative philosophical and organizational difficulty is as follows:

#	Philosophically Relatively	Organizationally Relatively
1	Difficult	Easy
2	Difficult	Difficult
3	Easy	Easy
4	Difficult	Easy
5	Easy	Easy
6	Difficult	Easy
7	Difficult	Difficult
8	Difficult	Difficult
9	Easy	Easy
10	Easy	Difficult
11	Difficult	Easy
12	Difficult	Easy
13	Difficult	Difficult
14	Easy	Difficult
15	Easy	Difficult

I fully accept that others may disagree on which of the fixes are easier and which are more difficult as it depends on your current situation and your principles. When we summarize, however, it provides useful information about where to start:

Easy	Easy	3 5 9
Easy	Difficult	7 10 15
Difficult	Easy	1 4 6 11 12
Difficult	Difficult	2 7 8 13

If you want easy wins, you would start with Easy Easy, but if you want to start with productive struggle, you would start with Difficult Difficult. You need to have an end in mind, which hopefully is implementing all the fixes, but I would not suggest implementing all the fixes at the same time unless you give stakeholders at least 18 months notification of the starting date for implementation. Communicating what will change is important but it is equally – or more – important to indicate what won't change.

Another structure that could be applied to grading reform to determine an implementation plan is provided by Birk and Larson (2019); they suggested that there are "three groupings of strategies approaches that represent High Value (Learning) Targets" (p. 86). They are as follows:

1. "Low Hanging Fruit" strategies – those with high observable impact and/or easy to implement; Fixes 3, 4, 5 and 9 may be in this category.
2. "Why are we Doing this" strategies – those with low observable impact and/or are difficult to implement; in my opinion, none of the fixes fit into this category, but I accept that there may be different views on this.
3. "Roll-Up Our Sleeves" strategies – high observable impact and hard to implement; Fixes 2, 7, 8, and 13 are definitely in this category. That leaves out Fixes 1, 6, 10, 11, 12, 13, 14 and 15 as easy to classify, but as they are all high impact and some are organizationally difficult, they probably are in the third category.

Wright (2021) used a protocol that may also be effective for initiating grading reform; it requires that teachers "dissect their practices, diagnose the root of the issue, and determine next steps" (p. 151).

Teachers, schools, and districts need to examine their current grading policy and procedures to see if they "fit" with what is required in standards-based systems. Changes in grading practices will occur effectively and efficiently when administrators mandate implementation of the basic principles and teachers engage in professional dialogue about the specifics and implementation of guidelines that avoid the inappropriate use and interpretation of grades. Fixes such as those described here can be the basis for such guidelines, and those guidelines can then be incorporated into school grading procedures (see Appendix 1). The approach suggested here is based on Douglas Reeves, "The Myth of Buy In" (Reeves, n.d.) and Lee Ann Jung's advocacy of "Disagree but Commit" (Jung, 2017).

It is my intent and hope in writing this book that teachers will become reflective practitioners in the area of grading and that the 15 Fixes will form the basis for grades that are consistent, accurate, learning focused, and meaningful. Resources apart from books and articles that will help you to move forward include:

- CVU Learns - http://cvulearns.weebly.com – the website for the Champlain Valley (VT) Union School district has a wealth of information and resources on standards-based learning and grading.
- Matt Townsley's website - http://mctownsley.net – Matt is a professor at the University of Northern Iowa and his website is packed with information about standards-based grading
- Standards-Based Learning and Grading Facebook group – you have to ask to join and answer some questions but once you are in you have access to rich dialogue and sharing of resources
- Tom Schimmer podcast - https://tomschimmerpod.podbean.com. – provides fascinating interviews about current topics of interest in K-12 education.
- Twitter Chats
    - #sblchat – Standards-Based Learning chat - 1st and 3rd Wednesdays at 9 PM ET
    - #ATAssessment – All Things Assessment – alternate Tuesdays at 9 ET
    - #TG2chat – Teachers Going Gradeless – Sundays at 9ET

The use of standards-based grading helped dedicated students learn, prompted them to be accountable for their own progress, relieved high-performing students from the necessity to complete unproductive "work", and made rigorous courses successful for struggling yet serious students. SBG prompted students to focus attention where they needed to be to be individually successful. It relied on reflection and student autonomy so students were responsible for their growth and results.

(Henderson, 2013, p.5)

REFERENCES

Alberta Assessment Consortium. (2008) *Successful learners.* https://aac.ab.ca/wp-content/uploads/2018/01/Successful_Learners_English.pdf.

Alexander, M. (2016). "The warm demander: An equity approach." *Edutopia.* https://www.edutopia.org/blog/warm-demander-equity-approach-matt-alexander

Anderson., M (2021). "6 intrinsic motivators to power up your teaching." *Educational Leadership, 79*(4), pp. 20-25 https://www.ascd.org/el/articles/6-intrinsic-motivators-to-power-up-your-teaching

Babcock Neighborhood School. (2020). *Babcock Neighborhood School Student and Parent Handbook 2020-2021.* http://www.babcockneighborhoodschool.org/_cache/files/1/f/1f019d0f-de3e-4620-8e57-7dc4333e1ad1/B4784C0943C712AD4AB2F38C3344EE27.final-bns-student-parent-handbook-guide-2020-2021.pdf

Birk, C., & Larson, G. (2019). *PLC 2.0; Collaborating for observable impact in today's schools.* First Educational Resources.

Black, P., & D., Wiliam. (1998) "Inside the black box: Raising standards through classroom assessment". *Phi Delta Kappan*, 80(2) pp. 139–148.

Boaler, J. (2016). *Mathematical mindsets.* Jossey-Bass.

Bowers, A. J. (2019). "Report card grades and educational outcomes" in T. R.

Guskey and S. M. Brookhart (Eds.), *What we know about grading; What works, what doesn't and what's next.* ASCD (pp. 32-56).

British Columbia Ministry of Education. (2020) *B.C. Performance Standards.* https://www2.gov.bc.ca/gov/content/education-training/k-12/teach/resources-for-teachers/curriculum/bc-performance-standards

British Columbia Ministry of Education. (n.d.). *Developing and Supporting K-12 Student Reflection and Self-Assessment of Core Competencies.* https://curriculum.gov.bc.ca/sites/curriculum.gov.bc.ca/files/pdf/assessment/developing-and-supporting-student-reflection-and-self-assessment-of-the-core-competencies.pdf

Brookhart, S. M., Guskey, T. R., McTighe, J., & Wiliam, D. (2020). Eight essential principles for Improving Grading. *Educational Leadership, 78*(1).

Brookhart, S. M., & Guskey, T. R. (2019). "Are grades reliable? Lessons from a century of research." *ASCD Education Update,* (5).

Brookhart, S. M. (2016). A Century of grading research: Meaning and value in the most common educational measurement. *Review of Educational Research, 86*(4), pp. 803-848.

Budrow, K., & Hillman, G. (2020). *Moving beyond classroom management.* FIRST Educational Resources.

Carnegie Mellon University Eberly Center. (n.d.). *Grading methods for group work.* https://www.cmu.edu/teaching/assessment/assesslearning/groupWorkGradingMethods.html

Chappuis, J., & Stiggins, R. (2020). *Classroom assessment for student learning: Doing it right—Using it well* (3rd ed.). Pearson.

Chappuis, J. (2015). *Seven strategies of assessment for learning.* Pearson Assessment Training Institute

Charlotte County Public Schools. (2020). *Code of student conduct.* https://www.

yourcharlotteschools.net/cms/lib/FL02211872/Centricity/ModuleInstance/9370/COSC%20Book%2019.20%20Final%204.16.19.pdf

Christel House Academy. (2018). *Assessing, scoring and reporting: Guidelines for Christel House Academy South and West.*

Clarke, S. (2021). *Unlocking learning intentions and success criteria: Shifting from product to process across the disciplines.* Corwin Press.

Comox Valley School District. (2015). *Communicating learning: Rethinking reporting: An overview for teachers, administrators, & parents.* https://portal.sd47.bc.ca/class/7fy46vr/Documents/Rethinking%20Reporting_Jaki.pdf

Cooper, D. (2022). *Rebooting assessment:* A practical guide for balancing conversations, performances, and products. Solution Tree.

Cooper, D. (2011). *Redefining fair.* Solution Tree.

Cooper, R. (2018). "How do we assess (and possibly, grade) project-based learning?" *Cooper on Curriculum* Blog. https://rosscoops31.com/2018/07/20/assesspbl/

Council of Chief State School Officers (CCSSO). (2018). *Revising the definition of formative assessment.* Washington, D.C. https://ccsso.org/sites/default/files/2018-06/Revising%20the%20Definition%20of%20Formative%20Assessment.pdf

Cutler, D. (2019). "Tips for allowing test retakes." *Edutopia.* https://www.edutopia.org/article/tips-allowing-test-retakes

Davenport, M. (2020). "Rethinking homework for this year – and beyond." *Edutopia.* https://www.edutopia.org/article/rethinking-homework-year-and-beyond

Dimich, N. (2021). "Time to change how we assess students, schools — Opinion." *Minnesota Reformer*, 10/1/21 https://minnesotareformer.

com/2021/10/01/time-to-change-how-we-assess-students-schools-opinion/

Dueck, M. (2021). *Giving students a say.* ASCD.

Dueck, M. (2014). *Grading smarter, not harder: Assessment strategies that motivate kids and help them learn.* ASCD.

Dwyer, W., & Hiscock., C. (2019) *Rethinking the American high school.* First Educational Resources

Edmonton Catholic Schools. (n.d.). *Assessment: Understanding the codes in grades and attendance.* https://www.ecsd.net/page/17856/understanding-the-codes-in-grades-and-attendance

Education World. (2022). *National standards.* https://www.educationworld.com/standards/

El Monte City School District. (2019). *Board policies and bylaws.* https://www.emcsd.org/apps/pages/index.jsp?uREC_ID=1566382&type=d&pREC_ID=1694704

El Segundo High School. (2020). *Absence policies.* https://www.elsegundohigh.org/apps/pages/index.jsp?uREC_ID=50481&type=d&pREC_ID=1773656

ExcelinEd. (2019). *Debunking the myth of seat-time: A national analysis of seat-time requirements for credit.* https://excelined.org/wp-content/uploads/2019/11/ExcelinEd.Innovation.NextGenerationLearning. SeatTimeReport.pdf

Fairfax County Public Schools. (n.d.). *Portrait of a graduate.* https://www.fcps.edu/about-fcps/portrait-graduate

Fannon, P. (2019). PCSD rollout of standards-based grading system gets an "F." *Park Record.* May 25th. https://www.parkrecord.com/opinion/guest-editorial-pcsd-rollout-of-standards-based-grading-system-gets-an-f/

Feldman, J. (2019). *Grading for equity: Why it matters and how it can transform schools and classrooms.* Corwin.

Ferriter, B. (2021a). "Punitive grading policies don't teach kids to act responsibly." *Building Confident Learners.* December 31st. https://buildingconfidentlearners.com/2021/12/punitive-grading-policies-dont-teach-kids-to-act-responsibly/

Ferriter, B. (2021b). "Our job is to build confident learners." *The Tempered Radical.* May 16. https://blog.williamferriter.com/2021/05/16/our-job-is-to-build-confident-learners/

Fisher, D., & Frey, N. (2019). "Getting started with restorative practices." *Educational Leadership*, 77(2), 84-85.

Francis, E. (2019). DOK and SBG: Levels of four are not equivalent to scales of four. *Knowledge is half the battle.* Blog August 24th. https://maverikeducation.com/blog/f/dok-and-sbg-levels-of-four-is-not-equivalent-to-scales-of-four

Freedman, M. K. (2020). *Grading, reporting, graduating . . . and the law.* Corwin.

Gathercoal, F. (2004) *Judicious Discipline.* Sixth Edition. San Francisco, CA. Caddo Gap Press

Goodwin, B. (2021). Zombie ideas in education. *Educational Leadership*, *78*(8), 44-49.

Gonser, S. (2021). Teachers opt for more leniency, and get better work. Edutopia, April 30th. https://www.edutopia.org/article/teachers-opt-more-leniency-and-get-better-work

Grand Erie District School Board. (2018). *Assessment, evaluation and reporting.* https://granderie.ca/application/files/5515/1740/8746/SO20_Assessment_Evaluation_and_Reporting.pd

Grant, A. (2016). "Why we should stop grading students on a curve." *New York Times.* September 10th. https://www.nytimes.com/2016/09/11/opinion/sunday/why-we-should-stop-grading-students-on-a-curve.html

Great Falls High School. (2020). *Student Condensed Handbook 2020-2021.* https://www.gfps.k12.mt.us/cms/lib/MT50000605/Centricity/Domain/429/2020-2021_Condensed_Student_Handbook.pdf

Greenstein, L. (2018) "9 ways for students to own the assessment." *Corwin Connect.* February 14th. https://corwin-connect.com/2018/02/9-ways-students-assessment/

Guskey, T. R., & Brookhart, S. (Eds). (2019). *What we know about grading: What works, what doesn't and what's next.* ASCD.

Guskey, T. R. (2021). Learning from failures; Lessons from unsuccessful grading reform initiatives. *NASSP Bulletin, 105*(3), 192-199.

Guskey, T. R. (2020). "Breaking up the grade." *Educational Leadership,* 78(1), 40-46.

Guskey, T. R. (2019). Grades versus comments: Research on student feedback. *Phi Delta Kappan, 101*(3), 42-47.

Guskey, T. R. (2017). New direction in the development of rubrics. *Corwin Connect.* http://tguskey.com/new-direction-in-the-development-of-rubrics/

Guskey, T. R. (2015). *On your mark: Challenging the conventions of grading and reporting.* Solution Tree.

Guskey, T. R. (2014). Why the label 'exceeds standard' doesn't work. *Education Week*, http://tguskey.com/why-the-label-exceeds-standard-doesnt-work/

Guskey, T. R. (2013). The case against percentage grades. *Educational Leadership, 71*(1), 68-72.

Guskey, T. R. (2005). Zero alternatives. *Principal Leadership, 5*(2), 49–53.

Guskey, T. R. (Ed.). (1996). Communicating student learning: The ASCD Yearbook 1996. ASCD.

Guskey, T. R., & Bailey, J. M. (2010). *Developing standards-based report cards.* Corwin.

Hattie, J. (2021). "What can we learn from COVID-era instruction." *Educational Leadership, 78*(8), 14-17.

Henderson, M. (2013). Standards-based grading promotes learning and accountability. *IB Journal of Teaching Practice, 1*(1), 1-10.

Hierck, T., & Larson, G. (2018). *Grading for impact; Raising student achievement through a target-based assessment and learning system.* Corwin.

Hill, D. (2021). *The power of ICU* (2nd ed.). Power of ICU.

Hill, D., & Hillman, G. (2018). *The grade cleanse: A roadmap to healthy grading.* Power of ICU.

Hong Kong International School. (2018). *HKIS high school assessment & grading philosophy & practice.* https://www.hkis.edu.hk/uploaded/documents/dragonnet/High_School/T_L_Reference_Documents/03_Learning_Philosophy/HKIS_HS_Assessment_and_Grading_Philosophy_and_Practice_2018-19_1.pdf

ICAI (International Center for Academic Integrity). (2022). *Facts and statistics.* https://academicintegrity.org/resources/facts-and-statistics

ICAI (International Center for Academic Integrity). (2021). *The fundamental values of academic integrity.* https://academicintegrity.org/images/pdfs/20019_ICAI-Fundamental-Values_R12.pdf

ISG Jubail. (2019). *MS/HS Assessment procedures & protocols.* https://jubail.isg.edu.sa/information/assessment-testing

International School of Kazan. (2021). *Assessment policy.*

Jung, L. A. (2021). Lesson planning with universal design of learning. *Edu-*

cational Leadership, 79(9), 38-43 https://12d6f56f-39f6-78c7-947d-e1b724f7a8d4.filesusr.com/ugd/5c0950_5cc5a32f73c340269f01de7a1f57a62c.pdf)

Jung, L. A. (2020). Does this count. *Educational Leadership, 78*(1), 34-38.

Jung, L. A. (2017). How to keep mutiny from sinking your change effort. *Educational Leadership*, 74. 28-32 https://www.ascd.org/el/articles/how-to-keep-mutiny-from-sinking-your-change-effort

Kagan Online. (2022). *Kagan cooperative learning chapter one.* https://www.kaganonline.com/catalog/BKCLW_Chapter_1/grading_rewards.php

Kagan, S. (1995). Group grades miss the mark. *Educational Leadership, 52*(8), 68–71.

Kirschenbaum, H., Napier, R., & Simon, S. B. (1971, 2021). *Wad-ja-get? The grading game in American education.* 50th Anniversary Edition. Maize Books.

Klein, T. (2020). Grades fail at motivating students. Intrinsic motivation works better. *EdSurge.* https://www.edsurge.com/news/2020-05-21-grades-fail-at-motivating-students-intrinsic-motivation-works-better

Kohn, A. (1993). Punished by rewards: The trouble with gold stars, incentive plans, A's, praise and other bribes. Houghton Mifflin.

Langley School District. (2021). *CSL and rethinking aassessment guide - Elementary and middle schools.* Langley, B.C. https://instructionalservices.sd35.bc.ca/wp-content/uploads/sites/76/2021/10/CSL-and-RETHINKING-ASSESSMENT-GUIDE-Elem-and-Mid-2021Oct.pdf

Lambton Kent District School Board. (2021). *Assessment, evaluation and reporting: Expected practices: Grades 9 – 12.* Chatham, ON.

Levine, E. (2021). *Habits of success: Helping students develop essential skills for learning, work, and life.* Aurora Institute. https://aurora-institute.org/

resource/habits-of-success-helping-students-develop-essential-skills-for-learning-work-and-life/

Link, L. J., & Kauffman, K. D. (2021). Are your grading policies legally sound? *School Administrator, 78*(5), 45-48

Manitoba Education. (2021). *Manitoba provincial report card policy and guidelines partners for learning Grades 1 to 12*, Government of Manitoba. https://www.edu.gov.mb.ca/k12/assess/docs/report_card/full_doc.pdf

McDowell, M. (2021). *The busy teacher: Differentiation for every classroom.* First Educational Resources.

McTighe, J., & Ferrara, S. (2021). *Assessing student learning by design: Principles and practices for teachers and school leaders.* Teachers College Press.

Meyer, A., Rose, D., & Gordon, D. (2014). *Universal design for learning: Theory and practice.* CAST Professional Publishing.

Michigan Assessment Consortium (MAC). (2020). *Assessment literacy standards: A national imperative.*

Minnetonka Public Schools. (2007). *Policy #636: Secondary academic integrity policy.* https://www.minnetonkaschools.org/uploaded/Documents/Policy/636.pdf

Minnetonka Public Schools. (2002). *Policy #506: Student discipline and code of conduct.* https://www.minnetonkaschools.org/uploaded/Documents/Policy/506.pdf

National Association of Colleges and Employers (2022) *NACE's diversity, equity, and inclusion statement.* https://www.naceweb.org/about-us/naces-diversity-equity-and-inclusion-statement

New Zealand Ministry of Education. (2021). *Assessment online: Moderation purposes.* https://assessment.tki.org.nz/Moderation/Moderation-purposes

North East School Division. (2017). *Assessment and evaluation handbook.* https://curriculum.nesd.ca/Resources/NESD-Handbooks/NESD%20ASSESS%20and%20EVAL%20Handbook%20September%202017.pdf

Novak, K. (2021). If equity is a priority UDL is a must. *Cult of Pedagogy.* https://www.cultofpedagogy.com/udl-equity/

Novak, K. (n.d.). *UDL Flowchart.* https://www.novakeducation.com/hubfs/ Resources/UDL_FlowChart.pdf

O'Connor, K. (2018). *How to grade for learning: Linking grades to standards* (4th ed.). Corwin.

O'Connor, K. (2013) *The School Leader's Guide to Grading.* Bloomington, IN. Solution Tree.

O'Connor, K. (2009) *How to grade for learning: Linking grades to standards* (3rd ed.). Thousand Oaks, CA: Corwin

O'Connor, K. (2002) *How to grade for learning: Linking grades to standards* (2nd ed.). Thousand Oaks, CA: Corwin

O'Connor, K. (1999) *How to grade for learning: Linking grades to standards* (1st ed.). Arlington Heights, IL: Skylight

O'Connor, K. (1995). Guidelines for grading that support learning and student success. *NASSP Bulletin, 79*(5), 91–95.

Ontario Ministry of Education. (2010). *Growing success: Assessment, evaluation, and reporting in Ontario schools.* Queen's Printer for Ontario.

Oregon Department of Education. (2015). *Standards for public elementary and secondary schools 581-022-1131 Credit options.* https://www.oregon.gov/ode/students-and-family/OregonDiploma/Documents/581-022-1131.pdf

Partnership for 21st Century Skills. (2012). *P21 framework definitions.* https://files.eric.ed.gov/fulltext/ED519462.pdf

Patrick, S., & Chambers, A. (2020). *Determining attendance and alternatives to seat-time.* Aurora Institute

Pewaukee High School. (2015). *Grading guidelines in a standards-based learning environment.*

Pink, D. (2009). *Drive: The surprising truth about what motivates us.* Riverhead.

Pittsford Central School District. (2019). *PCSD grading practices.* https://ny02205365.schoolwires.net/site/handlers/filedownload.ashx?moduleinstanceid=396&dataid=85603&FileName=PCSD%20Agreed%20upon%20grading%20practices%20updated%20August%202019.pdf

Prairie Spirit School Division. (2020). *Administrative procedures manual.* Warman, SK. https://www.spiritsd.ca/files/app/414%20Assessment.pdf

Price, D. (2021). *Laziness does not exist.* Atria Books.

Rasooli, A., & Brookhart, S. (2021). Planning for fair group work. *Educational Leadership,* 78, pp. 44-49 https://www.ascd.org/el/articles/planning-for-fair-group-work

Reibel, A., & Thede, M. (2020). *Small changes, big impact; 10 strategies to promote student efficacy and lifelong learning.* Solution Tree.

Reeves, D. (2016). *FAST grading: A guide to implementing best practices.* Solution Tree.

Reeves, D. (2004). The case against the zero. *Phi Delta Kappan, 86*(4), 324–325.

Reeves, D. (n.d.). *The myth of buy-in.* https://static1.squarespace.com/static/56a6ae1c22482e2f99869834/t/5c2d57af758d46dc8b0efec6/1546475442387/Reeves+The+Myth+of+Buy-In.pdf

Ripp, P. (2019). Using the single point rubric for better assessment conversations. Blog. https://pernillesripp.com/2019/02/24/using-the-single-point-rubric-for-better-assessment-conversations/

Ripp, P. (2017). The grading conversation we need to have. https://pernillesripp.com/2017/01/25/the-grading-conversation-we-need-to-have/

Rinkema, E., & Williams, S. (2019). *The standards-based classroom: Make learning the goal.* Corwin.

River East Transcona School Division. (2018). IKA-R *assessment roles and responsibilities.* https://www.retsd.mb.ca/yourretsd/Policies/Documents/IKA-R.pdf

Rivera, K. (2021). Spiral assessments: Why they are necessary. *1 stop teacher shop blog.* https://onestopteachershop.com/2016/08/spiral-assessments-quizzes-classroom.html

Rocky View School Division. (2022). *Real time reporting (RTR).* https://www.rockyview.ab.ca/21stC/assessing/real-time-reporting

Rocky View School Division. (2021). *Administrative procedure 360: Assessment & communication of student learning* https://www.rockyview.ab.ca/staff/admin_procedures/300-students/ap360-assessment-and-communication-of-student-learning/view

Roell, K. (2019). "What is grading on the curve?" *ThoughtCo.* https://www.thoughtco.com/grading-on-a-curve

Sackstein, S. (2015). *Teaching students to self-assess: How do I help students reflect and grow as learners?*. ASCD.

Saltzman, D. (2020). Distance learning pushed us to standards-based grading: We'll keep it. https://blog.betterlesson.com/distance-learning-pushed-us-to-standards-based-grading.-well-keep-it

Schimmer, T. (2020). Are you a tough grader or a 'tough grader?' *AllThingsAssessment* blog. https://allthingsassessment.info/2020/03/05/are-you-a-tough-grader-or-a-tough-grader/

Schimmer, T. (2018). 'It's okay NOT to reassess?' *AllThingsAssessment* blog.

https://allthingsassessment.info/2018/06/12/limiting-reassessment/

Schimmer, T. (2016). *Grading from the inside out; Bringing accuracy to student assessment through a standards-based mindset.* Solution Tree.

Schimmer, T., & SYS Education. (n.d.). *A guide to summative moments.* https://docs.google.com/presentation/d/1RED1iacKchaYNkVmRKO-q5MtDddi0NffQozNUT8092fg/

Schneider, J. (2020). Pass-Fail raises the question: What's the point of grades. *New York Times.* https://www.nytimes.com/2020/06/25/opinion/coronavirus-school-grades.html

Shattuck St. Mary's Forest City International School. (2021). *SSM-FC standards based grading and reports guidebook* (Draft).

Shaw, B. P. (2018). *Music assessment for better ensembles.* Oxford University Press.

Silver, D. (2021). Empowering our kids to motivate themselves. *Middleweb.* https://www.middleweb.com/45523/how-to-motivate-kids-my-two-word-answer/

Silver Spring International Middle School. (n.d.). *Academic honesty policy.* https://www2.montgomeryschoolsmd.org/contentassets/466ae9c6d-65745c8b311187a63ffa44d/academic-honesty-policy-ssims.pdf

Solon Community School District. (2012). *Standards-based grading at SCSD.* https://sites.google.com/a/solon.k12.ia.us/standards-based-grading/purpose-guidelines

South Koochiching-Rainy River School District. (n.d.). *Indus magnet school K-12 student handbook.* https://mlpp.pressbooks.pub/indus/chapter/attnedance/

Stack, B. M., & Vander Els, J. G. (2018). Breaking with tradition: The shift to competency-based learning in PLCS at work. Solution Tree.

Starr, J. (2021). Too much autonomy can mean too little equity. *Kappan, 102*(8), 60-61.

Syme, R. (2021). What deadlines do to timelines. *The New Yorker.* https://www.newyorker.com/magazine/2021/07/05/what-deadlines-do-to-lifetimes

Tamony, A. (2021a). The case against zeros in grading. *Edutopia.* https://www.edutopia.org/article/case-against-zeros-grading

Tamony, A. (2021b). Are all zeros created equally [YouTube video]. https://www.youtube.com/watch?v=adzARR3vjdk

The Institute for Habits of Mind. (n.d.). *Habits of mind chart.* https://www.habitsofmindinstitute.org/wpcontent/uploads/2018/10/HabitsofTheMind-Chartv2.pdf

Thomas Jefferson Middle School. (2021). *Academic integrity: International Baccalaureate Middle Years Programme.* https://jefferson.apsva.us/wp-content/uploads/sites/22/2021/03/Academic-Integrity-Policy.pdf

Texas Association of Public School Boards. (2022). *My Texas public schools; Attendance requirements in Texas schools.* https://www.mytexaspublicschool.org/preparing-and-enrolling-your-child/attendance-requirements.

Tomlinson, C. A., & Sousa, D. A. (2020). *The sciences of teaching.* https://jmss.vic.edu.au/wp-content/uploads/2020/12/The-Sciences-of-Teaching.pdf

Townsley, M., & Wear, N. L. (2020). *Making grades matter: Standards-based grading in a secondary PLC at work.* Solution Tree.

Townsley, M. (2019). *SBG in Iowa.* https://sites.google.com/view/iowasbg/

Tucker, C. (2020). *Balance with blended learning: Partner with your students to reimagine learning and reclaim your life.* Corwin.

Vanhala, M. (2020). How I revamped my grading system. *Educational Leadership, 78*(1), 67-70.

Urbana City Schools. (2015). *Grading and assessment guidelines.* https://www.urbanacityschools.org/docs/district/forms&documents/grading%20&%20assessment%20guidelines%202018-2019.pdf?id=1176

Westerberg, T. R. (2016). *Charting the course to standards-based grading: What to stop, what to start and why it matters.* ASCD.

Westman, L. (2017) "Standards-based grading made my kid average." In P DeWitt's "Finding Common Ground, *Education Week.* March 14. https://www.edweek.org/education/opinion-standards-based-grading-made-my-kid-average/2017/03

Westwood Community High School. (n.d.). *Academic integrity.* https://westwood.fmpsdschools.ca/senior-high/student-services/academic-integrity

Wiggins, G. (1997). Feedback: How learning occurs. *The American Association for Higher Education Bulletin, 50*(3), 7-8.

Winneconne School District. (2022). *Grading and reporting.* http://www.winneconne.k12.wi.us/district/curriculum___instruction/grading_and_reporting

White, K. (2022). *Student self-assessment: Data notebooks, portfolios, & other tools to advance learning.* Solution Tree

White, K. (2020). Next generation assessment: Increasing student voice and choice. *AllThings Assessment* blog. https://allthingsassessment.info/2020/03/23/next-generation-assessment-increasing-student-voice-and-choice/

White, K. (2017). *Softening the edges: Assessment practices that honor k-12 teachers and learners.* Solution Tree.

Willis, J. (2018). *Awesome insights about learning from brain-savvy teens.* Radical Teaching, Psychology Today blog. https://www.psychologytoday.com/ca/blog/radical-teaching/201809/awesome-insights-about-learning-brain-savvy-teens

Wolcott, G. (2019). *Significant 72: Unleashing the power of relationships in today's schools.* First Educational Resources

Wormeli, R. (2019). *Redos, retakes and do-overs.* Part1. https://www.schooltube.com/media/Rick-Wormeli-Redos-Retakes-and-DoOvers-Part-One/1_2nfrrlgq

Wormeli, R. (2018). *Fair isn't always equal: Assessing and grading in the differentiated classroom* (2nd ed.). Stenhouse.

Wormeli, R. (2016). *The right way to do redos.* Middleweb. https://www.middleweb.com/31398/rick-wormeli-the-right-way-to-do-redos/

Wormeli, R. (2010). *Redos, retakes and do-overs.* Part 2. https://www.youtube.com/watch?v=wgxvzEc0rvs

Wright, J. (2021). *What's our response? Creating systems and structure to support ALL learners.* First Educational Resources

Yukon Education. (n.d.). *For teachers: Yukon education grade conversion guide (Grades 10-12).*

Zerwin, S. M. (2020). *Pointless: An English teacher's guide to more meaningful grading.* Heinemann.

APPENDICES

Appendix 1

THE FIFTEEN FIXES AS PROCEDURES

1. a. Individual achievement of stated learning goals (standards, target, outcomes, etc.) shall be the only basis for grades.

   b. Behaviors/learning skills shall not be included in grades unless they are a stated part of a published learning goal.

   c. The 3-6 (?) most valued behaviors/learning skills shall be reported separately.

2. Late submission of evidence of learning shall be handled as follows:

   a. Teachers may set due dates and deadlines for all marked evidence of learning that will be part of a student grade.

   b. There shall be no mark penalties for late submission of assessment evidence.

   c. Late submission of evidence of learning may lead to parent contact and will be noted for inclusion in comments and/or learning skills section of the report card.

   d. Late submission of evidence of learning shall lead to an invitation or the requirement to attend a support session during the school day, before school, at lunchtime, or after school hours.

   e. Students may request and receive extensions of timelines.

3. Extra credit and bonus points/questions will not be used.

4. Academic dishonesty will be dealt with

   a. As set out in the Code of Conduct without any mark reductions.

   b. Students will be required to resubmit any assessment identified as academically dishonest, certifying that it was completed honestly.

5. Absences shall be handled as follows:

a. Students shall not be penalized only for absence.

b. Absent students shall be given makeup opportunities for all missed summative assessments (marked evidence of learning that will be part of student grades) without penalty

c. Any identification of excused and unexcused absences will be only for behavioral, legal, or financial reasons

6. a. No group marks will be included in grades unless collaboration is required by the standard being assessed.

   b. If group marks are to be included in grades, parents and students shall be notified in advance of why and how group marks will be used.

7. Grading procedures shall be related directly to stated learning goals.

   a. Grades will be determined for the learning goals selected for each subject K-12.

   b. There shall be no less than three and no more than 10 reporting standards for each subject

   c. Subject grades will be determined for grades x to y (preferably 9-12 at the most).

8. Performance standards will be identified and described using a 2-7 levels of proficiency.

9. Criterion-referenced standards shall be used to determine grades and marks.

10. a. Teachers shall use quality assessment instruments. Each assessment must meet standards of quality.

    i. It must arise from a clearly articulated set of achievement expectations,

    ii. serve an instructionally relevant purpose,

    iii. rely on a proper method,

    iv. sample student achievement in an appropriate manner, and

    v. control for all relevant sources of bias and distortion that can lead to inaccurate assessment.

b. All assessments must be reviewed regularly and adjusted as needed to meet these standards of quality

c. Teachers shall properly record evidence of student achievement on an ongoing basis.

11. a. Grading is an exercise in professional judgment wherein the educator seeks to ensure that the grade each student receives (for standards or subjects) is an accurate representation of his or her achievement as represented by a body of evidence.

b. Grades will be determined primarily by the most consistent level of achievement with emphasis on more recent evidence. (Mode +more recent + professional judgment.)

12. a. Teachers will record missing (M) or not submitted (NS) in their grade books for assessments that have not been received by the due date or the agreed upon extended date.

b. If a student has produced insufficient evidence to determine a grade for a standard or subject, the student's grade will be an "I" for Incomplete, until such time as sufficient evidence is provided.

c. If teachers are using percentages, zeros may not be used.

13. a. Teachers shall provide descriptive feedback orally or in writing on formative assessments.

b. Formal assessments used in the formative assessment process shall not be included directly in grades.

c. Marks from summative assessments shall be used primarily to determine grades.

14. a. Where repetitive measures are made of the same or similar knowledge, skills, or behaviors, the more recent marks shall be used for grade determination.

b. Reassessment opportunities shall be made available to students; students shall receive the more recent mark, not an average for any such multiple opportunities.

15. a. Teachers shall provide students and parents with a written overview of assessment in clear, easily understandable language, indicating how each summative assessment throughout the year/course will be evaluated before each such assessment is administered.

    b. Teachers shall discuss assessment with students, in an age-appropriate manner, near the beginning of instruction. Where feasible, students shall be involved in decisions about methods of assessment and scoring scales.

    c. Teachers will provide students with opportunities for self-assessment, reflection and goal setting, and will transition from parent teacher conferences to student-led conferences.

Appendix 2

SURVEY ON CURRENT TEACHER MARKING AND GRADING PRACTICES AND BELIEFS

Instructions:

There are two parts to the survey. The first part asks about your current grading practices. The second part asks about your beliefs about grading.

Definitions:

Mark/Score - the number or letter placed on any single student assessment (test or performance) to indicate the quality of achievement demonstrated

Grade - the symbol (number or letter) reported at the end of a period of time as a summary statement of student performance.

	Almost Always	Frequently	Sometimes	Never
1. I include one or more of the following in grades: effort, participation, tardiness, attendance, and/or adherence to class rules.				
2. I reduce points/marks on work submitted late.				
3. I give extra points for extra credit.				
4. I reduce marks/grades for cheating.				
5. I organize information in my grade book by source: homework, quizzes, tests, labs, etc				
6. I organize information in my grade book by learning goals or learning targets				
7. I include in grades zeros for missing assessments/ assignments.				
8. I provide students with scores and descriptive feedback on assessments for learning/formative assessments.				
9. I provide students with only descriptive feedback on assessments for learning/formative assessments.				
10. I provide students with only scores on assessments for learning/formative assessments.				
11. I provide students with only descriptive feedback on assessments of learning/summative assessments.				
12. I provide students with scores only on assessments of learning/summative assessments.				

	Almost Always	Frequently	Sometimes	Never
13. I include performance on homework in final grades.				
14. I keep separate information from formative and summative assessments in my grade book				
15. I determine grades by calculating the mean/average.				
16. I determine grades by emphasizing more recent assessment scores.				
17. I ensure that the students in my class(es) understand how grades are determined and what evidence will count and what won't count directly				
18. I include group scores in grades for individual students.				
19. I limit the number of students in my class(es) who receive the highest marks/grades (a or 4 or 100%)				

	Agree	Somewhat Agree	Somewhat Disagree	Disagree
20. The primary purpose for grades is to communicate student achievement at a point in time.				
21. Grades should be consistent				
22. Grades should be accurate				
23. Grades should support learning/be learning focused.				
24. Grades should be meaningful				
25. Students should be allowed to retake assessments with the reassessment score "counting" in my grade book.				
26. Marks and grades should show how students are doing relative to one another.				
27. It is most accurate to base grades on the mean (average) score rather than the more recent score(s).				
28. Peer and self- assessment should be limited to descriptive feedback with teachers determining the scores that go into the grade book				

Appendix 3

RUBRIC FOR EVALUATING GRADING PRACTICES

Criterion	Beginning	Developing	Fluent
1. Organizing the gradebook	The evidence of learning (gradebook) is entirely organized by sources of information (e.g., tests, quizzes, homework, labs, etc.).	The evidence of learning (gradebook) is organized by sources of information mixed with specific learning goals.	The evidence of learning (gradebook) is completely organized by student learning goals (e.g., content standards, targets, outcomes, etc.).
2 . Factors included in the grade	Overall summary grades are based on a mix of achievement and nonachievement factors (e.g., timeliness, attitude, effort, cheating). Non-achievement factors have a major impact on grades.	Overall summary grades are based on a mix of achievement and nonachievement factors, but achievement counts a lot more.	Overall summary grades are based on achievement only.
	Extra credit points are often given for actions with no connection to learning goals.	Extra credit points are occasionally given for actions with no connection to learning goals.	Extra credit points are never given for actions with no connection to learning goals.
	Tests often include bonus questions	Tests occasionally include bonus questions	Tests never include bonus questions
	Cheating, late work, and missing evidence of learning result in a zero (or a severely lowered score) in the gradebook. There is rarely any opportunity for make up evidence of learning.	Cheating, late work, and missing evidence of learning result in lowered scores (sometimes zeros) in the gradebook, but there are opportunities for make up evidence to raise the lower score or replace the zero.	Cheating, late work, and missing evidence of learning is recorded as "incomplete" or "not enough information" rather than as zero. There is an opportunity to replace an "incomplete" with a score without penalty.
	Borderline grade cases are handled by considering non-achievement factors.	Borderline cases are handled by considering a combination of non-achievement factors and collecting additional evidence of student learning.	Borderline grade cases are handled by collecting additional evidence of student achievement, not by counting non-achievement factors.

3. Considering assessment purpose	Everything each student does is given a score and every score goes into the final grade. There is no distinction between "scores" on practice (formative assessment/homework) and scores that demonstrate level of achievement (summative assessment).	Some distinctions are made between formative (practice such as homework) and summative assessment, but practice still constitutes a significant part of the grade.	Student evidence of is assessed frequently (formative assessment) and graded occasionally (summative assessment). Formative assessments and practice (e.g., homework) receive descriptive feedback to inform teachers and students of what has been learned and the next steps in learning. Grades are based primarily on summative assessments.
4. Considering most recent information	All assessment data is cumulative and used in calculating a final summative grade. No consideration is given to identifying or using the more recent information.	More recent evidence is given consideration at times, but does not entirely replace out-of-date evidence.	More recent evidence completely replaces out-of-date evidence when appropriate. For example, how well students write at the end of the grading period is more important than how well they write at the beginning, and later evidence of improved content understanding is more important than early evidence.

5. Summarizing information and determining final grade	The gradebook has a mixture of ABC, percentages, +|–, and/or proficiency levels, etc., with no explanation of how they are combined into a final summary grade.	The gradebook may or may not have a mixture of symbols, but there is some attempt, even if incomplete, to explain how to combine them into a final summary grade.	The gradebook only has proficiency levels and there is a sound explanation of how to combine them into a final summary grade
	Rubric scores are converted to percentages and averaged with other scores.	Rubric scores are not directly converted to percentages; some type of conversion scale is used	Rubric scores are converted to a final grade using a conversion scale that results in an accurate summary of the level of student attainment of the learning goals.
	Final summary grades are norm-referenced—a student's place in the rank order of student achievement.	Final grades are criterion referenced, not norm referenced. They are based on pre-set standards for proficiency levels, but there is no shared meaning of symbols—i.e., there is no clear description of each level.	Final grades are criterion referenced, not norm referenced. They are based on pre-set standards with clear descriptions of what each proficiency level means.
	Final grades for special needs students are not based on learning targets as specified in the IEP.	There is an attempt to base final grades for special needs students on learning targets in the IEP, but the attempt is not always successful; or, it is not clear to all parties that modified learning targets are used to assign a grade.	Final grades for special needs students are criterion referenced, and indicate level of attainment of the learning goals as specified in the IEP. The targets on which grades are based are clear to all parties.
	Final summary grades are based only on calculation of mean (average) with no use of professional judgment	Final summary grades are based primarily on calculation of mean (average) but with some adjustments using professional judgment	Final summary grades are based on mode + more recent + professional judgment

6. Verifying Assessment Quality	Quality standards for class- room assessment are not con- sidered and the teacher has trouble articulating standards for quality.	Some standards of quality are adhered to in judging the accuracy of the assessment results on which grades are based. The teacher can articu- late some of these standards; or, uses standards for quality assessment intuitively, but has trouble articulating why an assessment is sound.	The teacher can articulate standards of quality, and can show evidence of consider- ation of these standards in class- room assessments:
	Assessments are rarely modi- fied for special needs students when such modifications would provide much more accurate information about student learning.	Assessments are modified for special needs students, but the procedures used may not result in accurate information and/or match provisions in the IEP.	Assessments are modified for special needs students in ways that match instruction- al modifications described in IEPs. Such modifications result accurate information on student achievement.
7. Involving Students	Grades are a surprise to students because (1) students don't understand the base on which they are determined, (2) students have not been involved in their own assess- ment (learning targets are not clear to them, and/or they do not self-assess and track progress toward the targets); or (3) teacher feedback is only evaluative (a judgment of level of quality) and includes no descriptive component.	Grades are somewhat of a surprise to students because student-involvement practic- es and descriptive feedback are too limited to give them insights into the nature of the learning targets being pursued and their own performance.	Grades are not a surprise to students because (a) students understand the basis for the grades received, (2) students have been involved in their own assessment (they un- derstand the learning targets they are to hit, self-assess in relation to the targets, track their own progress toward the targets, and/or talk about their progress), and/or (3) teacher communication to students is frequent, descriptive, and focuses on what they have learned as well as the next steps in learning. Descriptive feedback is related directly to specific and clear learning targets.

INDEX